高等院校会计与财务系列教材

第4版

财务管理专业英语

刘媛媛 编著

Professional English For Financial Management

机械工业出版社
CHINA MACHINE PRESS

图书在版编目（CIP）数据

财务管理专业英语 / 刘媛媛编著 . —4 版 . —北京：机械工业出版社，2020.9（2025.6重印）
（高等院校会计与财务系列教材）

ISBN 978-7-111-66478-9

I. 财… II. 刘… III. 财务管理 – 英语 – 高等学校 – 教材 IV. F275

中国版本图书馆CIP数据核字（2020）第173261号

　　本书根据作者多年教学经验写就，涵盖财务报表、货币时间价值与估价、风险与收益、资本预算、资本市场与资金筹集、资本结构、股利政策、营运资本管理以及国际财务管理等内容。本书按照财务管理的课程架构分为12个专题，每个专题均由"新闻试听""名人名言"和饶有趣味的"微型案例"开始，"即时问答""思考与探索""知识扩展"和"相关网址"等内容为教学开拓了视野，也为促进教学互动提供了很好的方式，使学生能学以致用。

　　本书适用于财会专业英语课教学，适合广大财会专业教师、本科生及财务管理工作者和爱好者使用。

出版发行：机械工业出版社（北京市西城区百万庄大街22号　邮政编码：100037）
责任编辑：杜　霜　章集香　　　　　　　　　责任校对：殷　虹
印　　刷：北京联兴盛业印刷股份有限公司　　版　　次：2025年6月第4版第12次印刷
开　　本：185mm×260mm　1/16　　　　　　　印　　张：16.75
书　　号：ISBN 978-7-111-66478-9　　　　　　定　　价：49.00元

客服电话：(010) 88361066　68326294

版权所有·侵权必究
封底无防伪标均为盗版

推荐序

财务管理作为工商管理研究中最具活力的一门学科，在过去的一个世纪里取得了令人瞩目的发展。继莫迪利亚尼-米勒、马科维茨-夏普的财务革命之后，布莱克-斯科尔斯的期权定价模型与詹森-麦克林的代理成本理论使这一学科充满了生机和挑战，展现出无可限量的发展前景。伴随着财务学科的发展，财务管理的理论框架也在不断地更新与变革。从以筹资为核心研究公司财务问题的传统财务学派，到以资产定价为核心研究公司资源配置与财务决策的现代财务学派，财务管理研究的视角发生了很大的变化。

20世纪50年代，财务理论研究空前繁荣，形成了现代财务理论的许多思想和流派，尤其是以投资决策为研究对象的资本预算方法日益成熟。1951年，乔·迪恩（Joel Dean）出版了《资本预算》；F. 卢茨（F. Lutz）和V. 卢茨（V. Lutz）在《企业投资理论》中提出了投资决策的净现值法；1955年，洛里（J. Lorie）和萨维奇（L. Savage）发表了《资本限额的三个问题》等，这几部作品共同构成了现代企业投资决策理论学派。对财务理论影响最大的当属1990年诺贝尔经济学奖获得者们的理论贡献：马科维茨（Harry M. Markowitz）提出的证券组合理论（1952）；莫迪利亚尼（Franco Modigliani）和米勒（Merton H. Miller）提出的资本结构理论（1958）；夏普（William F. Sharpe, 1964）、林特纳（John Lintner, 1965）和特雷纳（Jack Treynor, 1966）等提出的资本资产定价模型。这些理论不仅丰富和发展了财务理论文库，也使金融学中原来比较独立的两个领域——投资学和财务管理相互融合，使财务管理跨入了投资管理的新时期。

20世纪70年代后，金融工具的推陈出新使公司与金融市场的联系日益加强，财务理论研究的视野不断拓宽。1973年，布莱克（F. Black）等人创立了期权定价模型；1976年，詹森（M. C. Jensen）和麦克林（W. H. Meckling）发表了《企业理论：管理行为、代理成本和所有权结构》，罗斯（S. Ross）提出了资本资产定价套利理论，并于 1977 年发表了《财务结构的决定：动机信号方法》；1977 年，利兰（H. E. Leland）和派尔（D. H. Pyle）发表了《信息不对称、财务结构和金融中介》；1995 年，哈特（Oliver Hart）出版了《企业、合同与财务结构》。这些名篇佳作借用"信号""动机""信息不对称"等信息经济学的概念以及"委托代理"和"激励"等代理理论，研究管理者行为和公司治理结构等问题，从而使财务理论研究空前丰富与充实。

从学科范畴看，财务管理与金融市场学、投资学一起，共同构成了金融学研究的三大领域。在这三大领域中，金融市场学主要是分析金融市场的组织形式和微观结构，考察不同的金融产品和它们的特征以及它们在实现资源配置过程中的作用。投资学是以投资者决策为出发点，研究金融市场和金融资产（包括股票、债券、期权和期货）的定价模式及其投资分析与组合管理的一门学科。财务管理则是以企业决策为出发点，研究企业稀缺资源的取得（筹资决策）和使用（投资决策），即公司实物投资与财务运作的决策过程。在这三者中，相比较而言，投资学与财务管理的关系更为紧密，投资学的理论只有通过企业财务活动才能真正与实物经济发生联系，与商品市场发生联系，而企业价值又要通过金融市场的交易才能得到正确的评估。据此，财务管理研究的框架主要包括两个方面：一是通过资源的流动和重组实现资源的优化配置和价值增值；二是通过金融工具的创新和资本结构的调整来实现资本的扩张和增值。

一位获得过诺贝尔奖的经济学家说过，21世纪人才的需求标准是懂得现代科技的金融人才或懂得现代金融的科技人才。从最近的发展动向看，财务管理的许多理论已走出学校的象牙塔，越来越广泛地运用到企业财务管理的实践中。为适应财务管理的发展，使学生"零距离"接触到国际一流的学术研究成果，一大批优秀的英文教材的翻译本或影印本被引入国内。然而对大多数读者来说，由于新术语层出不穷，无论是翻译本还是影印本，都不能将外语与专业知识很好地结合起来，而广大读者却迫切需要一本财务管理专业英语的指导读物。刘媛媛教授编写的《财务管理专业英语》正是从这一需要出发，旨在帮助读者轻松学习专业英语。本书作为一本财务管理的基础性教材，系统、简洁地介绍了财务报表、风险与收益、资本预算、资本市场与资金筹集、资本结构、股利政策、营运资本管理和国际财务管理等财务管理的基本理论和实用技术。本书突破了专业英语教材的传统模式与写作方法，每一专题以"新闻视听""名人名言"和"微型案例"为先导，引导读者分析财务管理中的成败得失、经验教训。每一专题后设置的"思考与探索""知识扩展"和"相关网址"等栏目，不仅丰富了教材的内容，拓展了读者的视野，更增加了教材的可读性。本书资料丰富、风格新颖，行文流畅、准确，既可满足财务管理、金融学、会计学等专业财务管理课程的教学需要，又可为从事相关方面研究的人员提供案头参考，为从事财务管理的实际工作者带来启发和裨益。

刘淑莲
2014 年 5 月于东北财经大学

前言

A journey of a thousand miles begins with a single step.

——Chinese proverb

The future is not what it used to be.

——Paul Valery

随着全球经济一体化进程的加快以及国家"一带一路"倡议的提出，社会相关行业需要大量国际化的复合型人才，要求他们具备扎实的专业知识、较高的信息素养和能在专业领域用外语进行交流沟通的能力。因此，学生个人的国际化发展诉求和社会相关行业的国际化人才需求共同对高校商科教育提出了更高的国际化建设要求。相比其他专业，财务管理专业人才国际化的特点更为突出。当前，我国日趋频繁的跨国并购、海外上市、国际工程招标等所需要的多元化英语交流团队，都不能缺少财务管理专业的国际化人才。作为一名财务管理专业和会计学专业教师，多年来，我一直采用国外原版教材从事财务管理专业和非财务管理专业的财务管理课程的双语教学。我深切体会到，虽然学生已经系统学习了大学基础英语，但由于缺乏专业英语基础，财务管理双语课程的教学效果并不尽如人意，因此很有必要在财务管理专业教学中设置财务管理专业英语课程。财务管理专业英语教学，作为从基础英语教学向专业课双语教学过渡的桥梁，是财务管理、会计学专业学生从基础英语学习过渡到专业领域英语应用不可或缺的中间环节。要对学生进行财务管理专业英语素养的培养，一本合适的财务管理专业英语教材无疑会起到不可或缺的作用。

本书是在《财务管理专业英语》原有版本的基础上修订而成的。在本书第1版发行期间，我作为东北财经大学刘淑莲教授带队的财务管理双语教学团队的主力成员，参与了财务管理双语课程建设。努力加幸运的结果是，该课程于 2008

年获得了教育部批准的国家级双语示范课程的殊荣。本着"在实践中求证、在探索中前行"的一贯思路，为了充分发挥该教学成果的示范、辐射和转化作用，且应出版社的邀请，我萌发了再版此书的想法。

党的二十大报告提出"两个相结合"，这意味着财务管理实务工作需要与企业实际相结合，与中国特色社会主义市场经济的实际情况相结合，才能有效地实现中华民族伟大复兴。财务管理专业英语课程，不仅要强化学生财务管理专业英语的听、说、读、写能力，更要以专业为本，以国内经济管理环境为背景，为学生营造一个在国际视野下用英语思考财务问题和解决财务问题的环境。第4版秉承以前版本的写作思路，从财务管理专业培养目标出发，并采用有助于提高学生专业知识和实际运用能力的编写形式，力求使其成为一本实用的财务管理专业英语教材，以期能使学生成为满足日益激烈的国际竞争和频繁的国际交流需求的高素质财务管理人才。

本书按财务管理专业主干课程的架构分为12个专题，分别介绍财务管理专业各个方面的专业英语基础知识和拓展知识。每一专题均先以"新闻视听""名人名言"和"微型案例"开始，以激发学生的兴趣，使其去主动获取知识、拓宽视野，正文尽量体现财务管理专业的基本理念与核心内容，每一专题还设有"知识扩展""相关网址"等，进一步丰富了教学内容。另外，"即时问答""思考与探索"和"汉译英"的练习内容很好地帮助学生巩固和消化每一专题的内容。本书为财务管理、会计学专业的学生而写，采用的是导读式的教材风格，而非包罗万象的财务辞典。

根据数年的教学经验，我建议财务管理专业英语教师在使用本书时，除了教给学生阅读专业英语、掌握专业英语术语和翻译的技巧之外，更重要的是要培养学生把所学到的专业知识转化为财务管理专业英语的实际运用能力，将专业英语学习重点置于地道的表达之中。教师要注意由浅入深，引导学生顺利地从基础英语学习过渡到专业英语学习，防止学生在还没有掌握多少专业知识的情况下就被一大堆专业词汇压得喘不过气来，令学生学而生厌。个人建议在课堂上采用渗透型双向式的教学模式并辅之以案例教学，将专业英语学习置于真实再现的商业情境中。通过渗透型双向式教学，加强学生在课堂教学的双向互动，努力营造学生积极参与课堂教学的氛围，激发学生的学习兴趣。通过案例教学，教师结合教学内容和进度，精心安排案例演示、分析讨论，引导学生逐步学会运用英语并结合专业知识对实际问题进行思考与分析，努力将思辨能力提升置于专业英语学习之中。

为了更好地辅助教学，机械工业出版社提供了本书的辅助资料，包括"教材配套 PPT 课件""'新闻视听'栏目的音频材料"和"教师用书"，请任课教师自行联系机械工业出版社获取。

本书写作的目的不仅在于提供一本与时俱进的财务管理专业英语教材，还在于为财务管理国际化的实践者们提供一本饶有趣味的案头书。本书力求传递财务管理专业英语知识，也注重财务管理理论与实践的介绍。本书可以作为财务管理专业英语教材，建议于大学本科二年级下学期或三年级上学期开设此课程，课时在 36 学时左右。

在本书的成稿过程中，我参阅了大量的素材，并尽量在网上搜索相关的视听资料以利于教学。我的学生罗样样对本书第 2 版、赵欣宇对本书第 3 版、侯梦宇等对本书第 4 版都做了大量的工作，在此表示感谢。尽管力图精益求精，但在经历了漫长的写作过程之后，在本书即将付梓再版之际，我仍感觉有太多地方值得雕琢。"闻道有先后，术业有专攻"，诚挚希望各位读者对本书中的错误及不当之处提出批评和建议，我将在今后适时更正。如果您觉得这是一本较好的财务管理专业英语教材，也请您不吝推荐和分享给有兴趣和需要的读者。

刘媛媛

目　录

推荐序
前言

第 1 章　财务管理概述（1）

TOPIC 1　Introduction to Financial Management (1) ·· 1

　　新闻视听 News in Media ·· 1
　　名人名言 Wisdom ··· 1
　　微型案例 Mini Case ·· 1
　　概览 Overview ··· 2
　　正文 Text ·· 2
　　　1.1　Financial Management and Financial Manager ··· 2
　　　1.2　Financial Management Decision ·· 3
　　　1.3　Risk-Return Tradeoff ··· 7
　　核心词汇 Core Words and Expressions ··· 7
　　即时问答 Quick Quiz ··· 8
　　思考与探索 Thinking and Exploration ·· 8
　　汉译英 Translation ·· 8
　　知识扩展 More Knowledge ··· 9
　　相关网址 Useful Websites ·· 12

第 2 章　财务管理概述（2）

TOPIC 2　Introduction to Financial Management (2) ·· 13

　　新闻视听 News in Media ·· 13
　　名人名言 Wisdom ··· 13
　　微型案例 Mini Case ·· 14

概览 Overview	14
正文 Text	15
2.1 Types of Business Organization	15
2.2 Corporate Structure of the Company	17
2.3 Objectives of Financial Management	19
2.4 Separation of Ownership and Control	21
2.5 Agency Relationships	22
核心词汇 Core Words and Expressions	24
即时问答 Quick Quiz	25
思考与探索 Thinking and Exploration	26
汉译英 Translation	26
知识扩展 More Knowledge	27
相关网址 Useful Websites	34

第3章 诠释财务报表
TOPIC 3 Interpreting Financial Statements ······ 35

新闻视听 News in Media	35
名人名言 Wisdom	35
微型案例 Mini Case	35
概览 Overview	36
正文 Text	36
3.1 Basics of Annual Reports and Financial Statements	36
3.2 Balance Sheet	39
3.3 Income Statement	42
3.4 Statement of Retained Earnings	45
3.5 Statement of Cash Flow	46
核心词汇 Core Words and Expressions	49
即时问答 Quick Quiz	51
思考与探索 Thinking and Exploration	51
汉译英 Translation	52
知识扩展 More Knowledge	52
相关网址 Useful Websites	55

第 4 章 财务比率分析
TOPIC 4 Financial Ratio Analysis ··· 57

新闻视听 News in Media ·· 57
名人名言 Wisdom ··· 57
微型案例 Mini Case ··· 57
概览 Overview ··· 58
正文 Text ··· 58
    4.1   Financial Ratio Analysis ·· 58
    4.2   Liquidity Ratios ·· 60
    4.3   Debt Management Ratios ·· 63
    4.4   Asset Management Ratios ··· 66
    4.5   Profitability Ratios ·· 71
    4.6   Market Value Ratios ··· 74
    4.7   Uses and Limitations of Financial Ratio Analysis ··· 76
核心词汇 Core Words and Expressions ··· 77
即时问答 Quick Quiz ·· 78
思考与探索 Thinking and Exploration ·· 79
汉译英 Translation ··· 79
知识扩展 More Knowledge ··· 79
相关网址 Useful Websites ·· 80

第 5 章 货币时间价值与估价
TOPIC 5 Time Value of Money and Valuation ·· 81

新闻视听 News in Media ·· 81
名人名言 Wisdom ··· 81
微型案例 Mini Case ··· 82
概览 Overview ··· 83
正文 Text ··· 83
    5.1   Central Concepts in Financial Management ·· 83
    5.2   Simple vs. Compound Interest Rates and Future vs. Present Value ······················· 84
    5.3   Annuity ·· 86
    5.4   Valuation Fundamentals ··· 90

  5.5 Bond Valuation ·· 94

  5.6 Common Stock Valuation ·· 99

 核心词汇 Core Words and Expressions ·· 103

 即时问答 Quick Quiz ·· 105

 思考与探索 Thinking and Exploration ·· 105

 汉译英 Translation ··· 106

 知识扩展 More Knowledge ··· 107

 相关网址 Useful Websites ·· 107

第 6 章 风险与收益
TOPIC 6 Risk and Return ·· 108

 新闻视听 News in Media ··· 108

 名人名言 Wisdom ·· 108

 微型案例 Mini Case ··· 109

 概览 Overview ·· 109

 正文 Text ··· 110

  6.1 Introduction to Risk and Return ··· 110

  6.2 Efficient Market Hypothesis (EMH) ··· 114

  6.3 Portfolio Theory ·· 118

  6.4 Beta and Capital Asset Pricing Model ··· 122

  6.5 Arbitrage Pricing Theory ··· 125

 核心词汇 Core Words and Expressions ·· 126

 即时问答 Quick Quiz ·· 127

 思考与探索 Thinking and Exploration ·· 128

 汉译英 Translation ··· 128

 知识扩展 More Knowledge ··· 128

 相关网址 Useful Websites ·· 131

第 7 章 资本预算
TOPIC 7 Capital Budgeting ··· 132

 新闻视听 News in Media ··· 132

 名人名言 Wisdom ·· 132

微型案例 Mini Case	132
概览 Overview	133
正文 Text	133
7.1　Capital Investment Decisions	133
7.2　Guidelines for Estimating Project Cash Flows	135
7.3　Investment Rules	137
7.4　Business Practice	140
7.5　Analyzing Project Risk	141
7.6　Project Selection with Resource Constrains	143
7.7　Qualitative Factors and the Selection of Projects	144
7.8　The Post-Audit	145
核心词汇 Core Words and Expressions	147
即时问答 Quick Quiz	147
思考与探索 Thinking and Exploration	147
汉译英 Translation	148
知识扩展 More Knowledge	148
相关网址 Useful Websites	148

第8章　资本市场与资金筹集
TOPIC 8　Capital Market and Raising Funds · 149

新闻视听 News in Media	149
名人名言 Wisdom	149
微型案例 Mini Case	149
概览 Overview	150
正文 Text	150
8.1　Financial Markets	150
8.2　Investment Banks	153
8.3　The Decision to Go Public	154
8.4　Cost of Capital Concept	157
核心词汇 Core Words and Expressions	160
即时问答 Quick Quiz	161
思考与探索 Thinking and Exploration	161

XIII

汉译英 Translation ··· 161

　　知识扩展 More Knowledge ··· 161

　　相关网址 Useful Websites ··· 164

第 9 章　资本结构
TOPIC 9　Capital Structure ··· 165

　　新闻视听 News in Media ··· 165

　　名人名言 Wisdom ··· 165

　　微型案例 Mini Case ··· 165

　　概览 Overview ·· 167

　　正文 Text ·· 167

　　　9.1　The Choices: Types of Financing ·· 167

　　　9.2　The Financing Mix ·· 172

　　　9.3　Understanding Financial Risk ··· 173

　　　9.4　Capital Structure and the Value of a Firm ·· 174

　　　9.5　Checklist for Capital Structure Decisions ·· 179

　　核心词汇 Core Words and Expressions ··· 182

　　即时问答 Quick Quiz ··· 183

　　思考与探索 Thinking and Exploration ··· 184

　　汉译英 Translation ··· 184

　　知识扩展 More Knowledge ··· 184

　　相关网址 Useful Websites ··· 186

第 10 章　股利政策
TOPIC 10　Dividend Policy ··· 187

　　新闻视听 News in Media ··· 187

　　名人名言 Wisdom ··· 187

　　微型案例 Mini Case ··· 188

　　概览 Overview ·· 188

　　正文 Text ·· 189

　　　10.1　Dividends and Dividend Policy ·· 189

　　　10.2　The Dividend Puzzle ·· 192

10.3	Factors Influencing the Dividend Decision	195
10.4	Dividend Policies	197
10.5	Stock Repurchases	199

核心词汇 Core Words and Expressions ········· 201
即时问答 Quick Quiz ········· 201
思考与探索 Thinking and Exploration ········· 202
汉译英 Translation ········· 202
知识扩展 More Knowledge ········· 202
相关网址 Useful Websites ········· 204

第 11 章　营运资本管理
TOPIC 11　Working Capital Management ········· 205

新闻视听 News in Media ········· 205
名人名言 Wisdom ········· 205
微型案例 Mini Case ········· 205
概览 Overview ········· 206
正文 Text ········· 206

11.1	Introduction to Working Capital Management	206
11.2	Cash Management	207
11.3	Accounts Receivable Management	212
11.4	Inventory Management	216

核心词汇 Core Words and Expressions ········· 220
即时问答 Quick Quiz ········· 221
思考与探索 Thinking and Exploration ········· 221
汉译英 Translation ········· 222
知识扩展 More Knowledge ········· 222
相关网址 Useful Websites ········· 224

第 12 章　国际财务管理
TOPIC 12　International Financial Management ········· 225

新闻视听 News in Media ········· 225
名人名言 Wisdom ········· 225

XV

微型案例 Mini Case ······ 225

概览 Overview ······ 226

正文 Text ······ 226

 12.1 Introduction ······ 226

 12.2 Foreign Exchange Market ······ 230

 12.3 Exchange Rate Parity ······ 234

 12.4 Multinational Capital Budgeting ······ 237

 12.5 International Financial Decision ······ 239

 12.6 Working Capital Management ······ 239

 12.7 Hedging Currency Risk ······ 241

核心词汇 Core Words and Expressions ······ 244

即时问答 Quick Quiz ······ 245

思考与探索 Thinking and Exploration ······ 245

汉译英 Translation ······ 245

知识扩展 More Knowledge ······ 246

相关网址 Useful Websites ······ 249

参考文献 ······ 251

第 1 章
TOPIC 1

Introduction to Financial Management (1)
财务管理概述（1）

新闻视听
News in Media

How much is a trillion?

CNN's Christine Romans speaks to a math expert to break down how big a trillion dollars is.

本章新闻视听资料请扫二维码收听。

名人名言
Wisdom

Money begets (or breeds or gets) money.

——Anonymous

Boundless risk must pay for boundless gain.

——William Morris（1834—1896，British poet）

微型案例
Mini Case

Gree Electric Appliances is a Chinese major appliance manufacturer that mainly offers air conditioners. The company sells goods with payment received in advance, at the same time gets credit out of its suppliers. This business model enables Gree to maximize its occupation of downstream customers' as well as upstream suppliers' money. In this way, Gree has grown quickly and has been able to finance that growth internally by its efficient use of working capital and its profitability.

概览 Overview

Business firms make decisions every day. Virtually all business decisions have financial implications. Consequently, finance matters to everybody. We start our study of financial management by discussing the meaning of financial management and the role of the financial manager. We then discuss three major types of decisions: long-term investment decisions, long-term financing decisions and working capital management decisions.

正文 Text

1.1 Financial Management and Financial Manager

Financial management is an integrated decision-making process concerned with acquiring, financing and managing assets to accomplish some overall goal within a business entity. Other names for financial management include managerial finance, corporate finance, and business finance. Making financial decisions is an integral part of all forms and sizes of business organizations from small privately-held firms to large publicly-traded corporations.

The person associated with the financial management function is usually a top officer of the firm such as a vice president of finance or **chief financial officer (CFO)**. This individual typically reports directly to the president or the **chief executive officer (CEO)**. In today's rapidly changing environment, the financial manager must have the flexibility to adapt to external factors such as economic uncertainty, global competition, technological change, the volatility of interest and exchange rates, changes in laws and regulations, and ethical concerns. As the head of one of the major functional areas of the firm, the financial manager plays a pivotal leadership role in a company's overall efforts to achieve its goals.

The duties and responsibilities of the financial manager are far reaching. In broad terms, the two main functions of the financial manager concern acquiring and allocating funds among a firm's activities. This individual has policy-making duties regarding these functions. The financial manager also acts as a liaison between others in the finance department and management personnel from other departments.

To enable you to better understand the role of a financial manager, we will let you know where the financial manager belongs in the organizational structure of a company in the next topic.

1.2 Financial Management Decision

Financial management involves three major types of decisions: long-term investment decisions, long-term financing decisions and working capital management decisions. These decisions concern the acquisition and allocation of resources among the firm's various activities. The first two decisions are long term in nature and the third is short term. Managers should not consider these decisions on a piecemeal basis but as an integrated whole because they are seldom independent of one another. Investment decisions typically affect financing decisions and vice versa. For example, a decision to build a new plant or to buy new equipment requires other decisions on how to obtain the funds needed to finance the project and to manage the asset once acquired.

1.2.1 Investment Decisions

Long-term investment decisions involve determining the type and amount of assets that the firm wants to hold. That is, investing concerns allocating or using funds. The financial manager makes investment decisions about all types of assets — items on the left-hand side of the balance sheet. These decisions often involve buying, holding, reducing, replacing, selling and managing assets. The process of planning and managing a firm's long-term investments is called capital budgeting. Common questions involving

long-term investments include:
- In what lines of business should the firm engage?
- Should the firm acquire other companies?
- What sorts of property, plant and equipment should the firm hold?
- Should the firm modernize or sell an old production facility?
- Should the firm introduce a more efficient distribution system than the current one?

Making investment decisions requires applying a key principle of financial management. The investment principle states that the firm should invest in assets and projects yielding a return greater than the minimum acceptable **hurdle rate**. A hurdle rate is the minimum acceptable rate of return for investing resources in a project. The financial manager should set the hurdle rate to reflect the risk of the project with higher hurdle rates for riskier projects.

1.2.2 Financing Decisions

Long-term financing decisions involve the acquisition of funds needed to support long-term investments. Such decisions concern the firm's capital structure, which is the mix of long-term debt and equity the firm uses to finance its operations. These sources of financing are shown on the right-hand side of the balance sheet. Firms have much flexibility in choosing a capital structure.

Typical financing questions facing the financial manager include:
- Does the type of financing used make a difference?
- Is the existing capital structure the right one?
- How and where should the firm raise money?
- Should the firm use funds raised through its revenues?
- Should the firm raise money from outside the business?
- If the firm seeks external financing, should it bring in other owners or borrow money?

The financial manager can obtain the needed funds for its investments and operations either internally or externally. Internally generated funds represent the amount of earnings that the firm decides to retain after paying a cash dividend, if any, to its stockholders. Dividend policy is intimately connected to a firm's investment and financing decisions because the dividend-payout ratio determines the amount of earnings that a firm can retain. According to the dividend principle, a firm should return cash to the owners if there are not enough investments that earn the hurdle rate. For publicly traded firms, a firm has the option of returning cash to owners either through dividends or stock repurchases. The form of return depends largely on the characteristics of the firm's stockholders.

If the firm decides to raise funds externally, the financial manager can do so by incurring debts, such as through bank loans or the sale of bonds, or by selling ownership interests through a stock offering. The choice of financing method involves various **tradeoffs**. For example, a firm must repay debt with interest over a specific period without typically sharing control with the lender. By issuing common stock, the firm dilutes the control of current owners but does not have to repay the funds obtained from the stock sale.

When making financing decisions, managers should keep the financing principle in mind. The financing principle states that the financial manager should choose a **financing mix** that maximizes the value of the investments made and matches the financing to the assets being financed. Matching the cash inflows from the assets being financed with the cash outflows used to finance these assets reduces the potential risk.

1.2.3 Working Capital Management Decisions

So far we have focused on long-term investment and financing decisions. Now we turn to the day-to-day investment and financing decisions of a firm. Decisions involving a firm's short-term assets and liabilities refer to **working capital management**. **Net working capital** is defined as current assets minus current liabilities. The financial manager has varying degrees of operating responsibility for current assets and liabilities. Some key questions that the financial manager faces involving working capital management include:

- How much of a firm's total assets should the firm hold in each type of current asset such as cash, marketable securities, and inventory?

- How much credit should the firm grant to customers?
- How should the firm obtain needed short-term financing?

In summary, some of the more important concerns of financial management can be distilled into three questions:

1. What long-term investments should the firm undertake? (Investment decisions)

2. How should the firm raise money to fund these investments? (Financing decisions)

3. How should the firm manage its short-term assets and liabilities? (Working capital management decisions)

The financial manager's role is to help answer these and other important questions facing the firm. The balance-sheet model shown in Figure 1-1 is one way to graphically portray the three major types of decisions facing the financial manager and their effects on the firm.

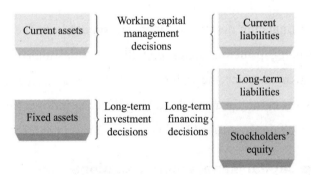

Figure 1-1 The balance-sheet model: Assets = Liabilities + Stockholders' Equity

As Figure 1-1 shows, the firm's long-term investment decisions concern the left-hand side of the balance sheet and the result in fixed assets. Fixed assets last for a long time and can result in tangible fixed assets, such as buildings, machinery and equipment, and intangible fixed assets, such as patents and trademarks. The firm's long-term financing decisions concern the right-hand side of the balance sheet. That is, the financial manager can obtain funds to pay for investments from creditors (long-term liabilities) or owners (stockholders' equity). Decisions involving short-lived assets and liabilities are working capital management decisions.

1.3 Risk-Return Tradeoff

At the heart of most financial decisions is the concern about two specific factors: risk and return. An underlying assumption of finance is that investors should demand compensation for bearing risk. According to the concept of **risk aversion**, investors should expect a higher return for taking on higher levels of risk. Although considerable debate exists over the precise model for estimating risk and return, few contest the notion of a **risk-return tradeoff**. When making financial decisions, managers should assess the potential risk and rewards associated with these decisions. In fact, the foundation for maximizing shareholder wealth lies in understanding tradeoffs between risk and return.

核心词汇 Core Words and Expressions

financial management 财务管理
decision-making 决策，决策的
acquire 获得，取得（在财务中有时指购买；名词形式是 acquisition，意为收购）
publicly traded corporations 公开上市公司、公众公司、上市公司（其他表达法如 listed corporation，public corporation，etc.）
vice president of finance 财务副总裁
chief financial officer (CFO) 首席财务官
chief executive officer (CEO) 首席执行官
pivotal 关键的，枢纽的
allocate （资源、权利等）配置（名词形式是 allocation，如 capital allocation，意为资本配置）
volatility 易变性，不稳定性（形容词形式是 volatile，意为可变的、不稳定的）
balance sheet 资产负债表

capital budgeting 资本预算
working capital management 营运资本管理
hurdle rate 门槛利率，最低报酬率
capital structure 资本结构
mix of debt and equity 负债与股票的组合
cash dividend 现金股利
stockholder 股东（也可以用 shareholder）
dividend policy 股利政策
dividend-payout ratio 股利支付比率
stock repurchase 股票回购（也可以用 stock buyback）
stock offering 股票发行
tradeoff 权衡，折中
common stock 普通股
current asset 流动资产
current liability 流动负债
marketable security 流动性证券，有价证券

inventory　存货
tangible fixed assets　有形固定资产
intangible fixed assets　无形固定资产
patent　专利
trademark　商标

creditor　债权人
stockholders' equity　股东权益
financing mix　融资组合（指负债与所有者权益的比例关系）
risk aversion　风险规避

即时问答 Quick Quiz

1. What are the responsibilities of the major financial managers?
2. What are the two major decisions made by financial managers?
3. Please explain the term of "finance". Explain how this field affects every organization.
4. What is the financial services area of finance?
5. Describe the fields of managerial finance. Compare and contrast this field with financial services.
6. Why is the study of managerial finance important regardless of the specific area of responsibility one has within the business firm?

思考与探索 Thinking and Exploration

Foreign Company A and Chinese company C planed to establish a joint venture B. A would invest US$3.5 million, while C US $1.5 million. The products of B would be exported totally with a foreign brand. To express its sincerity, C decided to give company D to B as a gift, which C had operated over ten years. Though similar to what B would produce, D's products were mainly sold on the domestic market. In addition, D's financial statements showed that the total assets were RMB100 million Yuan, among which accounts receivable were 40 million, and the rate of recovery estimated was 50%; the total liability was RMB–130 million Yuan. Besides, the manager of D claimed that the true value of D was higher than its book value because of its brand, distribution network, governance model, technique and so on. If you were in charge of company A, would you accept such a gift?

汉译英 Translation

如果你要创立一家生产皮鞋的公司，那么你首先要明确以下四个基本的公司财务问题。

第一，公司的目标是什么？

第二，公司将要采取怎样的长期投资战略？

第三，怎样筹措投资所需的资金？

第四，公司运营所需的短期现金流量是多少？

知识扩展 More Knowledge

与 Finance 有关的词汇和术语的解释

韦氏词典将"to finance"定义为"筹集或提供资本"（to raise or provide funds or capital for）。《华尔街日报》在其 Corporate Finance 的固定版面中将 Corporate Finance 定义为"为企业提供融资的业务"（business of financing businesses），这一定义基本上代表了金融实业界的看法。代表学界对 finance 的权威解释可参照《新帕尔格雷夫经济学大辞典》（The New Palgrave: A Dictionary of Economics）的"finance"词条。该词条由美国著名财务专家斯蒂芬·A. 罗斯（Stephen A. Ross）撰写，该词条称"finance"以其不同的中心点和方法论而成为经济学的一个分支，其中心点是资本市场的运营、资本资产的供给和定价；其方法论是使用相近的替代物给财务契约和工具定价。罗斯概括了"finance"的四大主题：有效市场、收益和风险、期权定价理论和公司理财。罗斯的观点集中体现了西方学者界定"finance"倚重微观内涵及资本市场的特质。

在英文中，"finance"一词与不同的修饰词搭配，翻译成中文时有不同的译法。现归纳如下。

finance 通常有三种译法：财务、金融、财政。

（1）一般情况下，与企业相关的理财范畴翻译成"财务"，相关的术语如下：

financial management　　财务管理　　　　corporate finance　　公司理财

managerial finance　　管理财务　　　　　business finance　　企业财务

（2）一般情况下，与货币市场、资本市场等相关的理财范畴翻译成"金融"，相关的术语如下：

financial market　　金融市场　　　　　　financial institution　　金融机构

financial instrument　　金融工具　　　　financial derivative　　金融衍生工具

（3）一般情况下，与宏观经济政策有关的理财范畴翻译成"财政"，相关的术语如下：

public finance　　公共财政

用英文表达"融资"这一行为时，用 finance 的动名词形式：financing。

Finance 的学科领域划分

按照理财主体的不同，理财学科可以划分为：①公共理财，或者叫财政，其主体是政府（作为公共事务管理者），一般称为公共财政（public finance）；②公司理财，研究的是营利性组织的理财，一般称为企业理财、公司理财等；③非营利组织的理财，研究的是不以营利为目的的组织的理财活动，一般称为非营利组织理财或者非营利组织财务管理；④家庭或者个人理财（personal finance）。

目前，西方企业理财学界一般把理财学科分为以下三个部分：金融市场学、投资学和公司理财学。其中，金融市场学是研究市场经济条件下金融市场运行机制及各主体行为规律的学科；投资学是专门研究资金投放的学科，它是不同主体理财中共有的一个环节；公司理财学是专门研究公司如何有效地筹集和配置财务资源和公正地处理财务关系的学科。

财务经济学（financial economics）与财务管理学（financial management）

财务学作为研究企业自身独立的资本配置活动的学科，主要包括两个分支：作为理论基础的财务经济学和作为应用技术和方法的财务管理学（或者称为管理财务学，managerial finance）。

财务经济学作为企业财务的基础理论，凸显出微观经济学的基本属性，它主要借助微观经济学的基本原理和分析方法，研究企业资本筹措和投放及其配置效率的问题。在企业财务理论中，作为主体的公司属于微观经济学中"厂商"的范畴，它被置于一种特殊的市场——金融市场，通过在供给、需求、竞争、成本、定价和效用等领域的分析和决策，最终完成有限的财务资源的合理配置。

财务管理学则涉及理财中的政策和控制问题，包括财务经济学基本原理的实际应用。财务管理学属于企业管理学的分支，与企业生产与运作管理、企业营销管理和企业人力资源管理等并列。企业财务管理实际上就是企业的理财行为，即为了实现企业资本有效配置而努力的过程。

国际上通行的财务管理与会计资格认证

1. 美国特许金融分析师（Chartered Financial Analyst，CFA）

美国特许金融分析师是指从事证券投资决策管理的从业人员，主要包括基金经理、证券分析师、财务总监、投资顾问、投资银行家和交易员等。特许金融分析师资格被称为"华尔街的入场券"。

相关网址：https://www.cfainstitute.org/

2. 国际财务管理师（International Finance Manager，IFM）

国际财务管理师是国际财务管理专业领域的一套职业资格认证体系，由国际财务管理协会（International Financial Management Association，IFMA）创建并在全球推行。

相关网址：http://www.fma.org

3. 英国会计师

英国会计师是指属于英国本土会计师专业团体的会员统称。英国是世界上最早创立会计师制度的国家，早在1854年，苏格兰特许会计师协会（Institute of Chartered Accountants of Scotland，ICAS）便在英国苏格兰的爱丁堡市创立。

除此之外，英国也是会计师专业发展最发达的地区。由于英国政府采用会计师专业团体多元竞争的特色，促使在英国境内出现了世界上两大会计师公会：欧洲最大的会计师公会——英格兰及威尔士特许会计师协会（ICAEW）；世界上规模最大的国际专业会计师公会——特许公认会计师公会（Association of Chartered Certified Accountants，ACCA）。

英国特许公认会计师公会成立于1904年，是目前世界上领先的专业会计师团体，也是国际上海外学员最多、学员规模发展最快的专业会计师组织。英国立法许可ACCA会员从事审计、投资顾问和破产执行的工作。ACCA会员资格得到欧盟立法以及许多国家公司法的承认。

相关网址：https://www.accaglobal.com/uk/en.html

4. 加拿大特许专业会计师（Chartered Professional Accountants of Canada，CPA Canada）

它是由加拿大特许专业会计师协会颁发的。目前，加拿大特许专业会计师协会是加拿大唯一的专业会计师团体，于2014年10月完成了本国会计师行业的整合。其前身是加拿大原三大会计师协会：加拿大特许会计师协会（CICA）、加拿大注册会计师协会（CGA-Canada）、加拿大管理会计师协会（CMA Canada）。现在的加拿大特许专业会计师协会是全球规模最大的会计师团体之一，拥有超过20万会员。CPA Canada是加拿大会计行业的唯一专衔。

相关网址：https://www.cpacanada.ca/

5. 中国注册会计师（Chinese Institute of Certificate Public Accountants，CICPA）

中国注册会计师是指依法取得中国注册会计师证书并接受委托从事审计和会计咨询、会计服务业等的执业人员。中国注册会计师目前还不是国际上通行的会计资格，但是中国注册会计师协会目前正在与国际公认的会计组织进行合作，并取得了一些进展。

相关网址：https://www.aicpa.org/

6. 美国注册管理会计师（Certified Management Accountant，CMA）

美国注册管理会计师是美国管理会计师协会（Institute of Management Accountants，IMA）所建立的专业认证制度，是全球针对管理会计及财务管理领域的权威认证。美国注册管理会计师（CMA）与美国注册会计师（USCPA）、金融特许分析师（CFA）一起并称为美国财会领域的国际三大黄金认证。

相关网址：https://www.imachina.org.cn/

7. CIMA 特许管理会计师

它是由特许管理会计师公会（The Chartered Institute of Management Accountants，CIMA）颁发的。CIMA 是全球最大的国际性管理会计师组织，同时它也是国际会计师联合会（IFAC）的创始成员之一。CIMA 专注于管理会计师的培养和发展，重在面向未来，履行预测、决策、规划、控制和考核的职能，在企业界享有很高的声望，被誉为 21 世纪最完善的商业培训体系。

相关网址：https://www.cimaglobal.com/

会计师、注册会计师与财务领域专业资格的区别

会计师的服务对象是企业外部的资产委托人，其总体目标是满足外部利益相关人对企业财务状况和经营成果信息的需要，会计师的主要职责是定期编制会计报告，侧重于经济活动的核算与披露。

注册会计师的工作是一种社会公信行为，其主要职责是鉴证企业的财务报告，出具审计报告，判断企业财务报告是否符合公认的会计准则。

以国际财务管理师为例，服务对象是企业经营决策者，总体工作目标是通过资金运作来提高企业的总体价值。而美国特许金融分析师则主要服务于证券投资的分析、决策与管理。

相关网址
Useful Websites

一些实务类英文杂志网址：
Financial Management（FM） https://www.fm-magazine.com/
Journal of Applied Corporate Finance（JACF） http://jacf-pub.com/
Strategic Finance（SF） https://sfmagazine.com/

第 2 章
TOPIC 2

Introduction to Financial Management (2)
财务管理概述（2）

新闻视听
News in Media

If people have money, they may buy shares of a company. This means they have a stake in that company. They become stakeholders. Why people want to invest in the stock market? Please listen to the radio.

本章新闻视听资料请扫二维码收听。

名人名言
Wisdom

How do we want the firms in our economy to measure their own performance? How do we want them to determine what is better versus worse? Most economists would answer simply that managers have a criterion for evaluating performance and deciding between alternative courses of action, and that the criterion should be the maximization of the long-term market value of the firm . . . This Value Maximization proposition has its roots in 200 years of research in economics and finance.

——Michael C Jensen.
Value Maximization, Stakeholder Theory, and the Corporate Objective Function[J]. *Journal of Applied Corporate Finance*, 2001(14):8.

It seems that Wang Jianlin only owns 0.24% of Wanda Group. According to the equity structure, Dalian Hexing Investment Co. directly holds 99.76% of the total issued equity of Wanda Group. As we can see that Wang Jianlin holds 98% of the equity of Dalian Hexing, and the remaining 2% is held by Wang Sicong, the son of Wang Jianlin. So Wang's family indirectly owns 99.76% of Wanda Group through the control of Dalian Hexing. It means that the Wang's family control 100% of Wanda Group.

It is an example of the separation of cash flow and voting rights. Under the normal shareholding structure, the parent company's cash flow rights and voting rights to the subsidiaries are consistent. However, when there is a pyramid-shaped holding or cross-holding, the separation of cash flow and voting rights will occur. The ultimate controller can use less cash flow to achieve substantial control over the target company, thus creating a strong incentive to infringe the minority shareholders. Therefore, the greater the separation of the two powers, the more serious the implicit agency conflict.

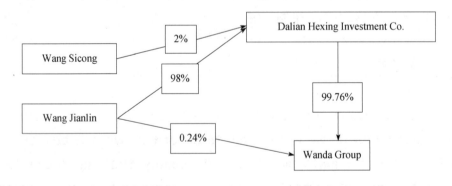

On the basis of understanding the definition of financial management and financial decision, we then turn to the forms of business and organizational structure of a company. To make effective business decisions, the financial manager should have a single-valued objective function. Thus, we advocate the maximization of shareholder wealth as the goal of financial management. Finally, we discuss potential agency problems involving the separation of ownership and management and mechanisms for aligning the interests of owners and managers.

正文 Text

2.1 Types of Business Organization

When a business is being established, it is important to consider how it will be structured in terms of the law. This is an important decision as the legal structure affects the financial risk faced by the owners of the company.

There are three possible legal structures of an organization.

2.1.1 Sole Proprietorship

This is the simplest form of business structure. A **sole proprietorship** is an unincorporated business owned by one person. Sole proprietorship includes small services run by an individual, retail stores and professional practices. The advantage of this structure is that it is easy to form and there is no double taxation. The drawbacks are that it is non-transferable, has a limited life and a limited pool of funds, and the proprietor has unlimited liability, which can result in losses that exceed the money he or she invested in the company (creditors may even be able to seize a proprietor's house or other personal property).

2.1.2 Partnership

A **partnership** is a business owned by two or more individuals (called **partners**). Partnerships may operate under different degrees of formality, ranging from informal, oral understandings to formal agreements filed with the secretary of the state in which the partnership was formed. Partnership agreement, whether formal or informal, define the ways any profits and losses are shared between partners. Partners have unlimited liability and their ownership in the partnership is not transferable. Partnerships have a limited life in that the death or departure of a partner dissolves the partnership structure.

Regarding liability, the partners can potentially lose all of their personal assets, even if the assets are not invested in the business, because under partnership law, each partner is liable for the business's debt. Therefore, if any partner is unable to meet his or her prorate liability in the event that the partnership goes bankrupt, the remaining partners must make good on the unsatisfied claims, drawing on their personal assets to the extent necessary. To avoid this, it is possible to limit the liabilities of some of the partners by establishing a **limited partnership**, wherein certain partners are designated as **general partners** and others as **limited partners**. In a limited partnership, the limited partners are liable only for the amount of their investment in the partnership, while the general partners have unlimited liability. However, the limited partners typically have no control, which rests solely with the general partners, and their returns are likewise limited.

2.1.3 Corporation

A **corporation** is a legal entity separate from its owners. This means that the corporation can own assets, enter into contracts, sue and be sued. Being a separate legal entity also implies that corporate income is taxable, thus giving rise to double taxation, i.e., corporate tax on profits plus personal tax on after-corporate-tax profits distributed to shareholders (the exception being a full imputation system). There is a **separation of ownership** (shareholders) **and control** (managers). Shareholders who hold shares in a corporation own the corporation. Shares represent a claim to corporate profits, which are distributed in the form of dividends, share repurchases, or acquisition payout, (e.g., **management buyouts** and **tender offers**). Shareholders have limited liability.

There are different types of corporations, depending on how their shares are exchanged:

- Shares in some corporations are traded in an organized equity market, such as the New York Stock Exchange. Companies that are traded in such a market are called public corporations since shares can be bought by anyone in the public. To be traded in an exchange, companies must meet certain financial standards and must provide financial information to the public. Public corporations have previously issued securities through **Initial Public Offerings (IPO)**, and these are subsequently traded on the open market.

- Corporations which do not wish to provide financial information to the public or which do not need or want to sell their shares to the general public are called private corporations.
- Corporations whose shares are held by a few individuals are called closely held corporations.

There are actually several different types of corporations in western countries. In the US, professionals such as doctors, lawyers, and accountants often form a **Professional Corporation (PC)** or a **Professional Association (PA)**. These provide most of incorporation's benefits but do not relieve the participants of professional malpractice. Indeed, the primary motivation behind the professional corporation is to provide a way for groups of professions to incorporate and thus avoid certain types of unlimited liability, yet still being held responsible for professional liability.

2.2 Corporate Structure of the Company

As a Finance Manager, in order to understand what your role is, you need to know where you belong in the **organizational structure** of a company.

Most large corporations have the following basic structure.

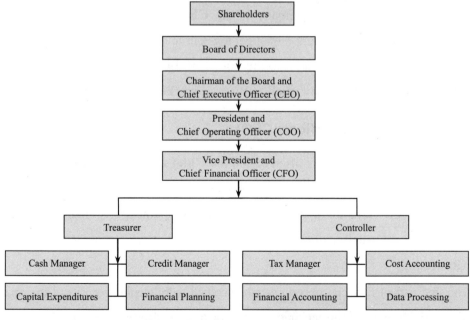

Figure 2-1 Corporate Structure of the Company

2.2.1 Shareholders

At the top of the company structure are the shareholders who are the owners of the company. For a small company, the owners of the company are often also the managers of the company. If you own a small business you are likely to be involved in the day-to-day operations of the company. However, for large companies, there is typically a separation of ownership from management. For example, while the millions of shareholders of Singapore Airlines are the owners of the company, they are not involved in the decisions such as which routes to fly on and how much to charge customers for each trip. In effect, they hire managers to run the company for them.

2.2.2 Board of Directors

The **board of directors** do not take part in the day-to-day activities of the company, but supervise management as representatives of the shareholders. The board includes some members of top management (**executive directors**), but should also include individuals from outside the company (**non-executive directors**). The board will elect a **Chairperson**.

2.2.3 Chief Executive Officer (CEO)

The top manager of the company is the **Chief Executive Officer (CEO)**. Of course, the millions of shareholders cannot get together to decide on who to hire, so instead, they choose a board of directors to do this for them. Below the CEO are the managers for various parts of the company, such as finance, marketing and operations.

2.2.4 Chief Financial Officer (CFO)

The manager for finance is often called the **Chief Financial Officer (CFO)**. This individual is responsible for all financial aspects of the company and for the financial implications of the company's strategy. For large companies, the financial operations of the company are usually split into two parts: Controller and Treasurer.

Controller

The first part of financial operations is concerned with keeping records of the financial activities of the company. The accounting department is headed by the **Controller**. Because the accounting function requires specialized knowledge of financial records, most individuals in the accounting department have majored in accounting.

Treasurer

The other part of financial operations is the financial management of the company, which includes cash management, securities issuance, investor relations, capital expenditure and financial planning. The treasury department is headed by the Treasurer. Those in the Treasury Department often major in finance or accounting, or have an advanced business degree, such as a **Master of Financial Management**, a Master of Accounting, or a **Master of Business Administration (MBA)**.

2.3 Objectives of Financial Management

So far we have seen that financial managers are primarily concerned with long-term investment and financing decisions as well as with working capital management decisions within a firm. To make effective decisions, the financial manager needs a clear objective or goal to serve as a standard for evaluating performance and deciding between alternative courses of actions. Without such a criterion, the financial manager would be unable to keep score — that is, to measure better from worse.

What should be the fundamental purpose of a business firm, specifically a corporation? More directly, what should be the goal of financial management? The number of potential goals is extensive. A few possibilities include maximizing revenues, profits, earnings per share, returns, market share, or social good; minimizing costs; maintaining steady earnings growth; avoiding financial distress and bankruptcy; and surviving. Each of these possibilities has serious defects as a corporate goal. For example, profit maximization focuses on accounting profits, lacks a time dimension, and ignores risk. Although much division of opinion exists on the goal of financial management, two leading contenders are stakeholder theory and value (wealth) maximization.

2.3.1 Stakeholder Theory

Stakeholder theory is the main contender to value maximization as the corporate goal. Stakeholder theory asserts that managers should make decisions that take into account the interests of all of a firm's stakeholders. Such stakeholders include not only financial claimholders but also employees, managers, customers, suppliers, local communities, and the government. The major problem with stakeholder theory is that it involves multiple objectives. Telling the financial manager to maximize multiple objectives, some of which may be conflicting, would leave that manager with no way to make a reasoned decision. That is, corporate managers cannot effectively serve many masters. Purposeful behavior requires the existence of a single-valued objective function.

2.3.2　Value or Wealth Maximization

Most corporate financial theorists agree that the primary corporate goal is to maximize long-term firm value or wealth. Some dissertation exists on whether the criterion should be the maximization of market value of the stockholders or that of the firm. Maximization of shareholder wealth focuses only on stockholders whereas maximization of firm value encompasses all financial claimholders including common stockholders, debt holders, and preferred stockholders.

Because common stockholders are the firm's most important stakeholders, the financial manager has a fiduciary responsibility to act in their best interests. From the stockholders' perspective, a good management decision would lead to an increase in the value of the stock. This is because investors generally prefer more wealth to less. Thus, the financial goal of the firm is to maximize shareholders' wealth as reflected in the market price of the stock. The term "shareholders" refers to the firm's current owners or stockholders. For non-publicly traded firms, the objective in decision making is to maximize firm value.

In practice, this goal means that the financial manager can best serve business owners by identifying goods and services that add value to the firm because the marketplace desires and values the firm's offerings. This single-valued objective serves as a prerequisite for rational behavior within an organization. In fact, maximizing shareholders' wealth has become the premier business mantra.

Why focus on maximizing **share price**? First, using stock price maximization as an objective function permits making definitive statements about the best way to allocate resources and to finance them. Second, stock prices are a highly observable measure that can be used to evaluate the performance of publicly held corporations. No competing measure can provide as comprehensive a measure of a firm's standing. Stock price takes into account present and future earnings per share; the timing, duration and risk of these earnings; the firm's dividend policy; and other factors affecting the stock price. The market price of the firm's stock is a measure of the owners' economic well-being. Finally, stock prices reflect the long-run effects of decisions made by the firm.

Does a short-term increase or decrease in a firm's stock price mean that management is doing a good or poor job? Not necessarily. Many factors that influence stock prices are beyond management's control. Thus, management can only partially influence the stock price of the firm. Despite this difficulty, managers can still strive to maximize stockholders' wealth in the context of the current economic and social environment.

Shareholders' wealth maximization rests on several assumptions. The corporate objective function assumes that managers operate in the best interests of stockholders, not themselves, and do not attempt to expropriate wealth from lenders to benefit stockholders.

Shareholders' wealth maximization also assumes that managers do not take actions to deceive financial markets in order to boost the price of the firm's stock. Another assumption is that managers act in a socially responsible manner and do not create unreasonable costs to society in pursuit of shareholders' wealth maximization. This implies that the financial manager should not take illegal or unethical actions to increase the value of the equity owners. Given these assumptions, shareholders' wealth maximization is consistent with the best interests of stakeholders and society in the long run.

2.4 Separation of Ownership and Control

Modern-day companies are characterized by a separation of ownership and control. That is, the entity which owns the company (shareholders) is often not the one that controls the company's resources (management).

- Professional managers would be expected to have specialized knowledge and therefore **superior ability** to run the business (theory of specialization).

- To grow to an optimal size in terms of business **efficiency**, the financial resources of many households may have to be pooled.
- In an uncertain economic environment, owners will prefer to **diversify** their risks across many companies. Efficient diversification is difficult to achieve without separation of ownership and management.
- The "**learning curve**" or "**going concern**" effect. If the business was sold and the previous owner was not the manager, the management staff will continue in their position and work for the new owner. If the owner is also the manager, the new owner will have to obtain detailed knowledge of the business from the previous owner in order to manage the business competently.

The four major downsides of the separation of ownership and management are:

- The **agency problem**—the costs incurred in aligning the objectives of management with those of the owners.
- The **free-riding** problem—shareholders leave it to others to collect information and incur the cost thereof.
- Shareholders typically own only a small fraction of the company, which also leads to increased costs of information gathering.
- The increased **information asymmetry** between management and shareholders and between various shareholder groups, such as retail investors and institutional investors. Regulation (e.g. "timely and public disclosure of share price sensitive information") is vital in reducing such information asymmetries.

2.5 Agency Relationships

Due to the separation of ownership and control, there is an **agency relationship** between the shareholders and the management of the company. Shareholders (as owners) essentially give management the authority to represent them in dealing with others. This relationship is known as the **principal-agent** or agency relationship, which is an explicit or implicit arrangement where an agent acts on behalf of a principal. Managers (agents) are entrusted to look after the interests of shareholders (principals).

2.5.1 What is an agency problem

The separation of management from ownership in a company could result in conflicts of interest as managers make decisions that are not in line with the goal of shareholders' wealth maximization. In reality, managers may ignore the interests of shareholders, and choose instead to make investment and financing decisions that benefit themselves. Agency problems are said to result from this divergence in interest. Some examples of agency problems are:

- Managers may waste corporate cash and resources by engaging in negative **net present value (NPV)** acquisitions or investments to satisfy their desire to build an empire.
- Less ominous, but no less costly, managers may squander corporate funds on excessively lavish corporate offices and jets.
- More recently managers have been known to increase share prices (not value) by using "**creative accounting**", so as to exercise their **stock options** (e.g. Enron).

These types of managerial actions are directly attributable to the separation of ownership and control. Given widely dispersed share ownership in today's modern company, it is virtually impossible for shareholders to monitor the day-to-day actions of managers.

2.5.2 What are agency costs

Agency costs are the total costs resulting from the agency problem. Agency costs are incurred when:

- management takes actions that negatively influence the wealth of shareholders, or when.
- the shareholders monitor the management's actions to ensure compliance.

As defined by Jensen and Meckling (1976), agency costs comprise the following:

- **Bonding costs**   costs of contractual agreements between shareholders and management (such as the cost of preparing periodic financial reports).
- **Monitoring costs**   costs associated with monitoring management (such as the cost of employing auditors).
- **Residual costs**   any other costs associated with the agency problem.

2.5.3 Practical solutions to the agency problem

There are several mechanisms that help to ensure that managerial actions are consistent with shareholders' interests. These are just some examples:

- Equity-based managerial compensation schemes such as stock options and shares. However, options have recently been blamed for accounting irregularities in the case of companies such as Enron, Merck, Xerox and WorldCom.
- Election of independent outside members to the board of directors to ensure that the board represents the interests of shareholders.
- Threat of dismissal of management.
- As a last resort, the threat of a **hostile takeover**. Inefficient management usually leads to a falling stock price which, in turn, encourages outside investors to take over the company and replace management.

核心词汇
Core Words and Expressions

business　企业、商业、业务
financial risk　财务风险（有时也指金融风险）
sole proprietorship　私人业主制企业
partnership　合伙制企业
limited partnership　有限合伙制企业
partner　合伙人
limited partner　有限责任合伙人
general partner　一般合伙人
separation of ownership and control　所有权与经营权分离
claim　（根据权利提出）要求，要求权，主张，要求而得到的东西
management buyout　管理层收购
tender offer　（美）要约收购（美国称 tender offer；英国称 takeover bid）

New York Stock Exchange　纽约股票交易所
financial standards　财务准则
initial public offering (IPO)　首次公开发行
private corporation　私募公司，未上市公司
closely held corporation　控股公司
shareholder　股东（也可以是 stockholder）
board of directors　董事会
executive director　执行董事
non-executive director　非执行董事
chairperson　主席（chairman or chairwoman）
controller　主计长
treasurer　司库
Master of Financial Management　财务管理专业硕士
Master of Accounting　会计学硕士

Master of Business Administration (MBA)
　工商管理硕士
revenue　收入
profit　利润
earnings per share　每股盈余
return　回报
market share　市场份额
social good　社会福利
financial distress　财务困境
stakeholder theory　利益相关者理论
value (wealth) maximization　价值（财富）
　最大化
common stockholder or shareholder　普通
　股股东（也可以是 ordinary stockholder
　or shareholder）
debt holder　债权人（也可以是 creditor）
preferred stockholder or shareholder　优先
　股股东（英国人用 preference stockholder
　or shareholder）
well-being　福利
diversify　多样化

learning curve　学习曲线
going concern　持续的
agency problem　代理问题
free-riding problem　搭便车问题
information asymmetry　信息不对称
retail investor　散户投资者（为自己买卖
　证券而不是为任何公司或机构进行投
　资的个人投资者）
institutional investor　机构投资者
agency relationship　代理关系
principal-agent or agency relationship
　委托-代理关系（代理关系）
net present value (NPV)　净现值
creative accounting　创造性会计，寻机性
　会计
stock option　股票期权
agency cost　代理成本
bonding cost　契约成本
monitoring costs　监督成本
takeover　接管

即 时 问 答
Quick Quiz

1. What are the advantages and disadvantages of corporate organization?
2. Explain the differences between the CFO's responsibilities and the treasurer's and controller's responsibilities?
3. Explain why each of the following may not be appropriate corporate goals:
　a. Increase market share
　b. Minimize costs
　c. Underprice any competitors
　d. Expand profits

4. Vocabulary test. Explain the differences between:

   a. Real and financial assets.

   b. Capital budgeting and financing decisions.

   c. Closely held and public corporations.

   d. Limited and unlimited liabilities.

   e. Corporation and partnership.

5. In most large corporations, ownership and management are separated. What are the main implications of this separation?

6. What are agency costs and what causes them?

7. What are the three basic forms of business organization? Which form is most common? Which form is dominant in terms of business receipts and net profits? Why?

8. List three reasons why profit maximization is not consistent with wealth maximization.

9. What is risk? Why must both risk and return be considered by the financial manager?

思考与探索
Thinking and Exploration

How do financial managers create value? What personalities should one possess to be a successful CFO?

Try to search the profiles of some successful CFOs in the real business world and discuss skills and capacities needed for their positions.

汉译英
Translation

格力电器混合所有制改革落地，治理结构优化

2019年4月1日，格力电器发布公告，控股股东格力集团拟转让公司总股本15%的股票。10月29日，公司确定最终受让方为高瓴资本旗下的珠海明骏。12月2日，公司发布临时停牌公告，与最终受让方珠海明骏签署股权转让协议。该公告称，高瓴资本一贯坚持以原有管理层为主导，预计新的大股东将与原核心管理层较快融合，展开紧密合作。同时，公司原国企性质变更，在充分竞争的家电行业，公司在资本市场上将更加灵活多元。公告中还称，预期公司较竞争对手稍弱的治理结构及激励机制将得到优化。

第2章 财务管理概述(2)
TOPIC 2 Introduction to Financial Management(2)

知识扩展
More Knowledge

IPO

首次公开发行（Initial Public Offerings，IPO）又称"首次公开募股"，指企业通过证券交易所首次公开向投资者出售股票，以期募集用于企业发展资金的过程。通常，上市公司的股份是根据向相应证券委员会出具的招股书或登记声明中约定的条款，通过经纪商或做市商进行销售。一般来说，首次公开上市完成后，这家公司就可以申请到证券交易所或报价系统挂牌交易。

Board of Directors

董事会（Board of Directors）是管理公司事务的领导机构，它通常由公司的投资者（股东）选举产生。董事会的主要成员一般由公司的内部成员出任，有时也特邀公司的外部成员参加。董事会受投资者（股东）委托对外代表公司，对内有权任免公司的高级职员、决定公司的重大事务。董事会由董事组成，其成员为3~13人。董事的任期由公司章程规定，各个公司可能有所不同，但每届任期不得超过3年。董事任期届满，连选可连任。董事在任期届满前，股东大会不得无故解除其职务。

董事会行使的职权包括：①负责召集股东大会，并向股东报告工作；②执行股东大会的决议；③决定公司的经营计划和投资方案；④制订公司的年度财务预算方案、决算方案；⑤制订公司的利润分配方案和弥补亏损方案；⑥制订公司增加或者减少注册资本的方案；⑦拟订公司合并、分立、变更公司形式、解散的方案；⑧决定公司内部管理机构的设置；⑨聘任或者解聘公司经理（总经理），根据总经理的提名，聘任或者解聘公司副经理、财务负责人，决定其报酬事项；⑩制订公司的基本管理制度。

独立董事、执行董事与非执行董事

董事会代表公司全部所有者掌握着任命经理、重大投资、合并和收购等一系列重大公司决策的控制权，但董事多由控股股东或其代表担任，他们实际上听命于内部股东，而做出有损外部股东利益的事情，这样的董事会不能有效地代表全体所有者的利益。为了在董事会中建立起对大股东产生抗衡作用的力量，独立董事（independent director）制度就应运而生了。1977年经美国证监会批准，纽约股票交易所引入一项新条例，要求本国的每家上市公司"在不迟于1978年6月30日以前，设立并维持一个全部由独立董事组成的审计委员会，这些独立董事不得与管理层有任何会影响他们作为委员会成员独立判断的关系"。之后，英国于1991年、中国香港特别行政区于1993年分别引入了独立董事制度。

针对我国上市公司长期受计划经济的影响和其特殊的股权结构，法人治理结构很不完善，中小股东的利益得不到有效保护，所有者缺位导致经营者的监督流于形式，中国证监会于 2001 年 8 月正式发布了《关于在上市公司建立独立董事制度的指导意见》（证监发〔2001〕102 号），正式引入独立董事制度。文件要求，上市公司董事会成员中应当有 1/3 以上为独立董事，其中应当至少包括一名会计专业人士；各境内外上市公司应当在 2002 年 6 月 30 日前修改公司章程、聘任独立董事。独立董事理论上是指除了董事身份外与公司没有任何其他契约关系的董事，他们既不是公司的雇员或亲朋好友，也不是公司的供应商、经销商、资金提供者，或者向公司提供法律、会计、审计和管理咨询等服务的机构职员或代表。独立董事与公司没有任何可能影响其对公司决策和事务行使独立判断的关系，也不受其他董事的控制和影响。独立董事可以独立发表自己的观点，对公司的董事会决策包括一些重大的问题独立发表意见。

与独立董事概念相近的是外部董事和非执行董事，它们均是指本人目前不是公司雇员的董事。外部董事是美国的称谓，非执行董事是英国的称谓。与外部董事或非执行董事相对应的是那些既是董事会成员又在公司内担任管理职务的董事，这类董事被称为内部董事或执行董事。

外部董事或非执行董事并不都是独立的，只有那些满足独立董事条件的外部董事或非执行董事才属于独立董事。非执行外部董事和非执行董事称为关联外部董事，这些董事虽然不是公司雇员，但与公司存在这样或那样不符合独立性的关系，例如，他们可能是本公司的大股东、供货商或经销商的代表、退休不久的高级管理人员、董事长或总经理的亲戚和至交。

中外 CFO、总会计师与财务总监职位辨析[一]

在我国企业的高级财务管理职位中，首席财务官（Chief Financial Officer，CFO）、财务总监与总会计师这三种制度同时并存，经常有人混同使用，但实际上这三者不等同，并不是同义词，他们之间既有联系又有区别。他们不仅字面表述不同，而且各自的历史渊源、本质、在公司治理中的地位、职责定位等方面亦存在差别。

CFO 源自一些国外企业，最早出现于 20 世纪 70 年代。CFO 是地位显赫的公司高级管理职位，在公司治理和价值创造中扮演着重要角色，他们同时进入董事决策层和经理执行层，以股东价值创造为基础参与公司战略的制定与实施。CFO 同时管辖首席信息官（Chief Information Officer，CIO）、主计长（Controller）和司库（Treasurer）。CFO 的重要职责就是通过资源配置实现企业的战略目标和长期发展，因此，CFO 应

[一] 刘媛媛. 中外 CFO、总会计师与财务总监职位辨析[N]. 财会信报，2006-7-5.

第 2 章 财务管理概述(2)
TOPIC 2 Introduction to Financial Management(2)

该是企业战略的管理者，代表出资者实施企业外部资本控制并向股东和董事会负责。在美国发生了安然、世通、安达信等系列财务丑闻之后，美国的有关法规规定 CFO 应当分别向 CEO 和审计委员会汇报工作。美国企业的 CFO 在制定和实施公司战略方面发挥着极其重要的作用。由于美国公司的财务管理已经达到相当高的水平，已没有降低成本的空间，因此，CFO 的主要压力集中在为公司寻求进一步发展的良机而必须解决的一些财务问题上。相对而言，欧洲企业的 CFO 仍然将成本控制列为首要任务。对我国来说，CFO 是舶来品，采用 CFO 这一称谓的主要是一些网络公司和高新技术企业，目前越来越多的国内公司采用 CFO 这一称谓。

总会计师的提法源自苏联的计划经济体制，当时总会计师是一个既对国家负责又对厂长（经理）负责的职位。进入市场经济之后，我国企业一般都是在对总经理负责这一含义上定位总会计师的职责。国务院 1990 年发布的《总会计师条例》对总会计师的定位是"总会计师是单位行政领导成员，协助单位主要行政领导人工作，对单位主要行政领导负责。凡设置总会计师的单位，在单位行政领导成员中，不设与总会计师职权重叠的副职"。《中华人民共和国会计法》（以下简称《会计法》）明确规定，国有独资和国有资产占控股地位或主导地位的大中型企业必须设置总会计师。总会计师制度是中国经济管理的重要制度。总会计师制度的建立是企业经营管理、经济核算的自然需要。随着企业的建立、经济核算工作的开展，就必然会有会计，会计的总管即总会计师。总会计师是总经理的理财助手、经营参谋，他由总经理提名，通过一定程序任命，与经营者利益完全一致。总会计师代表企业管理当局，是经理级财务管理人员，由总经理任命，对总经理负责。总会计师的职能是负责企业的日常管理，负责企业内部管理控制。总会计师侧重于财务管理和会计核算。在西方国家，总会计师更多地被称为主计长、会计长、会计经理或会计负责人，这一职位的主要工作是主管企业会计工作，向财务总监汇报工作。

财务总监制度起源于西方国家。二战前后，西方国家的国有企业有了一定的发展，一般是能代表国家的财政部门或主管部门在人才市场上选择总经理，由总经理代为管理国有企业，并授权总经理选择合适的总会计师等高级管理人员组成经理层，负责管理生产经营。由于所有权与经营权的分离，这些高级管理人员作为经理层在目标、利益和行为等方面与所有者存在很大差异，当双方利益不一致时，经理层往往通过选择会计政策、会计方法和会计程序等来维护自身的利益，从而使所有者的利益受到损害。为了解决这个问题，西方国家通过建立财务总监制监督总经理及经理层，以有效避免内部人控制，保护所有者的利益，满足所有者对企业经营监控的要求。在我国，财务总监的提法是在总会计师之后。与西方国家相同，我国的财务总监制度源自政府委派财务总监对国有企业实施监督，其工作内容涉及财务监督的主要方面，实质上是对国有大中型企业总会计师制度和企业内部审计制度关于财务工作组织运行和财务监督上的更高层次的发展与完善，它吸收和集中了总会计师和内部审计中的部分财务管理与监督职能，也弥补了总会计师在企业组织中地位和职责权限上的不足。财务总监是经理层高级财务管理人员，主要承担内部受托责任。最初使用这一称谓的主要是上市公司和上海、深圳的一些国有企业及其他企业，基于良好的监督效果，财务总监制度逐渐得以推广。如今财务总监这一称谓已经很普遍，但是其定位在各个企业中的差异较大，有的企业的财务总监相当于国有企业对总经理负责的总会计师，有的财务总监则是指财务部门负责人，也有个别企业的财务总监相当于 CFO。财务总监有的对董事会负责，有的对总经理负责，还有的对监事会负责。

Stakeholder Theory

利益相关者理论（Stakeholder Theory）是 20 世纪 60 年代在美国、英国等长期奉行外部控制型公司治理模式的国家中逐步发展起来的。该理论针对股东利益至上的观点，否定了公司是由持有该公司普通股的个人和机构所有的传统概念，认为任何一个公司的发展都离不开各种利益相关者的投入或参与，比如股东、债权人、雇员、消费者、供应商等，该理论的关键论点是"现代公司由各个利益平等的利益相关者所组成，股东只是其中的一员，企业不仅要为股东利益服务，而且要保护其他利益相关者的利益"。

Free Riding

免费搭车原意指不付钱搭便车，后来作为经济学术语，描述的是资源配置低效的一种经济现象，即理性的个人会尽量逃避为集体的利益效力而力图不花费任何成本地享受集体的福利。简单说来，即使个人未支付费用，也享受到了团体所提供的服务。我们熟知的"吃大锅饭"问题就是典型的免费搭车现象。免费搭车者（Free-rider）表示不当得利者。

Information Asymmetry

信息不对称（Information Asymmetry 或者 Asymmetric Information）是微观经济学前沿研究的核心内容之一，其是指相关信息在交易双方的不对称分布对于市场交易行为和市场运行效率所产生的一系列重要影响。信息不对称的两个后果是逆向选择（adverse selection）和道德风险（moral hazard，也译为败德行为）。逆向选择和道德风险体现了人的机会主义行为倾向，逆向选择是事前机会主义行为，道德风险是事后机会主义行为。

- 逆向选择

美国经济学家乔治·阿克洛夫（George A. Akerlof）1970 年提出了著名的旧车市

第 2 章　财务管理概述(2)
TOPIC 2　Introduction to Financial Management(2)

场模型，开创了逆向选择理论的先河。

○ 相关人物

乔治·阿克洛夫，美国著名经济学家，2001 年诺贝尔经济学奖得主（与迈克尔·斯宾塞和约瑟夫·斯蒂格利茨共同获得），美国加州大学伯克利分校（UC Berkeley）经济学教授。

阿克洛夫 1940 年生于美国的纽黑文（New Haven）；1966 年获美国麻省理工学院经济学博士头衔；自 1980 年起，一直在美国加州大学伯克利分校任经济学教授。他的专业领域包括宏观经济学、贫困问题、家庭问题、犯罪、歧视、货币政策和德国统一问题。其代表作品有《资本、工资与结构失业》《一位经济理论家讲述的故事》。其提出的"劣势选择"概念和"柠檬市场"现象已经被写进大学本科的教科书中。

在旧车市场上，买者和卖者对汽车质量信息的掌握是不对称的。卖者知道所售汽车的真实质量。一般情况下，潜在的买者要想确切地辨认出旧车市场上汽车质量的好坏是困难的，他最多只能通过外观、介绍及简单的现场试验等获取有关汽车质量的信息，然而，从这些信息中很难准确判断出车的质量，因为车的真实质量只有通过长期使用才能得知，但这在旧车市场上又是不可能的，所以，旧车市场上的买者在购买汽车之前并不知道哪辆汽车是高质量的、哪辆汽车是低质量的，他只知道旧车市场上汽车的平均质量。在这种情况下，典型的买者只愿意根据平均质量支付价格，但这样一来，质量高于平均水平的卖者就会将他们的汽车撤出旧车市场，市场上只留下质量低的卖者。结果是，旧车市场上汽车的平均质量降低，买者愿意支付的价格进一步下降，更多的较高质量的汽车退出市场。在均衡的情况下，只有低质量的汽车成交；而在极端情况下，甚至没有交易。这就是"柠檬市场"（lemon market）现象，即由于卖方比买方对产品的质量有更多的信息，低质量的产品将驱逐高质量的产品，从而使市场上产品的质量持续下降的情形。

- 道德风险

道德风险这一专业术语来源于保险业。在保险市场上，购买了财产保险的人将不再像以前那样仔细地看管家里的财物。购买了医疗保险的人，可能让医生多开一些不必要的价格较高的药品。购买了汽车保险的人可能更不注意保管自己的汽车。

Agency Problem and Agency theory

经济学上的委托—代理关系泛指任何一种涉及非对称信息的交易。交易中有信息优势的一方称为代理人，另一方称为委托人。简单地说，知情者（informed player）是代理人，不知情者（uninformed player）是委托人。代理理论应用于财务管理的经典文献是 Michael C. Jensen 和 William H. Meckling（1976）的文章。

○ **相关人物**

迈克尔·詹森（Michael C. Jensen），美国著名经济学家，是横跨经济学和公司财务与治理两大领域的大师，代理经济学的创始人之一。

詹森生于1939年，1962年获得马卡莱斯特学院经济学学士学位；后来获得芝加哥大学金融学 MBA 和经济学、金融学、会计学博士学位。1967年起，詹森执教于美国罗切斯特大学（University of Rochester）管理学院；1984年起任该校金融和商务管理专业 IsClare 荣誉教授；1985年他加入哈佛大学管理学院，目前为该校退休之讲座教授。

詹森于1996年当选为美国科学与文学院院士。1990年，他被东部金融协会授予"年度学者"称号，同年入选《财富》杂志评出的"年度25位最杰出的商界人士"。1973年，他创建《金融经济学》期刊，如今这份杂志已成为金融经济学领域最有影响力的刊物之一。1994年，他与人合作创建了社会科学电子出版公司，致力于社会科学著作的电子出版事业，公司旗下的 SSRN 网站，包括会计、经济、金融经济学、法律、管理、信息系统、市场营销、谈判等8个专业研究网，已成为社会科学研究的重要平台。

迈克尔·詹森博士对于财务学界最大的贡献在于他将代理问题（Agency problems）引入到对公司财务问题的分析中。

威廉·麦克林（William H. Meckling，1922—1998），美国著名经济学家，管理学和政府政策教授，曾任罗切斯特大学西蒙商学院院长。麦克林于1942年在威斯敏斯特学院获得学士学位，并于1978年被授予荣誉管理学博士学位。他于1947年获得丹佛大学工商管理硕士学位，1952年在芝加哥大学获得经济学研究生学位。

麦克林在管理经济学和法律经济分析领域有着深入的研究，其中最为著名的是他与迈克尔·詹森在代理理论方面的合作。他们于1979年3月获得了第一个 Leo Melamed 奖，获奖论文是《企业理论：管理行为、代理成本和所有权结构》。

Stock Option

股票期权或认股权（Stock Option）授予公司经营者一定数量的认股权（executive stock option，ESO），一般就是允诺公司经营者在某一期限内，以一个固定的执行价，购买本公司股票的权利，这个购买的过程称为行权（exercise）。行使认股权后，股票出售价与行权价之间的差额就是认股权被授予者的收益。认股权计划最早于20世纪70年代起源于美国，20世纪80年代，特别是90年代以来被广泛推广。据统计，在《财富》（Fortune）杂志排名前1 000位的美国公司中有90%实施了认股权计划，管理人员从认股权中获得的收入越来越多。美国有许多企业还将该计划推向大多数甚至全体员工。

Creative Accounting 创造性会计，伪造账目

这一名词是由美国会计学者格里夫斯（Griffiths）提出的，创造性会计是指企业管理当局及其会计机构和人员针对会计规则的漏洞或缺陷（包括会计规则未涉及的领域），依据客观环境或出于自身需要，创造性地发明、尝试或选择会计程序和方法，以达到某种目的的会计活动。

美国重大财务丑闻公司：安然公司、世通、施乐和默克制药

- 安然公司（Enron）

安然公司曾是一家位于美国得克萨斯州休斯敦市的能源类公司。在2001年宣告破产之前，安然拥有约21 000名雇员，是世界上大型电力、天然气以及电信公司之一，2000年披露的营业额达1 010亿美元之巨。公司连续6年被《财富》杂志评选为美国最具创新精神的公司，然而真正使安然公司在全世界声名大噪的，却是这个拥有上千亿资产的公司在美国公司500强中名列第7。2001年年底，安然公司虚报近6亿美元的盈余和掩盖10亿多美元的巨额债务问题暴露，持续多年、精心策划，乃至制度化、系统化的财务造假丑闻公布于天下。12月2日，安然公司向纽约破产法院申请破产保护，并在几周内破产，创下美国历史上最大宗的公司破产案纪录。

因安然事件，美国颁布了《萨班斯-奥克斯利法案》，该法案被视为自20世纪30年代以来对美国证券法最重要的修改。

安达信公司自安然公司1985年成立伊始就为它做审计，做了整整16年。除单纯的审计外，安达信还提供内部审计和咨询服务。20世纪90年代中期，安达信与安然签署了一项补充协议，安达信包揽安然的内部审计工作。不仅如此，安然公司的咨询业务也全部由安达信负责。2001年，安然公司付给它的5 200万美元的报酬中一半以上（2 700万美元）是用来支付咨询服务的。

安然公司1997~2001年虚构利润5.86亿美元，并隐藏了数亿美元的债务。美国监管部门的调查发现，安然公司的雇员中居然有100多位来自安达信，包括首席会计师和财务总监等高级职员，而在董事会中，有一半的董事与安达信有着直接或间接的联系。

2001年10月安然公司财务丑闻爆发，美国证券交易委员会（SEC）宣布对安然进行调查。可就在同时，安达信的休斯敦事务所从 10 月 23 日开始的两个星期中销毁了数千页安然公司的文件，而公司在 10 月 17 日就已得知美国证券交易委员会对安然公司的财务状况进行调查，直到 11 月 8 日收到证券交易委员会的传票后才停止销毁文件。2001 年 12 月，安然宣布破产。2002 年 1 月，安达信承认销毁文件，安达信芝加哥总部提出这是休斯敦事务所所为。2002 年年初，安达信将负责安然审计的资深合伙人大卫·邓肯除名，而大卫·邓肯则申辩说这是总部的授意。在初步调查的基础上，司法部于 3 月 14 日对安达信提起刑事诉讼，罪名是妨碍司法公正，理由是该公司在安然丑闻事发后毁掉了相关文件和电脑记录，从而成为美国历史上第一家被判有罪的大型会计师事务所。

- 世通（WorldCom）

美国第二大长途电话公司世界通信公司于 2002 年 6 月 25 日发表声明，承认自 2001 年年初到 2002 年第一季度，通过将大量的费用支出计入资本项目的手法，共虚增收入 38 亿美元，虚增利润 16 亿多美元。为该公司提供财务报表审计的是当时已涉嫌安然公司造假案的安达信公司。

- 施乐（Xerox）

仅在世界通信公司事件曝光后的第三天，也就是 2002 年 6 月 28 日，美国媒体又揭露出全球最大的复印机制造商，曾是美国"最可信赖的 50 家公司"的施乐公司 1997～2001 年间虚报收入 60 多亿美元，虚增利润 14 亿美元。

- 默克制药（Merck）

2002 年 7 月 5 日，全球第三大药品制造商、美国制药巨头默克公司在向美国证券交易委员会递交的报告中承认，1999～2001 年，该公司把 124 亿美元作为经营收入入账，但该公司从未收过这些款项。

我国财务丑闻公司——银广夏、东方电子、郑百文、蓝田股份等

关于我国的财务丑闻公司，请有兴趣的读者阅读相关媒体的历史资料。

相 关 网 址
Useful Websites

美国 CFO　　www.cfo.com
中国 CFO　　www.chinacfo.net
中国公司治理网　　www.cg.org.cn
国际财务总裁联合会　　http://www.iafei.org/

第 3 章
TOPIC 3

Interpreting Financial Statements
诠释财务报表

新闻视听
News in Media

Enron scandal is always incredible. What on earth has happened and how did it occur? This report will give you an answer.

本章新闻视听资料请扫二维码收听。

名人名言
Wisdom

Financial statements are like fine perfume; to be sniffed but not swallowed.

——Abraham Briloff

微型案例
Mini Case

In early 2001, Enron appeared on the top of the world. The high-flying energy firm had a market capitalization of $60 billion, and its stock was trading at $80 a share. Wall Street analysts frequently touted its innovation and management success, and most strongly recommended the stock. Less than a year later, Enron had declared bankruptcy, its stock was basically worthless, and investors had lost billions of dollars. The dramatic and sudden collapse left many wondering how so much value could be destroyed in such a short period of time (to be continued in Topic 4).

概 览 Overview

Our objective in this topic is to show how to interpret the contents and to understand the limitations of the following financial statements — balance sheet, income statement, statement of cash flows and statement of retained earnings. Like a patient's medical report issued by a physician, the information in these statements can provide important information that helps us to better understand the firm's financial condition. We emphasize the need to understand the difference between the accounting net income reported on the firm's income statement and the actual net cash flow generated by the firm during that same period.

正文 Text

3.1 Basics of Annual Reports and Financial Statements

Knowing how to interpret **financial statements** is critically important to the stakeholders of the firm. Lenders carefully scrutinize a firm's statements to assess the likelihood that the firm can repay the principal and pay the interest when due over the life of a loan. Equity investors analyze financial statements to assess the long-term profitability of a firm. Suppliers use these statements to assess whether the company can fully pay its obligations on time. Customers are concerned with its continuing viability, both to supply new products and to maintain those already purchased. Employees may use their firm's financial statements to assess its future, knowing that their jobs depend on its immediate solvency, long-term debt-paying ability, and future long-term profitability. Employees are also concerned about whether the firm can meet its future pension obligations.

But we have left out perhaps one of the most important users of financial statements: the firm's management. Managers carefully assess data from these financial statements when making an important investment, financing and working capital policy decisions. Data from financial statements may be used to determine incentives and rewards for a firm's managers. These managers may use the financial data in these statements to allocate capital investments within a firm's various segments or divisions. Divisional managers use financial statement data to implement changes to improve the performance of their respective divisions.

Financial statements are probably the most important source of information from which these various stakeholders (other than management) can assess a firm's financial health. But it should be intuitively clear that it is not easy to assess a firm's real financial status. The numbers shown on balance sheet generally represent the historical costs of assets. However, inventories may be spoiled, obsolete or even missing; fixed assets such as machinery and buildings may have higher or lower values than their historical costs, and accounts receivable may be uncollectible. Also, some liabilities such as obligations to pay retirees' medical costs may not even show up on the balance sheet. Similarly, some costs reported on the income statement may be understated, as would be true if a plant with a useful life of 10 years were being depreciated over 40 years. When you examine a set of financial statements, you should keep in mind that a physical reality lies behind the numbers, and you should also realize that the translation from physical assets to "correct" numbers is far from precise.

3.1.1 Corporate Annual Reports

Of the various reports corporations issue to their stockholders, the **annual report** is probably the most important. Most public firms in the United States (US) prepare two annual reports. These include the annual report to the Securities and Exchange Commission (SEC) and the shareholder annual report. The annual report to the SEC provides both financial and non-financial information about a firm, including a comprehensive review of the company's business and a prospect of future operations. This report is much more comprehensive than the annual report to shareholders.

The shareholder annual report is the most widely read annual report. It contains financial and non-financial information that is important to the various users of financial statements discussed above. The information provided includes both aggregated financial information and sales and marketing information. The shareholder annual report typically includes a statement of corporate mission and strategy, an executive message, product information, a discussion of financial performance, comparative financial information, an audit report, and selected investor information. Both the SEC and shareholder annual reports contain the firm's financial statements, which are the focus of this topic.

Firms in the US prepare their financial statements according to **Generally Accepted Accounting Principles (GAAP).** GAAP provides the conventions, rules, and procedures that define how firms should maintain records and prepare financial reports. The **Financial Accounting Standards Board (FASB)**, the US accounting profession's rule-making organization, provides the guidelines upon which these rules and procedures are based. The FASB also sets forth the conceptual framework for understanding the information provided by financial statements. The qualitative characteristics of accounting information include relevance, timeliness, reliability, consistency and comparability.

3.1.2 Overview of Financial Statements

Public corporations in the US and many other countries are required to prepare and disclose the following financial statements to the public on a periodic basis:

- balance sheet.
- income statement.
- statement of cash flows.
- statement of retained earnings.

Taken together, these statements give an accounting picture of the firm's operations and financial position. The quantitative and verbal materials are equally important. The financial statements report what has actually happened to assets, earnings and dividends over the past few years, whereas the verbal statements attempt to explain why things turned out the way they did. The information contained in an annual report is used by investors to help form expectations about future earnings and dividends.

Firms typically prepare these statements quarterly, but many analysts and users of financial statements concentrate on a firm's fiscal year-end statements. Firms provide the annual statements in both the annual report to the SEC and the shareholder annual report.

New US legislation requires that annual statements be filed within 60 days of the company's year-end and quarterly statements within 35 days of the close of the quarter. Only three quarterly reports are required, as the firm's year-end annual report replaces the fourth quarterly report.

In the following sections, we look at these financial statements by using those for SunFood Products.

3.2 Balance Sheet

A **balance sheet** is an accountant's snapshot of the firm's accounting value on a particular date, as though the firm stood momentarily. The balance sheet reports a firm's assets, liabilities, and owners' (stockholders') equity as of a given date, usually at the end of a reporting period. A firm's assets represent its investments (what it owns), and the liabilities (what it owes), while owners' equity represents how the firm financed these investments (assets).

The accounting definition that underlies the balance sheet and describes the balance is

$$Assets = Liabilities + Owners'\ equity$$

Table 3-1 shows the balance sheets for SunFood Products at the fiscal year-end of 2001 and 2002. In the following sections, we briefly discuss the major areas within a balance sheet with SunFood Products' balance sheet.

Table 3-1 Balance Sheet of the SunFood Products: December 31

(Millions of Dollars)

ASSETS	2018	2017	LIABILITIES AND EQUITY	2018	2017
Cash and marketable securities	$ 10	$ 80	Accounts payable	$ 60	$ 30
Accounts receivables	375	315	Notes payable	110	60

(续)

ASSETS	2018	2017	LIABILITIES AND EQUITY	2018	2017
Inventories	<u>615</u>	<u>415</u>	Accrues	<u>140</u>	<u>130</u>
Total current assets	$ 1 000	$ 810	Total current liabilities	$ 310	$ 220
Property, plant and equipment	1 100	960	Long-term bonds	<u>754</u>	<u>580</u>
Less accumulated depreciation	100	90	Total liabilities	$ 1 064	$ 800
Net property, plant and equipment	$ 1 000	$ 870	Preferred stock(400 000 shares)	40	40
			Common stock(50 000 000 shares)	130	130
			Retained earnings	<u>766</u>	<u>710</u>
			Total common equity	$ <u>936</u>	$ <u>880</u>
Total assets	$ <u>2 000</u>	$ <u>1 680</u>	Total liabilities and equity	$ <u>2 000</u>	$ <u>1 680</u>

  Let's look at the asset side of SunFood Products' balance sheet. The assets, which are the "things" the company owns, are listed in the order of decreasing liquidity or length of time it typically takes to convert them to cash at **fair market values**, beginning with the firm's current assets. SunFood Products' current assets include its cash and cash equivalents, accounts receivables, inventories and other current assets such as prepaid expenses. Current assets are those assets in the form of cash or that are expected to be converted into cash within 1 year. Cash and **marketable securities** include cash and other negotiable instruments such as checks and money orders that the bank does not have the legal right to demand notice before withdrawal. The accounts receivables represent those credit sales that the firm has not yet collected. They are reported on a net basis, which excludes credit sales that are overdue and unlikely to be ultimately collected. Inventories represent those items that remain unsold as of the balance sheet reporting date, but are likely to be sold within the next year. Other current assets such as prepaid expenses include payments made for benefits to be received within 1 year, such as payments for rent or insurance premiums.

  The next section of SunFood Products' balance sheet contains its property, plant and equipment (PPE). Rather than treat the entire purchase price of PPE as a capital expense in the purchase year, accountants "spread" the purchase cost over the asset's useful life. The amount they charge each year is called the **depreciation** expense. SunFood Products reports PPE on a net basis by subtracting the **accumulated depreciation** and amortization that has been taken as an expense on the income statement.

Intangible assets, which have no physical substance, include items such as patents, copyrights and trademarks.

The right side lists the claims that various groups have against the company's value, listed in the order in which they must be paid. The liability section of the balance sheet consists of current liabilities and long-term liabilities. Current liabilities include a firm's short-term maturing obligations. SunFood Products' current liabilities include its accounts payable, note payable and accrued expenses. SunFood Products expects to pay these liabilities within 1 year.

The long-term liabilities for SunFood Products include the firm's long-term debt, other long-term liabilities and deferred taxes. The long-term debt includes only the debt due for longer than 1 year.

The stockholders' equity section lists preferred stock, common stock and capital surplus and accumulated retained earnings. Preferred stock is a **hybrid** or a cross between stock and debt. In the event of bankruptcy, preferred stock ranks below debt but above common stock. Also, the preferred dividend is fixed, so preferred stockholders do not benefit if the company's earnings grow. When a company sells shares of stock, the proceeds are recorded in the common stock account. Accumulated retained earnings represent the firm's cumulative net income that has been reinvested back into the firm and not distributed to shareholders as cash dividends. Treasury stock represents shares of common stock that SunFood Products repurchased from shareholders.

Historical Cost versus Current Market Value

The values of most items reported on a firm's balance sheet are reported in terms of their accounting **book values**, which are based on **historical cost** or original value. The historical cost of an asset is the price paid when the firm acquires the asset. The historical cost of a liability is the amount involved when the firm incurs the liability.

Financial managers and analysts recognize that these historical values may differ substantially from their **current market values**. This is especially true for real estate and stockholders' equity. The reported value may understate the true market value of these assets. This understatement problem is avoided with the long-term investments reported on the balance sheet. Long-term investments are reported at their fair market value.

The total value of stockholders' equity reported on a firm's balance sheet might also differ substantially from the current market value of the firm's equity. The market value of a firm's equity is equal to the number of shares of common stock outstanding times the price per share, while the amount reported on the firm's balance sheet is basically the cumulative amount the firm raised when issuing common stock and any reinvested net income (retained earnings).

3.3 Income Statement

An **income statement**, also called a statement of earnings or a profit and loss statement, summarizes the total revenues earned and the total expenses incurred to generate these revenues over a specified period of time. The difference between total revenues and total expenses during a given period is referred to as the firm's **net income** for that period, also commonly referred to as the firm's net earnings or profits. The accounting definition of income is

$$Revenue - Expenses = Income$$

If the balance sheet is like a snapshot, the income statement is like a video recording of the people did between two snapshots.

An income statement is usually divided into two sections: operating and non-operating. Firms report the revenues and expenses that correspond to day-to-day operations in the operating section. Subtracting operating expenses from operating income or revenue yields the **operating income (or loss)** for the firm. This is an important profitability measure of a firm's business operations. The non-operating section includes income and expense items and gains and losses that are routine to most types of businesses, but viewed as peripheral to day-to-day business operations.

Non-operating items include dividend and interest income earned, interest expense, and gains or losses associated with the disposal of assets or the elimination of liabilities. Table 3-2 shows the income statement for SunFood Products for the fiscal year 2017 and 2018.

Table 3-2 SunFood Products: Statement of Retained Earnings for Year Ending, December 31, 2017
(Millions of Dollars)

	2018	2017
Net sales	$ 3 000	$ 2 850.0
Operating costs excluding depreciation and amortization	2 616.2	2 497.0
Earnings before interest, taxes, depreciation, and amortization(EBITDA)	$ 383.8	$ 353.0
Depreciation	100	90.0
Amortization	0.0	0.0
Depreciation and amortization	$ 100.0	$ 90.0
Earnings before interest and taxes(EBIT, or operating income)	283.8	263.0
Less interest	$ 88.0	$ 60.0
Earnings before taxes(EBT)	$ 195.8	$ 203.0
Taxes	78.3	81.2
Net income before preferred dividends	$ 117.5	$ 121.8
Preferred dividends	4.0	4.0
Net income available to common shareholders	$ 113.5	$ 117.8
Common dividends	57.5	53.0
Addition to retained earnings	56.0	64.8

Analysts and investors pay close attention to the **earnings per share** reported on a firm's income statement. The presentation of earnings per share figures depends on whether the firm has a simple or complex capital structure. A **simple capital structure** occurs when a firm is financed only with common stock and other non-convertible senior securities. That is, the firm's financing structure does not contain any potentially dilutive securities. This firm will report basic earnings per share, which is calculated by dividing the net income less any preferred dividends paid out by the weighted average number of outstanding shares of common stock.

Firms with **complex capital structures** have potentially dilutive securities such as convertible securities, options, and warrants that could potentially dilute **earnings per share** (**EPS**). These firms must report both basic and **diluted earnings** per share figures. The diluted earnings figure per share provides a more conservative earnings estimate by assuming that the total shares of common stock in the denominator include all shares of common stock plus future potential shares from the likely future conversion of outstanding convertible securities, stock options, and warrants.

The calculation of diluted EPS includes potential future common shares from the likely future conversion of outstanding stock options and warrants in the denominator of the EPS calculation.

Net Income versus Cash Flow

The net income reported on a firm's income statement typically does not equal the actual net **cash flow** generated by that firm over the particular time period. Net income and actual net cash flow may differ because accountants use an accrual accounting process for recognizing revenues and expenses, and because of the treatment of depreciation and taxes. We discuss each of these items in the following sections.

Accrual accounting

Revenue is recognized in an income statement when the earnings process is virtually completed and the exchange of goods or services has occurred. Accountants refer to recognizing the timing of revenues and expenses in this manner as **accrual accounting**. Under an accrual accounting process, for a given reporting period, the cash receipts from sales will not equal the revenue reported, nor will the cash disbursed equal the expenses recognized. Therefore, the unrealized appreciation in owning property will not be recognized as income. This provides a device for smoothing income by selling appreciated property at convenient times. For example, if the firm owns a tree farm that has doubled in value, then, in a year when its earnings from other business are down, it can raise overall earnings by selling some trees. The matching principle of GAAP dictates that revenues should be matched with expenses. Thus, income is reported when it is earned, or accrued, even though no cash flow has necessarily occurred.

Depreciation

An income statement usually includes several non-cash expenses of which the most common include **depreciation** and **amortization.** When a firm makes capital expenditures for long-term fixed assets, such as for plant and equipment, it normally cannot include the entire expense for these purchases during the year in which the capital expenditures are incurred.

Taxes

Many differences exist between treatments of items under tax and book accounting. These differences are reflected in what is shown on the financial statements and what is paid to the Internal Revenue Service (IRS). One example is the different depreciation methods allowed for tax purposes as opposed to book (financial statement) purposes:

The choice of depreciation methods affects both the income statement and balance sheet, especially for capital intensive companies. When compared to accelerated methods, straight-line depreciation has a lower depreciation expense in the early years of asset life, which tends to lead to a higher tax expense but higher net income. On the balance sheet, both assets and equity are higher under straight-line depreciation versus accelerated methods during the early years of an asset. Toward the end of an asset's life, these relationships reverse.

3.4 Statement of Retained Earnings

A firm's **statement of retained earnings**, also known as its statement of changes in shareholders' equity, provides additional information on the composition of the owners' equity accounts. Specifically, for the particular reporting period, it shows:

- the retained earnings balance at the start of the period.
- how much the firm earned (net income).
- how much dividends the firm paid.
- how much net income was reinvested back into the firm (retained earnings).
- any repurchases of the firm's stock.

- any new issues of the firm's stock.
- the retained earnings balance at the close of the period.

Table 3-3 SunFood Products: Statement of Retained Earnings for Year Ending, December 31, 2018
(Millions of Dollars)

Balance of retained earnings, December 31, 2017	710.0
Add: Net income, 2018	113.5
Less: Dividends to common stockholders	(57.5)
Balance of retained earnings, December 31, 2018	766.0

3.5 Statement of Cash Flow

A firm's **statement of cash flows** summarizes changes in its cash position over a specified period of time. A firm's cash position may change during a year as it collects revenues, pays operating expenses, and generates income (or loss). Cash also decreases as the firm buys fixed assets, increases inventories, finances additional accounts receivable, reduces outstanding debt obligations, pays dividends, or buys back shares of its stock. Its cash position will improve as it generates net income, finances additional accounts payable, sells assets and investments, and issues long-term debt and stock. The statement of cash flows helps us understand how these various activities change the firm's cash position during the year.

The statement of cash flows consists of three sections: operating cash flows, investing cash flows, and financing cash flows. Activities in each area that bring in cash represent **sources of cash** while activities that involve spending cash are **uses of cash**.

3.5.1 Operating Cash Flows

Cash flow from operations (CFO) reports the cash generated from sales and the cash used in the production process. Such items flow through the firm's income statement and working capital items. Under US GAAP, typical operating activities include cash collections from sales, cash operating expenses, cash interest expense, and cash tax payments.

There are two ways to calculate cash flow from operations: (1) the direct method and (2) the indirect method. Both methods result in the same cash flow from operations.

Direct method

The direct method, also called the top-down approach, derives operating cash flows by taking each item from the income statement and converting it to its cash equivalent by adding or subtracting the changes in the corresponding balance sheet accounts.

Indirect method

The indirect method, also called the bottom-up approach, involves several steps. This approach begins with the firm's net earnings (income) for the period, and then subtracts gains or adds losses that result from financing or investment cash flows. Next, the approach adds back any non-cash charges such as depreciation and amortization it subtracted to arrive at net income. Net income is further adjusted by accounting for any cash that the firm used to fund increases in current assets or decreases in current liabilities. As we will soon see, SunFood Products uses the indirect method to calculate cash flow from operations.

3.5.2 Investing Cash Flows

Cash flow from investing (CFI) reports the cash used to acquire and dispose of non-cash assets. Firms acquire such assets with the expectation of generating income. Such items are found in the non-current portion of the asset section of the balance sheet. Investing activities often include purchases of property, plant, and equipment, investments in joint ventures and affiliates, payments for businesses acquired, proceeds from sales of assets, and investments in or sales of marketable securities.

3.5.3 Financing Cash Flows

Cash flows from financing (CFF) reports capital structure transactions. These items are located in the long-term capital section of the balance sheet and the statement of retained earnings and involve activities related to contributing, withdrawing, and servicing of funds to support the firm's business activities. Financing activities include new debt issuances, debt repayments or retirements, stock sales and repurchases, and cash dividend payments.

The first section provides details on the net cash provided from operations. To arrive at its net cash provided by operations, SunFood Products adds back to its net income the depreciation and amortization expense for fiscal year 2002. Remember that depreciation and amortization are non-cash expenses that SunFood Products subtracted on the income statement to determine the net income. Thus, to convert net income to actual cash flow requires adding back these non-cash expenses.

SunFood Products makes further adjustments to account for the accrual accounting process that causes net income to deviate from cash flows that we discussed previously. Specifically, increases (decreases) in current asset accounts such as receivables and inventories are subtracted from (added to) net income, and increases (decreases) in current liability accounts such as accounts payable and taxes payable are added to (subtracted from) net income. Analysts pay close attention to the operating cash flow section of the cash flow statement because large, positive cash flows provided by operations are an initial sign of good health and liquidity for a firm. Table 3-4 shows the SunFood Products cash flow for fiscal year 2018.

Table 3-4　SunFood Products: Statement of Cash Flows for Fiscal Year 2018

(Millions of Dollars)

Operating Activities	
Net income before preferred dividends	117.5
Additions (Sources of Cash)	
Depreciation and amortization [①]	100.0
Increase in accounts payable	30.0
Increase in accruals	10.0
Subtractions (Uses of Cash)	
Increase in accounts receivable	(60.0)
Increase in inventories	(200.0)
Net cash provided by operating activities	(2.5)
Long-term Investing Activities	
Cash used to acquire fixed assets [②]	(230.0)

	（续）
Financing Activities	
Increase in notes payable	50.0
Increase in bonds	174.0
Payment of common and preferred dividends	(61.5)
Net cash provided by financing activities	162.5
Net decrease in cash and marketable securities	(70.0)
Cash and securities at the beginning of the year	80.0
Cash and securities at the end of the year	10.0

① Depreciation and amortization are non-cash expenses that were deducted when calculating net income. They must be added back to show the actual cash flow from operations.

② The net increase in fixed assets is $130 million; however, this net amount is after deducting the year's depreciation expenses. Depreciation expense must be added back to find the actual expenditures on fixed assets. From the company's income statement, we see that the 2002 depreciation expense is $100 million; thus, expenditures on fixed assets were actually $230 million.

The second section details SunFood Products' cash flow from investing activities, which includes investments in or sales of fixed assets.

The third section provides details about SunFood Products' financing activities, which includes raising cash by selling short-term investments or by issuing short-term debt, long-term debt, or stock. Also because both dividends paid and cash used to buy back outstanding stock or bonds reduce the company's cash, such transactions are included here.

Accounting texts explains how to prepare the statement of cash flows, but the statement is used to help answer questions such as: Is the firm generating enough cash to purchase the additional assets required for growth? Is the firm generating any extra cash that can be used to repay debt or invest in new products? Such information is useful both for managers and investors, so the statement of cash flow is an important part of the annual report.

核心词汇
Core Words and Expressions

financial statement　财务报表
profitability　盈利能力
viability　生存能力
solvency　偿付能力

corporate annual reports　公司年报
balance sheet　资产负债表
income statement　利润表
statement of cash flows　现金流量表

statement of retained earnings　留存收益表
Securities and Exchange Commission (SEC)　（美国）证券交易委员会
Generally Accepted Accounting Principles (GAAP)　一般公认会计原则
Financial Accounting Standards Board (FASB)　（美国）财务会计准则委员会
fair market value　公允市场价值
marketable securities　流动性证券，有价证券
check　支票
money order　拨款单，汇款单，汇票
withdrawal　提款
accounts receivable　应收账款
credit sale　赊销
inventory　存货
property, plant, and equipment (PPE)　土地、厂房与设备
depreciation　折旧
accumulated depreciation　累计折旧
liability　负债
current liability　流动负债
long-term liability　长期负债
accounts payable　应付账款
note payable　应付票据
accrued expense　应计费用
deferred tax　递延税款
preferred stock　优先股
common stock　普通股
capital surplus　资本盈余
accumulated retained earnings　累计留存收益
hybrid　混合金融工具

treasury stock　库存股
book value　账面价值
historical cost　历史成本
current market value　现行市场价值
real estate　房地产（有时也用 real property 或者 property 表示）
outstanding　（证券等）发行在外的
a profit and loss statement　损益表
net income　净利润
operating income (loss)　经营收益（损失）
earnings per share　每股收益（盈余）
simple capital structure　简单资本结构
dilutive　（公司股票）冲减每股收益的
basic earnings per share　基本每股收益
complex capital structures　复杂资本结构
diluted earnings per share　稀释的每股收益
convertible securities　可转换证券
warrant　认股权证
accrual accounting　应计制会计
amortization　摊销
Internal Revenue Service (IRS)　美国国内税务署
accelerated methods　加速折旧法
straight-line depreciation　直线折旧法
statement of changes in shareholders' equity　股东权益变动表
source of cash　现金来源
use of cash　现金运用
operating cash flows　经营现金流
cash flow from operations　经营活动现金流
direct method　直接法
indirect method　间接法

bottom-up approach　倒推法
investing cash flows　投资现金流
cash flow from investing　投资活动现金流
joint venture　合资企业

affiliate　分支机构
financing cash flows　筹资现金流
cash flows from financing　筹资活动现金流

1. Give four examples of important assets, liabilities, or transactions which may not be shown on the company's books.
2. Describe the basic contents, including the key financial statements, of the stockholders' reports of publicly owned corporations.
3. What are Generally Accepted Accounting Principles (GAAP) and who authorizes them? What role does the Securities and Exchange Commission (SEC) play in the financial reporting activities of U.S. corporations?
4. What basic information is contained in:
   (a) the income statement
   (b) the balance sheet
   (c) the statement of retained earnings?
   Briefly describe each.
5. What is a source of cash? Give three examples.
6. Why is accounting income not the same as cash flow? Give two reasons.

In the 2016 Annual Report of Berkshire Hathaway, Inc., Warren E. Buffett, chairman of the board, said to shareholders as follows.

Berkshire's gain in net worth during 2016 was $27.5 billion, which increased the per-share book value of both our Class A and Class B stock by 10.7%. Over the last 52 years (that is, since present management took over), per-share book value has grown from $19 to $172,108, a rate of 19% compounded annually.

Charlie Munger, Berkshire's Vice Chairman and my partner, and I expect Berkshire's normalized earning power per share to increase every year. Actual earnings, of course, will sometimes decline because of periodic weakness in the U.S. economy. In addition, insurance mega-catastrophes or other industry-specific events may occasionally reduce earnings at Berkshire, even when most American businesses are doing well.

Due to the increase in investment income, the fourth-quarter profit increased by 15%, net profit climbed to 6.29 billion US dollars, and earnings per share was 3,823 US dollars, compared with a net profit of 5.48 billion US dollars in the same period last year, and earnings per share of 3,333 US dollars. Operating profit after deducting part of the investment income was $2,665 per share, and the average estimate of three analysts surveyed by Bloomberg was $2,717 per share.

Please find the 2016 Annual Report of Berkshire Hathaway and discuss the following questions:

1. What are the business activities of Berkshire Hathaway?
2. Explain the corporate performance of Berkshire Hathaway.

江苏雅百特科技股份有限公司是金属屋面围护系统行业的首家 A 股上市公司。雅百特于 2015 年 8 月成功"借壳上市"，2015 年年报显示，雅百特在与巴基斯坦木尔坦市开展的城市快速公交专线项目实现收入超过 2 亿元，占年度销售总额的 21.8%。然而，证监会调查人员发现，雅百特的回款主要来源于本身控制的公司以及其他的一些中国境内公司，雅百特根本就没有参与项目的建设，只是通过海外的一个公司伪造了一个虚假的工程建设合同，向海外出口了一批建筑材料，对外声称用于巴基斯坦木尔坦公交车站的建设，实际上并没有运到巴基斯坦，通过第三方的公司又把材料进口回来。经确认，雅百特在 2015 年至 2016 年 9 月，通过虚构海外工程项目、虚构国际贸易和国内贸易等手段，累计虚增营业收入约 5.8 亿元，虚增利润近 2.6 亿元，其中 2015 年虚增利润约占当期利润总额的 73%。雅百特财务造假案是继首例沪港通跨境操纵案件——唐汉博操纵市场案后，证监会查处的又一例跨境违法案件。

我国上市公司信息披露的指定媒体

在我国，投资者和社会公众可以通过指定报刊和网站找到自己需要的信息。我国上市公司披露信息的平面媒体主要是《中华人民共和国证券法》规定的七报一刊：《中国证券报》《上海证券报》《证券时报》《证券日报》《金融时报》《中国改革报》《中国日报》和《证券市场周刊》。

从 1999 年起，上市公司的定期报告全文在上海证券交易所网站（www.sse.com.cn）、深圳证券交易所网站（www.szse.cn）和巨潮资讯网（www.cninfo.com.cn）上发布。上市公司的临时报告也可以在这三个网站上找到。

我国上市公司信息披露的要求

上市公司应当披露的信息包括首次披露——招股说明书、上市公告书、定期报告（年度报告、中期报告、季度报告）和临时报告。

具体而言，上市公司的信息披露主要分为定期报告和临时报告两类。定期报告包括年度报告和中期报告。中期报告分为前半个会计年度的半年度报告和季度报告。季度报告分为一季度（春季度）报告和三季度（秋季度）报告。临时报告包括的内容和形式较为广泛，较为常见的有股东大会决议公告、董事会决议公告、监事会决议公告。其他重大事项也会由一些中介机构同时发布信息，如回访报告、评估报告和审计报告、律师见证报告，等等。

上市公司的信息披露在内容和格式上有一系列的要求。1993 年 6 月 10 日，中国证监会《公开发行股票公司信息披露实施细则（试行）》出台，这是涉及上市公司信息披露内容与格式的第一个部门规章。此后，有关招股说明书、上市公告书、年度报告、中期报告等文件的内容与格式的规定相继发布。相关的规章名称中通常有"公开发行证券公司信息披露内容与格式准则第×××号"字样。发行证券公司包括上市公司、暂停上市公司和拟上市公司。

交易所对上市公司定期报告实行事后审核，对临时报告实行事前审核。

关于我国发行证券公司的监管信息可以在中国证券监督管理委员会（中国证监会）网站上找到，网址是 http://www.csrc.gov.cn。

GAAP——一般公认会计原则

一般公认会计原则是被会计界普遍接受并有相当权威支持的，用以指导和规范企业财务会计行为的各项原则的总称。它大致包括三个层次：①会计核算的基本前提和会计原则，即会计的基本原则，其是指会计实务中普遍运用的基本指导思想和约束条件的概括，是体现会计规律、基本特征的原理性规范，如会计主体、持续经营、会计分期、货币计量、权责发生制等；②对会计实际问题的方法指导和具体标准或准绳，通常由一系列只适应于某些工作环节或某一类问题的条文、示例构成，如财务会计要素的确认、计量与报告原则；③会计处理的方法程序，即具体的操作规程和技术要领，属于技术规范的范畴，通常具体说明某一步骤或某种具体操作方法，因而很少有自由选择的余地，如记账规则、改错规则等。

　　一般公认会计原则既可以由官方机构制定，也可以由民间机构制定。在美国，一般公认会计原则指那些受到美国注册会计师协会、财务会计准则委员会和证券交易委员会等权威团体支持认可的会计原则，主要包括财务会计准则委员会制定的《财务会计准则公告》（包括以前的会计程序委员会制定和发布的《会计原则意见书》）和一些公认的会计惯例。在英国，一般公认会计原则是指由英格兰和威尔士特许会计师协会等六个会计职业团体联合制定发布的《标准会计惯例公告》。日本的一般公认会计原则主要是指规范体系。我国企业基本会计准则的主要内容与公认的其他两个层次相当的内容则见于企业会计制度、具体会计准则及其他有关规定中。

FASB——美国财务会计准则委员会

　　美国财务会计准则委员会（Financial Accounting Standards Board，FASB）成立于 1973 年，目的是制定和监督美国的会计准则。http://www.fasb.org 是美国财务会计准则委员会的官方网站，你可以从中获取 FASB 的最新资讯，还可以从这里下载其公布的最新财务会计准则。

IFRS——国际财务报告准则

　　国际财务报告准则（International Financial Reporting Standards, IFRS）是国际会计准则理事会（IASB）颁布的易于各国在跨国经济往来时执行的一项标准的会计制度。IFRS 是全球统一的财务规则，是按照国际标准规范运作的财务管理准则，用于规范全世界范围内的企业或其他经济组织的会计运作，使各国的经济利益可以在一个标准上得到保护，不至于因参差不一的准则导致不一样的计算方式，从而产生不必要的经济损失。

　　IFRS 的前身是 IAS（International Accounting Standards），由于社会的不断进步以及经济业务的日趋多样和复杂，老版本的 IAS 已逐渐不适用于当下，因此 IFRS 应运而生并逐步替代 IAS 的内容（例如，新出的 IFRS15 Revenue from contract with customers 将最早于 2017 年替代现有的 IAS18 Revenue 以及 IAS11 Construction Contract）。IFRS 的内容共分六部分。

IASB——国际会计准则理事会

　　国际会计准则理事会（International Accounting Standards Board，IASB）的前身是国际会计准则委员会（International Accounting Standards Committee，IASC），IASC

是由来自澳大利亚、加拿大、法国、德国、日本、墨西哥、荷兰、英国和爱尔兰以及美国的会计职业团体于1973年发起成立的。IASC的目标是制定和发布国际会计准则，促进国际会计的协调。IASC的日常工作由秘书处负责，秘书处设在伦敦，由秘书长领导。作为国际民间组织，其成员也大多为民间会计团体。从1983年起，作为国际会计师联合会（International Federation of Accountants，IFAC）成员的所有会计职业团体均已成为IASC的成员。中国于1998年5月正式加入IASC和IFAC。到2000年，IASC已经拥有来自104个国家的143个成员。

2001年，国际会计准则委员会进行了战略性改组，改组后新的国际会计准则委员会在机构框架的设置上，全面借鉴美国会计准则制定机构的组织架构，分别设置提名委员会、管理委员会和新的国际会计准则理事会（IASB），其中国际会计准则理事会是制定会计准则的核心部门，全权负责国际财务报告准则及其他相关文件的制定。

国际会计准则委员会的官方网站是http://www.iasb.org，其主要介绍IASB召开的会议、新闻、工作日历以及最近的热点问题等。从该网站可以得到最新发布的国际会计准则。

CAS——中国会计准则

中国会计准则（China's Accounting Standards, CAS）是由中华人民共和国财政部基于中国的国情并广泛征求意见，于1997年开始陆续出台的具体准则。至2017年，中国的企业会计准则增加到43项，其中基本准则1项，具体准则42项，是我国会计人员从事会计工作必须遵循的基本原则，是会计核算工作的规范。它大致包括三个层次：①基本会计准则，明确了财务报告的目标是向财务报告使用者提供决策有用的信息，并反映企业管理层受托责任的履行情况，强调了企业会计确认、计量和报告应当以会计主体、持续经营、会计分期和货币计量为会计基本假设；②具体准则，是在基本准则的指导下，处理具体业务标准的规范，具体内容可分为一般业务准则、特殊行业和特殊业务准则、财务报告准则三大类；③应用指南，是从不同角度对企业具体准则进行强化，解决实务操作，包括具体准则解释部分、会计科目和财务报表部分。

1. 我国上市公司财务报告信息可以到以下网站查询：
   上海证券交易所　www.sse.com.cn

深圳证券交易所　www.szse.cn

巨潮资讯网　www.cninfo.com.cn

雅虎财经　http://finance.yahoo.com

东方财富　www.eastmoney.com

新浪财经　finance.sina.com.cn

2. 在 http://www.sec.gov 可以查到美国证券交易委员会（Securities and Exchange Commission，SEC）的相关文件。

第 4 章
TOPIC 4

Financial Ratio Analysis
财务比率分析

新闻视听
News in Media

Enron's story is continued here.
本章新闻视听资料请扫二维码收听。

名人名言
Wisdom

If you cannot measure it, you cannot improve it.
——Lord Kelvin（1824—1907）

微型案例
Mini Case

　　While Enron's stock fell steadily throughout the first part of 2001, most analysts voiced no concerns. The general consensus was that Enron was simply caught up in a sell-off that was affecting the entire stock market, and that the company's long-run prospects remained strong. However, a hint of trouble came when Enron's CEO, Jeffrey Skilling, unexpectedly resigned in August 2001 and was replaced by the company's chairman and previous CEO, Ken Lay. By the end of August, Enron's stock had fallen to $35 a share. Two months later, Enron stunned the financial markets by announcing a $638 million loss, along with a $2.2 billion write-down in its equity value. The write-down, which was later seen to be grossly inadequate, stemmed primarily losses the company had realized from a series of partnerships set up by the company's CFO, Andrew Fastow. Shortly thereafter it was revealed Enron had guaranteed debt taken on by the partnerships, so its true liabilities were considerably higher than the financial statements indicated. All of these revelations destroyed Enron's credibility, caused its customers to flee, and led directly to its bankruptcy. Not surprisingly, Enron's executives had realized some $750 million in salaries, bonuses and profits from stock options in the 12 months before the company went bankrupt. During that year, when the executives were bailing out of the stock as fast as they could, they were putting out misleading statements and touting the stock to their own employees and to outside investors. Lay, Skilling, and Fastow may ultimately face criminal charges for these actions.

概 览 Overview

In this topic, we show how lenders, investors, analysts, and managers can use information from a firm's balance sheet, income statement, and statement of cash flows to calculate financial ratios that provide useful insights into particular aspects of a firm's performance. These ratios allow the firm's stakeholders to better understand its liquidity and long-term debt paying ability, efficiency in employing its various assets, profitability, and how the market is valuing the firm relative to key financial variables. We show how to calculate and interpret various ratios related to each of the above areas. We discuss several uses and limitations of financial ratio analysis.

正文 Text

4.1　Financial Ratio Analysis

Many stakeholders analyze a firm's **financial ratios** before making important decisions involving the firm. A financial ratio is a mathematical relationship among several numbers often stated in the form of a percentage, times, or days. Lenders assess liquidity and debt ratios to determine whether to lend money to a firm and at what rate. Rating agencies, such as Moody's and Standard & Poor's, use financial ratios when assigning a credit rating to a firm's debt issues. Lenders try to protect the bondholders' interest by incorporating some ratios into the restrictive covenants in the firm's bond indenture to constrain some of its financial and operating activities. Other investors review certain financial ratios to assess the firm's future profitability when contemplating investment opportunities. Regulators often use financial ratios as performance targets when determining the appropriate prices that firms may charge in regulated industries.

Managers frequently use financial ratios to identify their own firm's strengths and weaknesses and to assess its performance. They may use certain financial ratios as targets to guide their firm's investment, financing, and working capital policy decisions and to determine incentives and rewards for managers.

Analyzing Financial Ratios

Before we turn our attention to defining, computing, and interpreting these ratios, some preliminary comments are warranted. First, financial ratios are not standardized. A perusal of the many financial textbooks and other sources that are available will often show differences in how to calculate some ratios. When comparing ratios provided by various financial services or your own computations, biases may occur if computational methods differ. We will point out a few of the more common computational differences.

Second, analyzing a single financial ratio for a given year may not be very useful. Analysts usually examine financial ratios over the most recent 3- or 5-year period and then compare them with industry averages or key competitors. Keep in mind the limitations of making comparisons with other firms, because many firms are diversified across different industry groups. Also, combining or decomposing ratios can be helpful in predicting bankruptcy or for assessing underlying strengths or weaknesses in certain ratios.

Third, some of a firm's financial accounting practices or choices such as inventory valuation method and depreciation will affect its financial statements and, finally, its financial ratios. As a result, firms with very similar operating and financial characteristics but with different accounting conventions will have income statements, balance sheets, and financial ratios that reflect these differences. Analysts often make appropriate adjustments in order to compare such ratios in a meaningful way.

Finally, financial ratios do not provide analysts with all of the answers about a firm's condition. Rather, this information provides important clues that the financial analyst, as a detective, uses to further investigate and ask pertinent questions about a firm's financial condition.

4.2 Liquidity Ratios

Liquidity ratios indicate a firm's ability to pay its obligations in the short run. Potential lenders carefully scrutinize these ratios before making short-term loans to the firm. Financial managers must pay close attention to liquidity ratios to ensure they reflect a high probability of the firm being able to promptly and fully pay its bills without undue stress.

The most commonly used liquidity ratios include the current ratio, quick ratio, cash ratio, and net working capital to total assets ratio. We discuss each in turn.

4.2.1 Current ratio

The most widely used liquidity ratio is the current ratio. The **current ratio** is computed by dividing the firm's current assets by its current liabilities.

$$Current\ ratio = \frac{Current\ assets}{Current\ liabilities}$$

The firm's current liabilities in the denominator show the amount of short-term obligations the firm faces at the balance sheet date; the current assets in the numerator indicate the amount of short-term assets the firm can use to pay these obligations. For example, a current ratio of 1.5 implies that a firm has $1.50 in current assets for every $1 in current liabilities and thus has 1.5 times the current assets, or has its current liabilities covered 1.5 times over. This does not necessarily mean, however, that the firm will be able to pay its debts when they come due because of the timing of the current assets and liabilities.

For example, a large portion of a firm's current liabilities may be due now but the company has much of its current assets tied up in accounts receivable and inventories, which take time to convert into cash in order to pay current obligations.

A declining current ratio may indicate a declining trend in a firm's liquidity. Excessively high current ratios, however, may indicate a firm may have too much of its long-term investor-supplied capital invested in short-term low-earning current assets.

A firm's accounting methods, particularly inventory valuation, may affect its current ratio. In an inflationary environment, firms that use **last-in, first-out (LIFO)** inventory valuation will likely have lower current ratios than firms that use **first-in, first-out (FIFO)**. With LIFO inventory valuation, firms determine the value of the cost of goods sold on the income statement by the cost of the inventory most recently produced; the value of the inventory reported on the balance sheet reflects the remaining inventory produced in prior periods. Except in some declining cost industries, inflation will likely cause the value of this "older" inventory carried on the balance sheet to be less than the more recent cost of producing that inventory. On the other hand, firms that employ FIFO inventory valuation will value the cost of goods sold on the inventory produced in the most distant periods. The value of inventory reported on the balance sheet is from more recent periods and will be based on more recent (higher) cost data than the inventory balance of similar firms that use LIFO.

Firms can also manage their current ratio to some degree. To illustrate, consider a firm that has $1.6 million in current assets, $1 million in current liabilities, and a resulting current ratio of 1.6. If the firm were to pay off $100, 000 in accounts payable with cash, it would then have $1.5 million in current assets, $0.9 million in current liabilities, and an apparently improved current ratio of 1.67. Yet, if a firm has a current ratio that is less than one, the same transaction would lead to a lower current ratio: If a firm with $0.8 million in current assets, $1 million in current liabilities, and a current ratio of 0.8 pays off $100, 000 in accounts payable with cash, its current ratio would decline to 0.78. This example serves as a caution for the analysis of other ratios. Equal absolute changes in the numerator and denominator may lead to apparent improvements or deterioration in ratios that do not reflect real changes in performance. Analysts should be aware that a firm's managers may undertake year-end transactions, such as the one described above, to make certain ratios appear better following a period of disappointing performance. This process is often called "window dressing" because it makes specific ratios from the financial statements look better than without making such changes.

Finally, current ratios may hide important liquidity differences among firms. For example, suppose two firms have identical current ratios. Should we conclude the firms have nearly identical liquidity positions? Not necessarily. One of the firms may have a substantial portion of its current assets tied up in inventories, while the other firm may have large cash and marketable securities. But the current assets in the numerator of the current ratio calculation would hide these important differences in liquidity. All else equal, the latter firm has stronger liquidity. Managers or analysts can examine a firm's common-size balance sheet over time to see relative changes in the composition of both current assets and current liabilities and assess changes or differences in liquidity.

4.2.2 Quick ratio

A more conservative measure of liquidity for a firm is the **quick ratio**, sometimes referred to as the **acid test ratio**. The quick ratio is similar to the current ratio except inventory is excluded from the current assets in the numerator:

$$Quick\ ratio = \frac{Current\ assets - Inventory}{Current\ liabilities}$$

The rationale for excluding inventory is that it is the least liquid of a firm's current assets and may not be as readily available to meet a short-term maturing obligation as the other more liquid current assets.

For any firm carrying an inventory balance, the quick ratio will be lower than the current ratio. Analyzing the current ratio and quick ratio together may allow analysts to understand how changes in relative inventory levels may affect a firm's liquidity. For example, suppose a firm's current ratio has been fairly stable and consistent with industry averages over the past three years. But during the same period, the firm's quick ratio has declined and is now below industry averages. Analysts would then logically focus on relative increases in the firm's inventory: whether the increase is likely temporary or permanent, how the firm finances the inventory, and how the relative increases in inventory will affect the firm's liquidity and overall performance.

4.2.3 Cash ratio

The **cash ratio** is a more conservative liquidity measure than the current or quick ratio. The cash ratio only includes cash and marketable securities in the numerator:

$$Cash\ ratio = \frac{Cash + Marketable\ securities}{Current\ liabilities}$$

The cash ratio is too conservative to accurately reflect a firm's liquidity position because it assumes that firms can fund their current liabilities with only cash and marketable securities. Analyzing a cash ratio, however, could be helpful for assessing a firm's liquidity when the firm needs to pay most or all of its current liabilities with cash in the near term. As with the other liquidity ratios, a higher cash ratio indicates a stronger liquidity condition.

4.3 Debt Management Ratios

Debt management ratios characterize a firm in terms of the relative mix of debt and equity financing and provide measures of the long-term debt paying ability of the firm. The two basic types of debt management ratios include the debt ratio and the long-term debt ratio, while the coverage ratios include the interest coverage ratio and the cash flow coverage ratio.

4.3.1 Debt Ratio

The ratio of total debt to total assets, generally called the **debt ratio**, measures the percentage of funds provided by creditors.

$$Debt\ ratio = \frac{Total\ liabilities}{Total\ assets}$$

Total debt includes both current liabilities and long-term debt. Creditors prefer a low or moderate debt ratio because it provides more protection if the firm experiences financial problems. Stockholders, on the other hand, may want more leverage because it magnifies expected earnings.

Two useful variations of the debt ratio are the debt-to-equity ratio and the equity multiplier. The **debt-to-equity ratio** is computed by dividing the firm's total liabilities by its total equity.

$$Debt\text{-}to\text{-}equity\ ratio = \frac{Total\ liabilities}{Total\ equity}$$

The **equity multiplier** is computed by dividing total assets by total equity.

$$Equity\ multiplier = \frac{Total\ assets}{Total\ equity}$$

4.3.2 Long-term Debt Ratio

Long-term debt ratio is computed by dividing a firm's long-term debt, usually defined as all non-current liabilities, by its total assets. By excluding current liabilities, this ratio may provide better insight into a firm's debt management policy. Some current liabilities, such as accounts payable, result from operations and may not be relevant to the firm's debt management policy.

$$Long\text{-}term\ debt\ ratio = \frac{Long\text{-}term\ debt}{Total\ assets}$$

When computing the debt ratio and the long-term debt ratio, some managers and analysts use total capital in the denominator in place of total assets. The resulting ratios are defined as the debt-to-total-capital and long-term debt to total capital ratios, respectively. Total capital includes all non-current liabilities plus equity, and thus excludes short-term debt. We exclude short-term debt because it usually does not represent a permanent source of financing and is thus constantly changing, and because some current liabilities, such as accounts payable, reflect the firm's trade practice more than its debt management policy.

Leverage ratios characterize a firm in terms of its relative amount of debt financing, but they do not indicate the firm's ability to meet its debt obligations. In fact, the possibility exists that a firm with a higher debt ratio could actually in a stronger position to service the firm's debt due to stronger earnings and cash flows than a firm with a lower debt ratio and weaker earnings. The next group of debt management ratios provides a measure of the firm's ability to meet its long-term debt obligations by relating them to earnings and cash flow measures.

4.3.3 Interest Coverage Ratio

The interest coverage ratio, also called times interest earned, is computed by dividing the firm's earnings before interest and taxes (EBIT) by its interest expense.

$$Interest\ coverage\ ratio = \frac{EBIT}{Interest\ expense}$$

The ratio measures the extent to which operating income can decline before the firm is unable to meet its annual interest costs. Failure to meet this obligation can bring legal action by the firm's creditors, possibly resulting in bankruptcy. Note that earnings before interest and taxes, rather than net income, is used in the numerator because interest is paid with pre-tax dollars, and the firm's ability to pay current interest is not affected by taxes.

4.3.4 Cash Flow Coverage Ratio

The **cash flow coverage ratio** is an earnings-based ratio, since firms pay debt and other financial obligations with actual cash (not earnings), cash flow ratios may provide a better indication of a firm's ability to meet these obligations. One version of a cash flow coverage ratio is computed by adding back depreciation to the firm's EBIT in the numerator.

$$Cash\ flow\ coverage\ ratio = \frac{EBIT + Depreciation}{Interest\ expense}$$

Depreciation is added back to EBIT to estimate cash flow because depreciation is a non-cash expense subtracted from revenues to calculate EBIT on the income statement.

4.3.5 Cash flow to debt ratio

The ratio of **cash flow to debt ratio** refers to the ratio of net cash flow from operating activities to total liabilities. It is the ability to measure the net cash flow from operating activities of enterprises and repay all debts. The formula is as follows:

$$Cash\ flow\ to\ debt\ ratio = \frac{Net\ cash\ flow\ from\ operating\ activities}{Total\ liabilities}$$

In general, the total liabilities in this ratio are based on the end of the period rather than the average, as the actual repayment is the ending amount, not the average amount.

4.4 Asset Management Ratios

Asset management ratios, also referred to as asset utilization or asset efficiency ratios, measure a firm's ability to manage the assets at its disposal.

4.4.1 Accounts Receivable Turnover Ratio

The **accounts receivable turnover ratio** is computed by dividing net credit sales by the average accounts receivable outstanding. When the financial statements do not separate cash and credit sales, total net sales are often used in the numerator. Technically, the numerator should only include credit sales because the accounts receivable in the denominator arise only from credit sales.

$$Accounts\ receivable\ turnover\ ratio = \frac{Net\ credit\ sales}{Average\ accounts\ receivable}$$

This ratio measures how many times a firm's accounts receivable are generated and collected during the year. In general, higher receivables turnover ratios imply that a firm is managing its accounts receivable efficiently. But a high accounts receivable turnover ratio may indicate that a firm's credit sales policy is too restrictive; managers should consider whether a more lenient policy could lead to enhanced sales. Managers should analyze the tradeoff between any increased sales from a more lenient credit policy and the associated costs of longer collection periods and more uncollected receivables to determine whether changing the firm's credit sales policy could increase shareholder's wealth.

A low or declining accounts receivable turnover ratio may indicate the firm is either becoming lax in its efforts to collect receivables or is not writing off receivables that are unlikely to be ultimately collected. By performing an aging of the receivables account, where receivables are sorted by the length of time outstanding, managers can assess likelihood of collecting outstanding receivables. Those receivables that have been outstanding the longest time often have the lowest likelihood of eventual collection.

Average accounts receivable is used in the denominator because the net credit sales is a cumulative sales number that reflects operations over one year, while a balance sheet item reflects the amount at the end of the fiscal year. Averaging a firm's monthly or quarterly receivables over the year typically yields a better estimate of the receivables outstanding during the year. One common approach to determine average accounts receivable is to add the beginning and ending amounts for the period and divide by two.

A variant of the accounts receivable turnover ratio is the receivables collection period which is computed by dividing 365 by the accounts receivable turnover ratio.

$$Receivables\ collection\ period = \frac{365}{Accounts\ receivable\ turnover\ ratio}$$

As its name suggests, the receivables collection period indicates how many days a firm takes to convert accounts receivable into cash. If the receivables collection period exceeds a firm's credit terms, this may indicate that a firm is ineffective in collecting its credit sales or is granting credit to marginal customers.

4.4.2 Inventory Turnover Ratio

The **inventory turnover ratio** is computed by dividing the cost of goods sold by the average inventory.

$$Inventory\ turnover\ ratio = \frac{Cost\ of\ goods\ sold}{Average\ inventory}$$

A high inventory turnover ratio, relative to some benchmark, suggests efficient management of the firm's inventory. A low, declining ratio may suggest the firm has continued to build up inventory in the face of weakening demand or maybe carrying and reporting outdated or obsolete inventory that could only be sold at reduced prices, if at all. On the other hand, a manager or analyst should check to make sure that a high ratio does not reflect lost sales opportunities because of inadequate inventory levels caused by production problems, poor sales forecasting, or weak coordination between sales and production activities within the firm. The advent of computer inventory systems in recent years has allowed many firms to keep inventory levels to a minimum.

The inventory processing period is computed by dividing 365 by the inventory turnover ratio.

$$Inventory\ processing\ period = \frac{365}{Inventory\ turnover\ ratio}$$

The inventory processing period indicates the average number of days a firm takes to process and sell its inventory.

4.4.3 Accounts Payable Turnover Ratio

The **accounts payable turnover ratio** is computed by dividing the cost of goods sold by the average accounts payable for the firm.

$$Accounts\ payable\ turnover\ ratio = \frac{Cost\ of\ goods\ sold}{Average\ accounts\ payable}$$

This ratio measures how many times a firm's accounts payable are generated and paid during the year. In general, as long as a firm pays its bills in a timely manner and satisfies its financial obligations to its suppliers, the lower the payables turnover ratio the better.

The accounts payable payment period can be computed by dividing 365 by the accounts payable turnover ratio.

$$Accounts\ payable\ payment\ period = \frac{365}{Accounts\ payable\ turnover\ ratio}$$

The accounts payable payment period measures how long, on average, a firm takes to pay its accounts payable. Think of the accounts payable payment period as the counterpart to the average collection period. In general, high accounts payable payment periods are beneficial to the firm as accounts payable are a low cost source of funds for the firm.

When a firm produces goods or acquires inventory for the sale and/or sells the items on a credit basis, it will need to have ample cash during the period between when the firm must pay for the raw materials, inventory and labor and when it receives cash from the sale of goods. The receivables, inventory, and payables "period" can be combined to determine the length of time that the cash is tied up in this cycle, i. e. a time period defined as the cash conversion cycle for the firm:

$$\begin{matrix} Cash \\ conversion \\ cycle \end{matrix} = \begin{pmatrix} Receivables \\ collection\ period \end{pmatrix} + \begin{pmatrix} Inventory \\ processing\ period \end{pmatrix} - \begin{pmatrix} Accounts\ payable \\ payment\ period \end{pmatrix}$$

Thus, the cash conversion cycle is the length of time a company's cash is tied up in the business. A firm's management can reduce its cash conversion cycle and free up cash for other activities by collecting its receivables more promptly, reducing the inventory processing time, or lengthening the time required to pay its suppliers. The cash conversion cycle increases when firms take longer to process inventory (buy and process raw materials, acquire inventory for sale, and make the eventual sale) and to collect the accounts receivable generated from credit sales. This cash conversion cycle correspondingly decreases by the amount of time the firm takes to pay its expenses associated with the sale of these goods (trades payable).

4.4.4 Non-current asset turnover rate

The **non-current asset turnover rate** is calculated by dividing the company's operating income by non-current assets.

$$Non\text{-}current\ asset\ turnover\ ratio = \frac{Operating\ income}{Non\text{-}current\ assets}$$

This ratio measures the number of times the company's annual non-current assets are turned over, that is, the operating income supported by each non-current asset. The non-current asset turnover rate reflects the management efficiency of non-current assets, mainly used for investment budget and project management, and it is determined whether the investment and competition strategy, acquisition and divestiture policies are consistent.

Non-current asset turnover days can be calculated by dividing 365 by the non-current asset turnover rate.

$$Non\text{-}current\ asset\ turnover\ period = \frac{365}{Non\text{-}current\ asset\ turnover\ ratio}$$

The working capital turnover days measure the time required for the turnover of non-current assets, that is, the average time required for non-current assets to be converted into cash.

4.4.5 Asset Turnover Ratios

Other asset management measures include two ratios that measure how efficiently management is using its fixed assets and total assets to generate sales. The fixed asset turnover and total asset turnover ratios are computed by dividing net sales by the appropriate asset figure:

$$Fixed\ asset\ turnover\ ratio = \frac{Net\ sales}{Average\ net\ fixed\ assets}$$

$$Total\ asset\ turnover\ ratio = \frac{Net\ sales}{Average\ total\ assets}$$

The **fixed asset turnover ratio** indicates how efficiently a firm's management uses its net fixed assets to generate sales. Similarly, the **total asset turnover ratio** indicates how efficiently management uses total assets to generate sales. For example, a fixed asset turnover of 2.0 times would indicate that the firm generates $2.00 of net sales for each dollar invested in net fixed assets. High asset turnover ratios generally indicate more efficient use of the firm's fixed assets. However, biases may occur due to the historic cost accounting principle used for a firm's fixed assets. A firm with old plant and equipment will have higher asset turnover ratios as the equipment is depreciated and reported on the balance sheet at low book value, especially under periods of high inflation. Thus, a high asset turnover ratio may simply indicate that a firm needs to replace the aging plant and equipment. Biases may also result from the depreciation method used and the extent to which a firm leases rather than owns its fixed assets.

4.5 Profitability Ratios

Profitability ratio measures the earning power of a firm. They measure management's ability to control expenses in relation to sales and reflect a firm's operating performance, riskiness, and leverage. Some of the most commonly used profitability ratios include the gross profit margin, operating profit margin, net profit margin, return on assets, total return on assets, return on total equity, and return on common equity.

4.5.1 Gross Profit Margin

The **gross profit margin** is computed by dividing a firm's gross profit by net sales.

$$Gross\ profit\ margin = \frac{Gross\ profit}{Net\ sales}$$

The gross profit margin indicates the gross profit generated per dollar of net sales. A firm with a gross profit margin of 30 percent generates $0.30 of gross profit per $1.00 of sales. Since the cost of sales is the only item subtracted from net sales to compute gross profit, the gross profit margin indicates the relationship between sales and manufacturing or production costs.

4.5.2 Operating Profit Margin

A firm's **operating profit margin** is computed by dividing its operating profit by net sales.

$$Operating\ profit\ margin = \frac{Operating\ profit}{Net\ sales}$$

Operating profit is computed by subtracting the cost of sales, selling, general and administrative expenses, and depreciation expenses from net sales. Thus, the operating profit margin, which indicates the operating profit generated per dollar of net sales, measures the firm's operating profitability before financing costs.

4.5.3 Net Profit Margin

The **net profit margin** measures the percentage of sales that result in net income, and is calculated as:

$$Net\ profit\ margin = \frac{Net\ income}{Net\ sales}$$

High net profit margins suggest a firm can control its costs or has a solid competitive position within its industry that is not threatened by cost-cutting competitors. Low net profit margins suggest a firm has not controlled its costs well or that other firms in the industry offer lower prices that threaten its competitiveness. Net profit margins vary widely by the type of industry. Firms in industries with high sales volumes (like retail grocery stores) can operate profitably with relatively low net profit margins because they experience a high turnover of their total assets, while firms in other industries require much higher margins to survive.

Using net income from recurring operations in the numerator avoids including changes in net profit margins caused by unusual or infrequent items, extraordinary items, discontinued operations, and changes in accounting principles. Analysts often exclude these nonrecurring items from net income to concentrate on income resulting from normal activities and operations.

4.5.4 Return on Assets

The **return on asset (ROA)** ratio measures the net income generated from each dollar invested in total assets, and is usually calculated as:

$$Return\ on\ assets = \frac{Net\ income}{Average\ total\ assets}$$

The net income should be from recurring operations, thereby excluding income or loss from transactions outside the ordinary course of business. Analysts often compute average total assets as the sum of the beginning and ending total assets for the period divided by two. ROA ratios are also affected by the age of a firm's plant and equipment, especially during periods of moderate to high inflation. If the firm's fixed assets are old and have been depreciated to low book value, and the assets have not lost their productive ability, the low figure in the denominator will inflate ROA.

4.5.5 Total Return on Assets

Since total assets are financed by both debt and equity and provide returns to both groups of investors, some analysts compute **total return on assets** by adding a firm's interest expense to the numerator.

$$Total\ return\ on\ assets = \frac{Net\ income + Interest\ expense}{Average\ total\ assets}$$

Without this adjustment, firms with high relative amounts of debt financing will have lower returns on assets.

4.5.6 Return on Equity

The **return on equity ratio(ROE)** measures the accounting return earned on the capital provided by the firm's preferred and common stockholders. The computation of ROE is:

$$Return\ on\ total\ equity = \frac{Net\ income}{Average\ total\ equity}$$

ROE indicates how well management has used shareholder resources to generate net income. This ratio is often referred to as **return on total equity (ROTE)** because the equity figure includes both common and preferred equity and the net income before any dividends paid to common or preferred shareholders.

4.5.7 Return on Common Equity

Return on common equity (ROCE) focuses on just the return to common shareholders and is computed by removing the dividends to preferred shareholders from net income and dividing by the capital provided by common shareholders. The computation of ROCE is:

$$Return\ on\ common\ equity = \frac{Net\ income - Preferred\ dividends}{Average\ common\ equity}$$

Both returns on equity ratios are accounting-based measures that do not typically represent the actual return earned by shareholders. Net income is an accrual-based accounting measure of profit earned during the period and may differ substantially from the net cash flow generated during the period. Also, the equity amount in the denominator represents the equity capital that has been invested in the firm, including reinvestment of retained earnings, but does not represent the current market value of the firm's equity investment.

4.5.8 DuPont Analysis of ROE

Analysts often examine the return on equity more carefully by breaking it down into other ratios using a traditional **DuPont analysis framework** where:

$$Return\ on\ equity = Profit\ margin \times Total\ asset\ turnover \times Equity\ multiplier$$

$$Return\ on\ equity = \frac{Net\ income}{Sales} \times \frac{Sales}{Average\ total\ assets} \times \frac{Total\ assets}{Equity}$$

By separating ROE into these three components, an analyst can determine whether changes in a firm's ROE are attributable to changes in the level of earnings generated from sales, the sales generated from total assets, or the equity multiplier (leverage factor) employed in the financing of the firm's assets.

4.6 Market Value Ratios

Market value ratios use market data such as stock price to provide useful information about the firm's relative value. Commonly used market value ratios include the price-to-earnings ratios, market-to-book value ratio, dividend yield, and dividend payout.

4.6.1 Price/earnings Ratio

The **price/earnings ratio (P/E)**, one of the most widely used financial ratios, is computed by dividing the market price per share of the firm's common stock by its earnings per share.

$$Price/Earings\ ratio = \frac{Market\ price\ per\ share}{Earnings\ per\ share}$$

The P/E ratio indicates how many investors are willing to pay per dollar of earnings for shares of the firm's common stock. It provides an important indication of how the market perceives the growth and profit opportunities of a firm. High growth firms with strong future profit opportunities will command a higher P/E ratio, but it has several potential shortcomings. For example, a firm can have negative earnings, which produces a meaningless P/E ratio. In addition, management can distort reported earnings because of the discretion allowed by accounting practices.

4.6.2 Price/Sales Ratio

The **price/sales ratio (P/S)** is calculated by dividing the stock price per share of the common stock by the operating income per share. The operating income per share is the ratio of the operating income to the weighted average number of shares of the common stock in circulation, indicating the operating income created by each common stock.

$$Price/Sales\ ratio = \frac{Market\ price\ per\ share}{Operating\ income\ per\ share}$$

The results of the market-to-sales ratio indicate the price that ordinary shareholders are willing to pay for each dollar of operating income.

4.6.3 Market-to-book Value Ratio

A firm's **market-to-book value ratio** is computed by dividing the market value of the firm's equity by its book value of equity.

$$Market\text{-}to\text{-}book\ value\ ratio = \frac{Market\ value\ of\ equity}{Book\ value\ of\ equity}$$

In this ratio, the book value of equity equals total assets minus total liabilities less preferred stock. The market-to-book value ratio measures how much value the firm has created for its shareholders.

4.6.4 Dividend Yield and Payout

Dividend yield is computed by dividing a firm's dividends per share by market price of its common stock.

$$Dividend\ yield = \frac{Dividends\ per\ share}{Market\ price\ per\ share}$$

Dividend yield represents parts of a stock's total return; another part of a stock's total return is price appreciation. The **dividend payout** is the percentage of a firm's earnings paid out as cash dividends.

$$Dividend\ payout = \frac{Cash\ dividend\ per\ share}{Earnings\ per\ share}$$

4.7 Uses and Limitations of Financial Ratio Analysis

Note, while ratio analysis can provide useful information concerning a company's operations and financial condition, it does have limitations that necessitate care and judgment. Some potential problems are listed below:

1. Many large firms operate different divisions in different industries, and for such companies, it is difficult to develop a meaningful set of industry averages. Therefore, ratio analysis is more useful for small, narrowly focused firms than for large, multidivisional ones.

2. Most firms want to be better than average, so merely attaining average performance is not necessarily good. As a target for high-level performance, it is best to focus on the industry leaders' ratios. Benchmarking helps in this regard.

3. Inflation may have badly distorted firm's balance sheets—recorded values are often substantially different from "true" values. Further, because inflation affects both deprecation charges and inventory costs, profits are also affected. Thus, ratio analysis for one firm over time, or a comparative analysis of firms of different ages, must be interpreted with judgment.

4. Seasonal factors can also distort ratio analysis. For example, the inventory turnover ratio for a good processor will be radically different if the balance sheet figure used for inventory is the one just before versus just after the close of the canning season. This problem can be minimized by using monthly averages for inventory (and receivables) when calculating turnover ratios.

5. Different accounting practices can distort comparisons. As noted earlier, inventory valuation and depreciation methods can affect financial statements and thus distort

comparisons among firms. Also, if one firm leases a substantial amount of its productive equipment, then its assets may appear low relative to sales because leased assets often do not appear on the balance sheet. At the same time, the liability associated with the lease obligation may not be shown as a debt. Therefore, leasing can artificially improve both the turnover and the debt ratios.

6. It is difficult to generalize about whether a particular ratio is "good" or "bad". For example, a high current ratio may indicate a strong liquidity position, which is good, and excessive cash, which is bad (because excessive cash in the bank is a non-earning asset). Similarly, a high fixed assets turnover ratio may denote either that a firm uses its assets efficiently or that it is undercapitalized and cannot afford to buy enough assets.

7. A firm may have some ratios that look "good" and others that look "bad", making it difficult to tell whether the company is, on balance, strong or weak. However, statistical procedures can be used to analyze the net effects of a set of ratios. Many banks and other lending organizations use discriminant analysis, a statistical technique, to analyze firms' financial ratios, and then classify the firms according to their probability of getting into financial trouble.

8. Effective use of financial ratios requires that the financial statement upon which they are based be accurate. Revelations in 2001 and 2002 of accounting fraud by such industry giants as WorldCom and Enron show that financial statements are not always accurate; hence information based on reported data can be misleading.

Ratio analysis is useful, but analysts should be aware of these problems and make adjustments as necessary. Ratio analysis conducted in a mechanical, unthinking manner is dangerous, but if it is used intelligently and with good judgment, it can provide useful insights into a firm's operations.

核心词汇
Core Words and Expressions

financial ratio　财务比率　　　　　　　　bond indenture　债券契约
restrictive covenants　限制性条款　　　　financial analyst　财务分析师

liquidity ratio　流动性比率
current ratio　流动比率
last-in, first-out (LIFO)　后进先出
first-in, first-out (FIFO)　先进先出
window dressing　账面粉饰（基金管理人的一种做法，即在季度末售出亏损股票，使其投资组合整个季度的回报率不会被这些不良资产所拖累）
marketable securities　有价证券
quick ratio　速动比率
cash ratio　现金比率
debt management ratios　债务管理比率
debt ratio　债务比率
debt-to-equity ratio　债务与权益比率
equity multiplier　权益乘数
long-term ratio　长期比率
debt-to-total-capital　债务与全部资本比率
long-term debt to total capital ratio　长期债务与全部资本比率
leverage ratios　杠杆比率
interest coverage ratio　利息保障比率
earnings before interest and taxes (EBIT)　息税前盈余
cash flow coverage ratio　现金流量保障比率
asset management ratio　资产管理比率
inventory turnover ratio　存货周转率
accounts receivable turnover ratio　应收账款周转率
inventory processing period　存货周转期
accounts payable turnover ratio　应付账款周转率
cash conversion cycle　现金周转期
asset turnover ratio　资产周转比率
total asset turnover ratio　全部资产周转比率
profitability ratio　盈利比率
gross profit margin　毛利
operating profit margin　经营利润
net profit margin　净利润
return on assets (ROA)　资产收益率
return on equity (ROE)　权益报酬率
return on total equity (ROTE)　全部权益报酬率
return on common equity (ROCE)　普通股权益报酬率
DuPont Analysis of ROE　权益报酬率的杜邦分析体系
market value ratio　市场价值比率
P/E ratio　市盈率
market-to-book value ratio　市场价值与账面价值的比率
dividend yield　股利收益率
dividend payout　股利支付率
discriminant analysis　判别分析

即 时 问 答

1. What is financial leverage? Which ratio can be used to measure a firm's degree of indebtedness? Which ratio can be used to assess the firm's ability to meet interest

payments associated with debt?
2. Financial ratio analysis is often divided into four categories: liquidity, activity, debt, and profitability ratios. Differentiate each of these areas of analysis from the others. Which is the greatest relative concern to present and prospective creditors?
3. Describe how you would approach a complete ratio analysis of the firm by summarizing a large number of ratios.
4. In what circumstances would a firm have a high gross profit margin and a low net profit margin?
5. Profitability ratios all have the same figure in the numerator. What is it? What do these ratios measure? How do you interpret the results?

思考与探索
Thinking and Exploration

Please find the 2018 Annual Report of Berkshire Hathaway, Inc., then read through it and make a financial ratio analysis report.

汉 译 英
Translation

客车生产制造商——宇通客车，2017年实现净利润31.68亿元，同比增长22.78%。同期，宇通客车的竞争对手金龙汽车，实现净利润10.33亿元，同比增长147.79%。以2017年每股收益和12月27日的收盘价计算，宇通客车的市盈率为17.01倍，而金龙客车的市盈率为17.37倍。请结合这两家公司的年度财务报告，判断到底哪一家公司在2017年表现得更好一些，是宇通客车还是金龙汽车？

知识扩展
More Knowledge

创造性会计（Creating Accounting）

创造性会计由美国会计学者格里夫斯（Griffiths）在1986年出版的《创造性会计》中提出，其是指企业管理当局及其会计机构和人员针对会计规则的漏洞或缺陷（包括会计规则未涉及的领域），依据客观环境或出于自身需要，创造性地发明、尝试或选择会计程序和方法，通过包装或粉饰公司财务报表，以达到某种目的的会计活动的会计处理方式，它的产生与当时的经济环境压力以及会计规范的灵活性和不完善性有关。不同于做假账，创造性会计是在不违背会计准则和有关会计法规的前提下，有意识地选择会计程序和会计方法，其本身并不是违法行为，但会使得公司的财务报表信息严重失实。

国外早期的创造性会计行为包括收益平滑（有意压低收益较高年度的报表利润并转移到亏损年度）和隐蔽准备金（认为的低估公司的资产或高估负债），常常同时被采用，此外还有窗饰、表外筹资、财务报告的扩展等方式。我国上市公司普遍使用的有滥用并购会计、任意变更计提方法、操纵合并财务报表、资产置换，等等。

公司的一切控制机制都依靠会计信息的可靠性，而创造性会计以各种障眼法，使公司控制者麻痹，导致控制机制失灵，许多公司因此陷入一蹶不振的境地或破产倒闭，如安然公司、世通公司。

关于财务分析学需要说明的若干问题

本部分所涉猎的财务比率分析仅仅是财务分析学内容的一小部分，也有学者将其称为传统的财务分析。传统的财务分析具体包括盈利能力分析、偿债能力或支付能力分析、营运能力分析（或投资分析、筹资分析、经营分析，或资产负债表分析、利润表分析、现金流量表分析）等，现在国内外越来越多的财务分析教材拓展了传统的财务分析的范畴，将战略分析、会计分析、价值评估分析、预测分析等涵盖进来。

关于财务分析学的体系问题请参考下列学者的书籍：

郭永清：《财务报表分析与股票估值》（2017）

姜国华：《财务报表分析与证券投资》（2008）

张然：《基本面量化投资：运用财务分析和量化策略获取超额收益》（2017）

肖星：《上市公司财务问题及其分析》（2002）

张新民：《战略视角下的财务报表分析》（2017）

张先治和陈友邦：《财务分析》（2019）

克雷沙·G. 帕利普、保罗 M. 希利：《经营分析与估值》（2014）

斯蒂芬 H. 佩因曼：《财务报表分析与证券估值》（2016）

相 关 网 址
Useful Websites

1. 以下网站可以查到美国股票市场的最新信息和华尔街的研究报告：

http://www.bloomberg.com/

2. 以下网站可以查到美国上市公司的财务报表和财务分析师的报告：

雅虎网财经频道　　http://finance.yahoo.com

第 5 章
TOPIC 5

Time Value of Money and Valuation
货币时间价值与估价

新闻视听
News in Media

Most of you have the experience of depositing money in the bank, but do you know how the bank calculates the interest? Please listen to the dialogue.

本章新闻视听资料请扫二维码收听。

名人名言
Wisdom

Time is money.

I will pay you Tuesday for a hamburger I can eat today.

——Wimpie, from the Popeye cartoon, E.C. Segar

A cynic is a man who knows the price of everything and the value of nothing.

——Oscar Wilde Lady Windermere's Fan

The problem in valuation is not that there are not enough models to value an asset. It is that there are too many. Choosing the right model to use in valuation is as critical to arriving at a reasonable value as understanding how to use the model.

——Aswath Damodaran, *Investment Valuation*

Receive $10, 000 now OR Receive $10 000 in Three Years

Congratulations!!! You have won a cash prize! You have two payment options:

A. Receive $10, 000 now; OR

B. Receive $10, 000 in three years.

Okay, the above offer is hypothetical, but play along with me here ⋯ Which option would you choose?

If you're like most people, you would choose to receive the $10, 000 now. After all, three years is a long time to wait. Why would any rational person defer payment into the future when he or she could have the same amount of money now? For most of us, taking the money in the present is just plain instinctive. So at the most basic level, the time value of money demonstrates that, all things being equal, it is better to have money now rather than later.

But why is this? A $100 bill has the same value as a $100 bill one year from now, doesn't it? Actually, although the bill is the same, you can do much more with the money if you have it now: over time you can earn more interest on your money.

Back to our example: by receiving $10, 000 today, you are poised to increase the future value of your money by investing and gaining interest over a period of time. For option B, you don't have time on your side, and the payment received in three years would be your future value. To illustrate, we have provided a timeline:

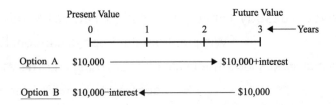

If you are choosing option A, your future value will be $10, 000 plus any interest acquired over the three years. The future value for option B, on the other hand, would only be $10, 000. But stay tuned to find out how to calculate exactly how much more option A is worth, compared to option B.

TOPIC 5　Time Value of Money and Valuation

概览 Overview

The time value of money serves as the foundation for all other notions in finance. It impacts business finance, consumer finance and government finance. Most of us would prefer to receive money today, so we can invest the money and expect to have an even greater sum in the future. The same reasoning suggests we should prefer to pay money we own later than sooner. Thus, the value of money depends on the time when it is paid or received. The principles of time value analysis have many applications, ranging from setting up schedules for paying off loans to capital investment decisions.

This topic covers an introduction to simple interest and compound interest, and then introduces the concepts of compounding, annuities due, and perpetuities.

This topic also deals with the mathematics of the time value of money and the techniques to value future cash flows. Then we show how to use these concepts and techniques to value a firm's long-term securities — bonds and common stock. In fact, of all the concepts used in finance, none is more important than the time value of money, also called discounted cash flow (DCF) analysis.

正文 Text

5.1　Central Concepts in Financial Management

An old saying is that "A bird in the hand is worth two in the bush". In a way, this expression refers to the time value of birds. That is, having a single bird in the hand today is worth more than the change of catching two birds in the future. The bird-in-hand expression reflects two central concepts in financial management: the risk-return tradeoff and the time value of money.

- **Risk-return tradeoff**: Investors will take on additional risk only if they anticipate high returns.
- **Time value of money**: A dollar available today is worth more than a dollar available at a future date. This is because a dollar today can be invested to earn a return.

Thus, investors require compensation for both risk bearing and the time value of money. These two principles lie at the heart of the financial decision-making concepts. We focus on the time value of money principles in this topic and discuss risk analysis in the next.

The notion that money has time value is intuitively appealing. Knowledge of the time value of money concept is essential to an understanding of money topics in financial management. In fact, most financial decisions at both the personal and business levels involve cash flows at different points in time. Here are a few examples.

- When firms issue bonds to investors in the capital markets, they should compare the value of future cash payments to the bondholders in exchange for the cash received from them today. Analysts and investors are using time value of money concepts to value many financial securities.

- Managers who make capital investments in long-lived fixed assets should compare the value of expected future cash flows to the present cash outlay need to undertake the investment.

5.2 Simple vs. Compound Interest Rates and Future vs. Present Value

The interest rate is in essence a specialized form of time value of money, and pertains generally to the use of debt instruments. Interest rates are also often used as riskless or base rates to draw comparison to alternative riskier investments.

There are two forms of interest rates: simple and compound.

5.2.1 Simple interest

Interest that is not added to the principal or capital in calculating subsequent interest payments is referred to as **simple interest**. Under the simple interest arrangement, the amount of interest paid does not vary and is based on the initial cash flow involved. If simple interest is paid on a **debt instrument** (such as bonds), it is generally referred to as an **annuity**. The present value of the annuity is the price at which the debt instrument trades in an efficient market.

Generally, the relationship between present and future values can be defined as:
$$FV = PV \cdot (1 + n \cdot i)$$

Where FV——Future Value.

PV——Present Value.

n——Number of periods of investment.

i——Interest rate.

Alternatively, if the future value is known and we wish to calculate the principal, we can rearrange the above equation to be:
$$PV = \frac{FV}{1 + n \cdot i}$$

5.2.2 Compound interest

Compounding involves calculating interest not only on the principal but also on the interest earned to date on that principal, assuming that the interest is reinvested. The so-called compounding effect therefore tends to increase the amount of interest paid (charged) as the principal increases due to the addition of previous interest payments (charges). Most personal loans, mortgages and credit cards operate on a compounding basis. Most credit card holders are acutely aware of the implications of missing an interest payment as this amount is then added to the outstanding balance to calculate the amended amount owing! The respective formulas for future value and present value calculation are shown below:

The future value using the **compound interest rate** is:
$$FV = PV \cdot (1 + i)^n$$

The present value at **compound interest** is:
$$PV = \frac{FV}{(1 + i)^n}$$

Where "n" refers to the number of compounding periods.

5.2.3 Future Value

Future value calculations answer the question: How much will an investment be worth at a specific time in the future, compounded at a specific rate of interest? Future value is a compounded value because of compounding of interest. Another common name for future value is **terminal value**.

The level of interest rate (i) and the length of the compounding term (n) affect future values. Specifically, future values increases as the compound interest rate increases and/or the compounding term becomes longer.

5.2.4 Present Value

The process of computing the present value of a future amount is called **discounting**. The interest rate used to compute the present value is called the **discount rate**, but may also be referred to as the **opportunity cost**, **required rate of return**, and the **cost of capital**. Regardless of the term used, it represents the compound rate of return that an investor can earn on an investment.

Present values decrease as the discount rate increases. Thus, present values are inversely related to interest rates.

5.3 Annuity

An **annuity** is a series of equal and periodic cash flows with two particular traits, namely:
- the **size** of the cash flow from the security is identical in each period.
- the **timing** of the cash flows is uniform, i.e., the cash flows occur at the same periodic interval (e.g., at the end of every month or year).

If these two traits are satisfied, then the instrument could safely be classed as an **annuity**. Because of the uniform structure of this form of financial instrument, it is common practice to reduce the volume of calculations and working by using **annuity factors** or **multipliers**. Note that the correct annuity factor to use depends on whether the calculation is for a future or a present value. A good example of an annuity is an interest-bearing bond. Bonds satisfy both criteria as they pay a set coupon rate based on the initial principal invested at uniform periods in time.

Generally, annuities are classified into four categories:
- **Ordinary annuity**, in which the first cash flow in the series is one period from today.

This is the most common form of annuity.

- **Annuity due**, in which the first cash flow in the series occurs at the beginning of each period.
- **Deferred annuity**, in which the first cash flow in the series occurs beyond one period from today.
- **Perpetuity**, in which the series of payments continues indefinitely.

5.3.1 Ordinary annuity

The cash flow pattern of an ordinary annuity consists of equal amounts, equal space in time. Note that annuities focus primarily on cash flow payments. To calculate this payment, the **Face Value** of the annuity — the total amount invested as principal — must be multiplied by the **Coupon Rate**, that is, the **prevailing** interest rate offered for the annuity at the time of purchase/sale.

Future value of an ordinary annuity

The future value of an ordinary annuity is given by:

$$FV = A\left[\frac{(1+i)^n - 1}{i}\right]$$

Where FV——Future value of the annuity.

　　　　A——Annuity payment at the end of each period.

　　　　n——Number of periods of annuity.

　　　　i——Interest rate.

$\dfrac{(1+i)^n - 1}{i}$, as the **FVIFA** (future value interest factor for annuities) annuity factor, is included in most quantitative financial texts. Their use will substantially reduce the complexity of calculations as well as the time taken to do them. To check that the correct annuity factor is being applied, make sure that the calculation form corresponds with the annuity factor form, e.g., for an **FV** calculation one should use the **FVIFA** annuity factor. To confuse matters further, most texts refer to the FVIFA as "sum of an annuity" rather than "future value of an annuity".

Present value of an ordinary annuity

The present value of an ordinary annuity is the sum of the present values of all the payments of an annuity. The present value of an ordinary annuity is given by:

$$PV = \frac{A}{i}\left[1 - \frac{1}{(1+i)^n}\right]$$

Where PV——Present value of the annuity.

  A——Annuity payment at the end of each period.

  n——Number of periods of annuity.

  i——Interest rate.

$\frac{1}{i}\left[1 - \frac{1}{(1+i)^n}\right]$, as the **PVIFA** (present value interest factor for annuities) annuity factor, is included in most quantitative financial texts. It is also contained in the financial tables of the financial management textbook. Unlike the FVIFA, you will notice that the PVIFA factors are much smaller multipliers. This is consistent with the view that future values must be discounted when scaled back to present time, whereas present or near present value must be magnified to correctly equate with future value.

5.3.2 Annuity due

The distinguishing factor with an annuity due is the fact that the first cash flow occurs on the valuation date, i.e., immediately. Thus the only material difference between an ordinary annuity and an annuity due is the **timing** of the cash flows.

The natural solution to this difference is to reduce the annuity period (the "n") by one, since the first cash flow is already in its present value form, i.e., it is paid immediately and thus requires no further discounting. Therefore, the correct adjustment for an annuity due is to reduce the discounting factor by one and to add to the reduced calculation a non-discounted cash flow stream.

5.3.3 Deferred annuity

If an annuity does not begin its payment in the first period, as with an ordinary annuity, or immediately, as with an annuity due, then it is classified as a deferred annuity:

an annuity that begins its cash flow stream **subsequent to the first period**. A common example is a superannuation (hence the annuity in superannuation). With this form of investment, cash flow is added, but no periodic cash outflow is exhibited for a number of years until retirement.

A simple two-stage discounting method is applied that combines the techniques employed above. Essentially, the periodic payments are discounted back to the first period prior to the beginning of the cash flow stream. This value is then discounted back to time 0.

5.3.4 Perpetuity

Because perpetuity continues necessarily into **eternity**, there cannot be a solution to its future value. However, calculating the present value is the simplest of all annuity problems. The equation is expressed as follows:

$$PV = \frac{P}{i}$$

Where   PV——Present Value.

   P——Payment into perpetuity.

   i——Discount rate.

5.3.5 Nominal and effective interest rates

When payments are made more or less frequently than the interest is compounded, this misspecification can be resolved by matching the payment period with the compounding period. There are two methods available:

Nominal interest rate

This is an interest rate where interest is charged more frequently than the quoted rate. For example, 4.5% per quarter payable monthly means that interest will be charged each month at 1.5% per month.

Effective (annual) interest rate

The effective (annual) interest rate is calculated to determine an effective rate (usually annual) from a rate with multiple compounding periods. To make a fair comparison between two interest rates when different compounding periods are used, you should first convert both nominal (or stated) rates to their equivalent effective rates, so the effects of compounding are clear.

The effective rate of an investment will always be higher than the nominal or stated interest rate when interest is compounded more than once per year. As the number of compounding periods increases, the difference between the nominal and effective rates will also increase. To convert a nominal rate to an equivalent effective rate:

$$Effective\ rate = \left(1+\frac{i}{m}\right)^m - 1$$

Where i——Nominal or stated interest rate.

m——Number of compounding periods per year.

5.4 Valuation Fundamentals

Valuation is the process that links risk and return to estimate the worth of an asset or a firm. The term value can have different meanings when applied to a financial asset or a firm. Broadly defined, a financial asset is a monetary claim on an issuer, typically a paper asset such as a bond, preferred stock, or common stock. These different types of value include:

5.4.1 Going-concern value

Going-concern value is the value of a firm as an operating business. This type of value depends on the firm's ability to generate future cash flows rather than on its balance sheet assets. Going-concern value is particularly important when one firm wants to acquire another.

5.4.2 Liquidation value

Liquidation value is the amount of money that a firm would realize by selling its assets and paying off its liabilities. A firm's assets are generally worth more as a going concern than they are worth separately. Liquidation value per share is the actual amount per share of common stock that stockholders would receive if the firm sells all assets, pays all its liabilities including preferred stock, and divides any remaining money among them.

5.4.3 Book value

Book value is the accounting value of a firm or an asset. Book value is a historical value rather than a current value. Firms usually report book value on a per share basis. Book value per share of common stock is the shareholders' equity — total assets less liabilities and preferred stock as listed on the balance sheet — divided by the number of shares outstanding. Book value per share may bear little relationship to liquidation value per share or market value per share.

5.4.4 Market value

Market value is the price that the owner can receive from selling an asset in the market place. The key determinant of market value is the supply and demand for the asset. For stocks and bonds, market values reflect current market prices.

5.4.5 Intrinsic value

Intrinsic value, also called fundamental value, is a measure of the theoretical value of an asset. Because determining the intrinsic value requires estimates, we may never know the "actual" or "true" intrinsic value of some financial assets. Nonetheless, intrinsic value serves as a basis for determining whether to buy or sell a financial asset when compared to its market value or price.

The various types of value — book value, market value and intrinsic value — can differ for the same financial asset. For example, in a market in which security prices rapidly reflect all information about securities, called an efficient capital market, the intrinsic value of a security is equal to its market value. In less than efficient markets, market value and intrinsic value may differ. Although controversy surrounds the degree of market efficiency, most experts agree that the capital markets are not perfectly efficient. Thus, mispricing may occur for financial assets.

We focus on estimating the intrinsic value of two types of financial assets — bonds and common stock. We do not examine the valuation of the overall firm.

Corporate managers, especially financial managers, need to know how to estimate the intrinsic value of financial assets to determine if the market properly prices these assets. Financial managers also need to estimate the price that their firms are likely to receive when issuing bonds or shares of common or preferred stock. In addition, financial managers need to understand how corporate decisions may affect the value of their firm's outstanding securities, especially common stock. For example, financial management decisions determine the risk/return characteristics of the firm. These decisions cause both cash flows and required rate of return to change, which in turn cause changes in the firm's stock price.

Analysts and investors often compare the current market price of a security to the intrinsic value they estimate from a security valuation formula. If the estimate of intrinsic value exceeds an asset's market value (price), investors would consider buying an asset. Conversely, if the market value (price) exceeds the estimated intrinsic value, investors would not consider buying the asset (or would consider selling if they own it). Because the financial rewards from identifying an undervalued or overvalued security can be great, many analysts and investors devote substantial time and resources to developing innovative security valuation models, especially for common stock.

5.4.6 Valuation Approaches

There are three basic approaches to valuing financial assets — discounted cash flow (DCF) valuation, relative valuation, and contingent claim valuation. DCF valuation and relative valuation are the standard approaches to valuation.

With discounted cash flow valuation, the estimated value of a financial asset is the present value of the asset's expected future cash flows. The discounted rate should reflect the riskiness of these cash flows. Thus, DCF valuation serves as a way to estimate the intrinsic value of a security. While DCF models are considered to be theoretically correct, they often provide intrinsic value estimates that differ from prevailing market prices. These differences are likely to result from the difficulty in estimating inputs for the models.

With relative valuation, the value of a financial asset is computed relatively to how the market prices similar assets. For example, relative valuation of common stock uses firm-specific multiples such as price-to-earnings, price-to-cash flows, price-to-book value, and price-to-sales ratios. This valuation method provides information on current valuation, but it does not provide guidance on the appropriateness of the current valuation. That is, the approach measures relative value, not intrinsic value. Relative valuation techniques are appropriate to consider when a good set of comparable entities is available and when serious undervaluation or overvaluation does not prevail in the market.

In some situations, option-pricing models may give more realistic estimates of value than those obtained using DCF valuation or relative valuation models. With contingent claim valuation, as asset with the characteristics of an option is valued using an option-pricing model. Some cases in which managers and analysts may view equity in a firm as an option include equity in a deeply troubled firm, natural resources firm, and firms deriving much of their value from product patents. In this topic, we focus only on DCF valuation.

5.4.7 Discounted Cash Flow Valuation

The valuation of any financial asset is a function of the:
- amount of the expected cash flows (returns) generated by the asset over its life.
- timing of the cash flows.
- riskiness associated with these cash flows as measured by the required rate of return.

The value of a financial asset is directly related to the amount of expected cash flows, but inversely related to the amount of risk. In addition, the timing of cash flows affects the value of a financial asset. The basic DCF valuation model combines these variables into the following formula, which shows that intrinsic value is the sum of an asset's discounted cash flows over the life of the security. With certain modifications and customization, this model serves as the basis for valuing bonds, preferred stock, and common stock.

$$V_0 = \sum_{t=1}^{n} \frac{CF_t}{(1+K)^t}$$

Where V_0 is the intrinsic value of an asset at time zero; CF_t is the expected future cash flow at the end of year t; K is the appropriate required rate of return (discounted rate); n is the remaining term to maturity; and t is the time period.

Applying the basic DCF model involves a three-step valuation process:

- Estimate the future cash flows expected over the life of the asset.
- Determine the appropriate required rate of return on the asset.
- Calculate the present value of the estimated cash flows using the required rate of return as the discounted rate.

5.5 Bond Valuation

A bond is a contract or a promissory note issued by a corporation or government promising to pay the owner of the bond a predetermined amount of interest each year. It can also be defined as a debt security that promises to make payments periodically for a specified period of time. Bond is a security that involves no ownership interest in the issuing entity.

5.5.1 Contractual Provisions of a Typical Bond

Par Value

Par value, also called the face value or maturity value, is the nominal value stated on the bond. Par value represents the amount of principal per bond that the corporation agrees to repay when the bond matures. The typical way of quoting the market value (prices) of a bond is as a percent of its par value.

The par value is not necessarily equal to the bond's market value or price. The price of a bond may rise above or fall below its par value due to differences between its coupon rate and prevailing market interest rates. If interest rates move above (below) the bond's coupon rate, the bond will sell below (above) its par value. A bond that trades below its par value sells at a discount; a bond that sells above its par value trades at a premium.

Coupon and Coupon Rate

Coupon is the interest on a bond that the issuer promises to pay the holder until maturity. **Coupon payment** is the periodic interest payment which is equal to the **coupon interest rate** as a percentage rate multiplied by the maturity or par value of the bond. The coupon interest rate, also called the nominal yield, face value, is the contractual rate of interest based on a bond's par value.

Maturity

Term to maturity or simply maturity of a bond is the length of time until the agreement expires. At maturity, the bondholder receives the last coupon interest payment and the bond's par value payment from the issuer.

Call Provisions

A **call provision** gives the issuer the right to buy back or "call" all or a part of a bond issue before maturity (under specified terms). With a call feature, the issuer may decide to retire bonds to take advantage of low interest rates, to get rid of restrictive indenture provisions, or to reduce indebtedness. Because a call provision is beneficial to the issuer, the issuer usually has to offer investors some enticements to sell such a bond. These enticements include a higher-than-normal coupon rate, a provision not to call the bond until after a specified period (called a deferred call provision), and a call premium. A call premium is an additional amount that the issuer agrees to pay above the bond's par value to repurchase the bond. The price at which the issuer may call a bond (par value plus any call premium) is termed as the call price.

Sinking Fund Provisions

A **sinking fund provision** permits the issuer to retire a bond through a series of predefined principal payments over the life of the issue. Sinking fund requirements often do not apply during the early years of a bond issue. Some bonds carry an accelerated sinking fund provision, which allows the issuer to retire a larger proportion of the issue at par, at its discretion.

Conversion Rights

Conversion rights give the bondholder the right to convert bond into a specified number of shares of common stock at a predetermined fixed price. Such bonds are called convertible debt because they offer the bondholder a chance for capital gains in exchange for lower coupon payments. This option benefits the bondholders if the equivalent value of the common shares from conversion is greater than the value of the bond. Almost all convertible bonds are callable.

Put Provisions

Some bonds have a **put provision**, which gives the bondholder the right to sell the bond stock back to the issuer at the put price on certain dates before maturity. The put price is a price at or near par. If interest rates increase, causing the bond price to fall below par, the bondholder may sell the bond back to the issuer at par or a higher price.

Indenture

An **indenture** is a legal document between the issuer and the bondholders detailing the terms and conditions of the debt issue. The purpose of this agreement is to address all matters pertaining to the bond.

An indenture generally contains protective covenants, which limit certain actions that the company might be taking during the term of the agreement. Two types of protective covenants are negative covenants and positive covenants. Negative covenants limit or prohibit the borrower from taking certain actions such as paying too many dividends, pledging assets to other lenders, selling major assets, merging with another firm, and adding more long-term debt. Positive or affirmative covenants are actions that the borrower promises to perform such as maintaining certain ratios, keeping collateral in good condition, and making timely payments of interest and principal. Failing to adhere to these covenants could place the bond issuer in default.

Trustee

The issuer must appoint a **trustee** for each bond issue of a substantial size. A trustee is the bondholders' agent, typically a bank, in a public debt offering. The issuer appoints the trustee before selling the bonds to represent the bondholders in all matters concerning the bond issue. This is necessary because some bond issues have many bondholders. The trustee monitors the issuer to ensure that he complies with all terms of the indenture. If the borrower violates the terms, the trustee initiates action against the issuer and represents the bondholders in this action.

Collateral

Corporations can issue bonds as secured or unsecured debt. **Secured debt** is a debt backed by the pledge of assets as collateral. These assets are typically in the form of real property such as land and buildings (mortgage bonds) or financial assets such as stocks and bonds (collateral trust bonds). **Unsecured debt**, also called a debenture, represents bonds raised without any collateral. In the case of unsecured debt, the bondholders have a claim on the assets that the issuer has not pledged to other securities. With a subordinated debenture, the claims against a firm's assets are junior to those of secured debt and regular debenture.

Bond Rating

A **bond rating** is an assessment of the creditworthiness of the issuer. Major rating services include Standard & Poor's Corporation (S & P), Moody's Investors Service, Inc. (Moody's) and Fitch Investor Services. The purpose of bond ratings is to help investors assess default risk, which has the possibility that the issuer will fail to meet its obligations as specified in the indenture. Bond ratings range from AAA (S & P) or Aaa (Moody's), the highest or prime grade, to D, debt in default. An inverse relationship generally exists between the rating and quality of a bond and its interest rate or yield to maturity. That is, high-quality (high-rated) bonds have lower yields than low-quality (low-rated) bonds. Lower ratings by these agencies mean more risk and higher required returns. Table 5-1 summarizes the bond categories and the corresponding ratings issued by S&P and Moody's.

Table 5-1　Bond Ratings by S&P and Moody's

Quality	S&P	Moody's
Prime	AAA	Aaa
High	AA	Aa
Upper Medium	A	A
Medium	BBB	Baa
Junk	BB, B, CCC, CC, C	Ba, B, Caa, Ca, C
In Default	D	D

Theory in Practice

The relationship between bond rating and financial crisis

In the development of global financial markets, bond rating agencies have gained wide recognition in the market by providing investors with objective and independent industry analysis and risk warnings. Until the outbreak of the US subprime mortgage crisis in 2007 and the global financial crisis that spread to the whole world, the first time the US bond rating agencies were truly introduced into the public's cause, and caused widespread criticism. Although the causes of the financial crisis are complex and diverse, the US bond rating agencies represented by Moody's, Standard & Poor's and Fitch are clearly blamed. In the process of securitization of subordinated loan assets, bond rating agencies are overly optimistic about the future cash flow forecast of structured financial products and give their financial derivatives a higher bond rating. This "rating expansion" effectively links subprime mortgage loans and secondary markets. Because investors lack sufficient understanding of complex financial derivatives, they rely too much on the bond rating of financial products to make investment decisions, which leads investors to irrational purchases of financial derivatives. When the subprime mortgage crisis broke out, the bond rating of financial derivatives such as substandard bonds, which were originally high, was greatly reduced in the short term. This "excessive" downgrade of the three major bond rating agencies in the United States increased the panic in the market. The procyclical effect has aggravated the turmoil in the financial market and eventually led to the evolution of the US subprime mortgage crisis into a global financial crisis.

5.5.2 The Bond Valuation Formula

A typical (coupon) bond pays coupon every six months and pays a principal value at maturity. If the coupon payment received every six months is denoted by C, the principal payment received at maturity denoted by F, the number of the six-month periods between today and maturity by t, and the appropriate discount rate by k_B, then the cash flows from the bond can be written as:

```
0       1       2       3                   t
|       |       |       |                   |
        C       C       C                  C+F
```

and the **Bond Valuation Formula** can be written as:

$$V_B = \frac{C}{k_B}\left[1 - \frac{1}{(1+k_B)^t}\right] + \frac{F}{(1+k_B)^t}$$

5.5.3 Bond Prices and Returns

Given a bond's price, its coupon, par value, and time to maturity, two types of bond returns can be calculated.

Current Yield

The **current yield** on a bond is defined as $\frac{C}{P}$. It is also called current return on a bond. Current yield is the annual coupon of a bond expressed as a percent of its market price, P. The current yield is limited in the sense that it reflects the return on the investment only in terms of the coupon interest payments, not on their timing, length or on the principal payment at maturity.

Yield to Maturity

Yield to maturity (YTM) is also called return-to-maturity (RTM) or internal rate of return (IRR). The yield to maturity is the required rate of return that equates the market price of a bond to its intrinsic value. You can also think of yield to maturity as the implicit rate of return the market has in mind when setting the market price of the bond, i.e., the implicit rate being used by the market to price the bond. Therefore, the YTM is the rate r which satisfies the equality:

$$P = V_B = \frac{C}{k_B}\left[1 - \frac{1}{(1+k_B)^t}\right] + \frac{F}{(1+k_B)^t}$$

5.6 Common Stock Valuation

5.6.1 Common Stock Characteristics and Features

Common stock is a form of equity that represents ownership of a corporation. Common stockholders are the residual owners because their claim to earnings and assets is what remains after satisfying the prior claims of various creditors and preferred stockholders. As the true owners of the corporation, they bear the ultimate risks and realize the rewards of ownership. Stockholders have limited liability because they cannot lose more money than their investment in the common stock.

Features

Common stock has several major features. Some involve accounting terminology, which helps to explain how to record common stock on the firm's balance sheet.

Par or No Par Stock

Corporations can issue common stock with or without par value, which is based on specifications in the corporation's charter. For common stock, par value is the stated value attached to a single share at issuance. Except for accounting and legal purposes, par value has little economic significance. If a company sells the stock for more than its par value, it records any issued price in excess of par as additional paid-in capital or capital in excess of par. If a company sells the stock for less than its par value, any discount from par represents a legal liability of the owners to the crediting in the event of liquidation. The issuer carries no-par stock on its books at the original market price or at some assigned or stated value, which is usually below the actual issuing price.

Authorized, Issued, Outstanding, and Treasury Shares

The charter of a corporation specifies the **authorized shares** of common stock, which are the maximum number of shares that the corporation may issue without amending its charter. Issued shares are the number of authorized shares sold by the firm. **Outstanding shares** refer to the number of shares issued and actually held by the public. The firm bases its earnings per share and dividends per share on the outstanding shares. If a firm repurchases its shares, the number of issued shares may exceed the number of outstanding shares. **Treasury shares** refer to common stock that the issuing company repurchases and holds. Companies often repurchase their stock when they believe that it is undervalued in the market.

Rights of Common Stockholders

As the ultimate owners of a company, common stockholders have certain rights and privileges that are unavailable to other investors.

Right to Vote

Common stockholders are typically the only ones who can vote on certain key matters concerning the firm. They have a voice in management through the board of directors whom they elect annually. Other issues on which common stockholders vote include amending the corporate charter and bylaws, selecting the firm's independent auditors, changing the amount of authorized shares, and approving the issuance of securities. They also have the right to proxy their vote to others. A proxy is a temporary transfer of the right to vote to another party.

Two common systems of voting for members of the board of directors are majority voting and cumulative voting. **Straight or majority voting** is a voting system that entitles each shareholder to cast one vote for each share owned. If a nominee receives 50 percent plus one vote, this person has a majority of the votes and becomes a director. **Cumulative voting** is a voting system that permits the stockholder to cast multiple votes for a single director. The cumulative voting system improves the chances of minority interests to obtain representation on the board of directors.

Right to Income

Common stockholders have the right to share in cash dividends only if the company's board of directors declares them. If the company does distribute dividends, common stockholders have the right to dividends only after the preferred shareholders receive their dividends.

Right to Residual Assets

In the event of liquidation, common stockholders have the right to share in any residual assets remaining after the firm satisfies the claims of all other parties such as creditors and preferred stockholders.

Right to Transfer Ownership

Common stockholders can sell their ownership in the firm to another party. This generally involves selling the stock in the secondary market where the company's stock trades.

Other Rights

Common stockholders have the right to inspect the corporation's books. In some instances, existing stockholders have the right, but not the obligation, to share proportionately in the purchase of all new shares of common stock that the company sells. Some corporations entitled existing stockholders privilege, called a preemptive right.

5.6.2 Common Stock Valuation

Compared with valuing bonds and preferred stocks, common stock valuation is more difficult because of the uncertainty associated with the size and timing of future cash flows and the unknown nature of the required rate of return. Future cash flows may be in the form of cash dividend payments and/or changes in the stock's price (gains or losses) over the holding period. Dividends are uncertain because corporations have no legal requirement to pay them unless declared by the board of directors. Because common stock is generally riskier than bonds, investors require a higher rate of return (k_s) to compensate for this risk.

Dividend Discount Models

The most basic models for valuing equity are the dividend discount models.

These models require two key inputs: expected dividends and required rate of return on equity. The attractions of these models stem from their simplicity and intuitive logic.

The following equation shows that the **intrinsic value** of a common stock is the present value of the expected dividends during the holding period plus the present value of the terminal price (P_n), which is the expected price of a stock at the end of a specified holding period.

$$Vs = \sum_{t=1}^{n} \frac{D_t}{(1+k_s)^t} + \frac{P_n}{(1+k_s)^n}$$

Analysts often estimate the required rate of return that stockholders demand for holding a stock based on a risk and return model called the **capital asset pricing model (CAPM)**, which will be discussed in Topic 6.

For investors who do not contemplate selling their stock in the near future, a model assumes an investor plans to buy a common stock and hold it indefinitely.

$$Vs = \sum_{t=1}^{n} \frac{D_t}{(1+k_s)^t}$$

This model applies both to firms that pay current dividends and to those that do not. It suggests investors must forecast dividends to infinite and then discount them back to present value at the required rate of return to estimate the value of a common stock. In practice, investors cannot accurately project dividends through infinity. This does not present an insurmountable problem if investors can efficiently model the expected dividend stream by making appropriate assumptions about future growth.

The Constant Growth Model

Commonly referred to as the **Gordon Growth Model**, the **constant growth model** assumes that dividends grow each period at a constant rate g, i.e., $D_t = D_1 (1+g)^{t-1}$ and that this growth rate g is less than the expected rate of return r. This means that, given the first period dividend D_1 and the growth rate g, all future dividends can be written. Notice that in this case the current share price is growth perpetuity, and so we have:

$$P = \sum_{t=1}^{\infty} \frac{D_0 \cdot (1+g)^t}{(1+k_s)^t} = \sum_{t=1}^{\infty} \frac{D_1 \cdot (1+g)^{t-1}}{(1+k_s)^t} = \frac{D_1}{k_s - g}$$

核心词汇
Core Words and Expressions

time value of money 货币时间价值	terminal value 终值
simple interest 单利	discounting 折现计算
debt instrument 债务工具	discount rate 折现率
annuity 年金	opportunity cost 机会成本
future value（FV） 未来值，终值	required rate of return 要求的报酬率
present value（PV） 现值	cost of capital 资本成本
compound interest 复利	ordinary annuity 普通年金
compounding 复利计算	annuity due 先付年金
principal 本金	deferred annuity 递延年金
mortgage 抵押	perpetuity 永续年金
credit card 信用卡	face value 面值

coupon rate 息票利率
nominal interest rate 名义利率
going-concern value 持续经营价值
effective (annual) interest rate 有效（年）利率
liquidation value 清算价值
book value 账面价值
market value 市场价值
intrinsic value 内在价值
mispricing 给……错定价格
valuation approach 估价方法
discounted cash flow (DCF) valuation 折现现金流量估价
undervaluation 低估
overvaluation 高估
option-pricing model 期权定价模型
contingent claim valuation 或有要求权估价
promissory note 本票，期票
contractual provision 契约条款
par value 票面价值
maturity value 到期价值
coupon 息票利息
coupon payment 息票利息支付
coupon interest rate 息票利率
maturity 到期日
term to maturity 到期时间
call provision 赎回条款
call price 赎回价格
sinking fund provision 偿债基金条款
conversion right 转换权
put provision 卖出条款

indenture 债务契约
covenant 条款
protective covenant 保护性条款
negative covenant 消极条款
positive covenant 积极条款
trustee 托管人
secured debt 有担保债务
unsecured debt 无担保债务
creditworthiness 信誉
collateral 抵押品
mortgage bonds 抵押债券
collateral trust bonds 抵押信托债券
debenture 信用债券
bond rating 债券评级
Fitch Ratings, Inc. 惠誉国际信用评级有限公司
Standard & Poor's Corporation (S&P) 标准普尔公司
Moody's Investors Service, Inc.(Moody's) 穆迪公司
current yield 当期收益率
yield to maturity (YTM) 到期收益率
default risk 违约风险
interest rate risk 利率风险
authorized shares 额定股份
outstanding shares 流通股
treasury share 库存股
repurchase 回购
right to vote 投票权
independent auditor 独立审计师
right to proxy 代理权
straight or majority voting 多数投票制

cumulative voting　累积投票制
liquidation　清算
right to transfer ownership　所有权转移权
preemptive right　优先认股权
dividend discount model　股利折现模型

capital asset pricing model (CAPM)
　资本资产定价模型
constant growth model　固定增长率模型
growth perpetuity　增长年金

即 时 问 答
Quick Quiz

1. What is the difference between future value and present value? Which approach is preferred by financial managers? Why?
2. How is the compounding process related to the payment of interest on savings? What is the general equation for the future value?
3. What effect would
   (a) a decrease in the interest rate has on its future value? Why?
   (b) an increase in the holding period of a deposit has on its future value? Why?
4. What is meant by "the present value of a future amount"? What is the equation for the present value?
5. What effect does increasing
   (a) the required return have on the present value of a future amount? Why?
   (b) the time period have on the present value of a future amount? Why?
6. What is perpetuity? How can the present value interest factor for such a stream of cash flows be determined?
7. What is valuation, and why is it important for the financial manager to understand the valuation process?
8. Explain the difference between accounting value and market value. Which is more important to the financial manager? Why?

思考与探索
Thinking and Exploration

Respond to the following comment: "It's no good just telling me to maximize my stock price. I can easily take a short view and maximize today's price. What I would prefer is to keep it on a gently rising trend."

汉译英

1. 复制的威力

有一个古老的故事，它显示了复利效果的威力。传说西塔发明了国际象棋这使国王十分高兴，国王决定要重赏西塔，西塔说："我不要您的重赏，陛下，只要您在我的棋盘上赏一些麦子就行了。在棋盘的第1个格子里放1粒，在第2个格子里放2粒，在第3个格子里放4粒，在第4个格子里放8粒，依此类推，以后每一个格子里放的麦粒数都是前一个格子里放的麦粒数的2倍，直到放满第64个格子就行了。"国王觉得很容易就可以满足他的要求，于是就同意了。但很快国王就发现，即使将国库所有的粮食都给他，也不够百分之一。因为即使一粒麦子只有一克重，也需要数十万亿吨的麦子才够。尽管从表面上看，他的起点十分低，从一粒麦子开始，但是经过多次乘方，形成了庞大的数字。

2. 诺贝尔奖奖金始终发不完的故事

诺贝尔基金会成立于1896年，由诺贝尔捐献980万美元建立。基金会成立初期，章程中明确规定这笔资金只能投资在银行存款与公债上，不允许用于有风险的投资。随着每年奖金的发放与基金会运作的开销，历经50多年后，诺贝尔基金的资产流失了近2/3，到了1953年，该基金会的资产只剩下300多万美元。而且因为通货膨胀，300万美元只相当于1896年的30万美元，原定的奖金数额显得越来越可怜，眼看着诺贝尔基金即将破产，诺贝尔基金会的理事们赶紧求教麦肯锡，将仅有的300万美元银行存款转成资本，聘请专业人员投资股票和房地产。新的理财观一举扭转了整个诺贝尔基金的命运，基金不但没有再减少过，而且到了2005年，总资产还增长到了5.41亿美元。从1901年至2012年的111年里，诺贝尔奖发放的奖金总额早已远远超过诺贝尔的遗产。诺贝尔基金会长线投资的历史是追求复利收益的历史，伴随着人类的各种天灾人祸和战争，可是一路走来，长线仍有可观复利收益。估算可知，从1953年到现在，诺贝尔基金的年平均复利速度超过20%。

3. 美国百岁老太180美元变成700万美元

美国伊利诺伊州森林湖市100岁老妪格蕾丝·格罗纳离开人世后，竟将700万美元的遗产都捐赠给了她的母校森林湖学院。据格蕾丝多年的好友披露，这名百岁老太的700万美元巨款，竟然全都来源于她在1935年购买的180美元美国雅培公司的股票。这个真实案例开始于1935年，其后也经历了一系列的战争，包括二战、美苏"冷战"和其他大大小小的局部战争，还同样经历了全球大大小小的金融危机、天灾人祸等，一路艰难走来，长线投资仍然达到16.3%的年化复利收益。人类的经济纵然有波动,但始终是向上的。科学技术的进步,社会的发展,总会带来一个又一个的地区或具体新兴产业的经济热点。经计算,70 年平均每年的复利收益是 16.3%。

知识扩展 More Knowledge

信用评级

信用等级反映借款人在还款上的信誉,为比较债务工具发行人和债券的信用品质提供了一个国际框架。评级机构的评级分为三类:对发行人、对长期债务和对短期债务的评级。其中对发行人的信用评级最受关注。这些评级反映债务人的信用程度,包括其履行金融债务的能力和意愿。最高的等级意味着债务人几乎没有无力偿还本息的风险。等级越高,债务人的举债成本(即需支付的利息水平)就越低。由主要的评级机构(如标准普尔、穆迪和惠誉国际)评定的最高信用等级为 AAA 或 aaa,只有少数的国家和公司可获得这种评级。各评级公司所评定的等级的名称和含义不尽相同,但均可分为两大类:投资级别(investment grade)和投机/垃圾级别(speculative/junk grade)。

中国信用评级现状

中国信用评级行业诞生于 20 世纪 80 年代末,它是改革开放的产物。最初的评级机构由中国人民银行组建,隶属于各省市的分行系统。20 世纪 90 年代以后,经过几次清理整顿,评级机构开始走向独立运营。目前,国内资本市场上的评级机构主要有大公国际资信评估有限公司、中诚信国际信用评级有限公司、中诚信证券评估有限公司、联合资信评估有限公司、联合信用评级有限公司、上海新世纪资信评估投资服务有限公司、东方金诚国际信用评级有限公司和鹏元资信评估有限公司。上述评级机构均为发行人付费模式的评级机构。此外,我国评级行业中有一家也是目前唯一一家投资者付费的评级机构——中债资信评估有限责任公司。

相 关 网 址 Useful Websites

国际上公认的主要评级公司的网址:

Standard & Poor's Corporation (S & P)　标准普尔公司　www.standardandpoors.com

Moody's Investors Service, Inc.(Moody's)　穆迪公司　www.moodys.com

Fitch Ratings, Inc.　惠誉国际信用评级有限公司　www.fitchratings.com

中国债券信息网　http://www.chinabond.com.cn

第6章
TOPIC 6

Risk and Return
风险与收益

新闻视听
News in Media

Apple and Google used to be close. Suddenly, Google became a competitor of Apple. Why did Google do so? What return would it have and what risk would it face? Please listen to the news.

本章新闻视听资料请扫二维码收听。

名人名言
Wisdom

Don't put all your eggs in one basket.

——Anonymous

My ventures are not in one bottom trusted, not to one place, nor is my whole estate upon the fortune of this present years; Therefore, my merchandise makes me not sad.

——Shakespear, Merchant of Venice

He is the part of wise man to keep himself today for tomorrow, and not venture all his eggs in one basket.

——Cervantes, Don Quixote

第 6 章　风险与收益
TOPIC 6　Risk and Return

The reason why corporations do not enter gambles with volatile payoffs and small positive expected returns is that managers know that generally volatility matters.

——René M. Stulz

微型案例
Mini Case

Risk and return are concepts that we deal with every day. For many people, it is quite acceptable to risk $20 every week in the lottery, in view of potential returns of hundreds of thousands (or even millions) of dollars. When you buy a lottery ticket, the risk of losing your $20 is very high (how often have you won anything at lotto).

In general, in order to take a higher risk, you would expect a much greater potential pay-off. Consider a lottery where each ticket costs $2,000. Would you buy a ticket if the odds were the same as in the lottery where the ticket costs $20? Probably not — you would expect much better odds of winning in order to risk such a big amount of money.

"Better odds" means that you would expect a much higher probability of winning back your bet. How much you will be willing to risk, given a set probability of winning or losing, depends on your character — you may be a risk-lover or you may be risk-averse.

概　览
Overview

In this topic, we start from the basic premise that investors like returns and dislike risk. Therefore, people will invest in riskier assets only if they expect to receive higher returns. We define precisely what the term risk means as it relates to investments. We examine how managers measure risk, and discuss the relationship between risk and return. Then we introduce Portfolio Theory and Capital Asset Pricing Model.

正文 Text

6.1 Introduction to Risk and Return

As you will see, risk can be measured in different ways, and different conclusions about an asset's risk can be reached depending on the measure used. Risk analysis can be confused, but it will help if you remember the following:

1. All financial assets are expected to produce cash flows, and the risk of an asset is judged by the risk of its cash flows.

2. Here are two assumptions about risk and return:

Assumption (1): The returns from investments are normally distributed.

Assumption (2): Investors are risk-averse.

3. The risk of an asset can be considered in two ways: on **a stand-alone basis**, where the asset's cash flows are analyzed by themselves, or in **a portfolio context**, where the asset's cash flows are combined with those of other assets, and then the consolidated cash flows are analyzed. There is an important difference between stand-alone and portfolio risk, and an asset that has a great deal of risk if held by itself may be much less risky if it is held as part of a larger portfolio.

4. In a portfolio context, an asset's risk can be divided into two components: **diversifiable risk**, which can be diversified away and thus is of little concern to diversified investors, and **market risk**, which reflects the risk of a general stock market decline and cannot be eliminated by diversification, and does concern investors. Only market risk is relevant — diversifiable risk is irrelevant to rational investors because it can be eliminated.

5. An asset with a high degree of relevant (market) risk must provide a relatively high expected rate of return to attract investors. Investors in general are averse to risk, so they will not buy risky assets unless those assets have high expected returns.

6.1.1 What is Return

A return expresses the financial performance of a financial asset (or investment), which might be above or below its value at the time of purchase/investment. You can think of it as the "pay-off" to your investment. A return can be expressed in either monetary ($) or percentage (%) terms and essentially has a difference between the initial purchase/investment cost and the market value at some later point. Returns to a financial asset or investment can be calculated over whatever time period annually, quarterly or even daily.

Expected return

Expected return refers to the expected change in the value of an asset over a given (future) time period. Since we cannot know the future, we have to make a guess as to what to "expect", based on what has happened to returns in the past. In order to make this guess as to what might happen in the future, we use an average of a series of the past returns from a financial asset over time. In this way, it is possible to estimate the expected (future) return from the past returns by computing the arithmetic mean.

6.1.2 What is Risk

Although the term "risk" is multi-faceted, we use risk in a general sense to refer to situations in which the outcomes are not known with certainty. Risk can be measured by the volatility or uncertainty of the returns to an asset over a given time period. It is the chance that the actual outcome will be lower or higher than the "expected" (possible) outcome. The greater the variability of the possible returns, the riskier the investment is. Under the normality assumption, the risk is usually estimated with the **standard deviation**, which is the square root of the variance of returns.

Stand-alone Risk

An asset's **stand-alone risk** is the risk an investor would face if he or she holds only this one asset. It disregards the fact that a project is only one asset within a firm's portfolio of assets and that a firm's stock is only one stock in most investor's portfolios.

Actually, no investment should be undertaken unless the expected rate of return is high enough to compensate the investor for the perceived risk of the investment. Risky assets rarely produce their expected rates of return — generally, risky assets earn either more or less than was originally expected. Indeed, if assets always produced their expected returns, they would not be risky. Investment risk, then, is related to the probability of actually earning a low or negative return — the greater the chance of a low or negative return, the riskier the investment.

Uncertainty

Using past prices we can easily compute the past returns of financial assets — these are known with certainty because they have already happened. However, what do these tell us about future returns? Future returns are random variables. A **random variable** is a value from a list of potential outcomes. It is possible to ascertain the likelihood of each outcome. Uncertainty in financial returns exists when there may be more than one possible outcome (if there is only one outcome then there is no uncertainty — an event will definitely happen).

Investors use various risk assessment methods, including **sensitivity analysis** and **scenario analysis**. Based on information obtained from various assessment methods, investors may be able to construct probability distributions about possible outcomes. If investors can estimate probability distributions, they can calculate several probability-based risk measuring stand-alone risk. These measures include the standard deviation of an asset's estimate cash flows or returns and the coefficient of variation.

Probability

Although we cannot know what the future returns are going to be, assuming that the future reflects the past, we can make some statement about possible future outcomes. The uncertainty of future outcomes is usually expressed in terms of **probability** and plotted in a **probability distribution** which can be expressed as an equation called the **probability distribution function**.

Probability is the likelihood that an event will take place, that is, the fraction of the time we would observe that particular outcome in the long run. The probability of an event is always a number between 0 and 1: zero probability implies that the event will not occur; one implies that the event will occur; 0.5 implies there is an equal chance that the event will and will not happen.

In corporate finance we almost always assume that financial returns can be described by a continuous normal distribution function — this is also called the **normality assumption**. This assumption greatly simplifies investment analysis, as two parameters, the expected return (mean) and the standard deviation (or variance), are sufficient to completely describe the probability distribution of all financial returns. This implies that investors live in a **mean-variance world**. In essence, this simplification signifies that investors choose financial assets exclusively on the basis of risk and return.

Normal distribution

Normal distributions are a family of distributions that have the same general shape. They are symmetrical with densities more concentrated in the middle than in the tails. Normal distributions are sometimes described as bell-shaped, with the height of a normal distribution specified mathematically in terms of two parameters: mean (μ) and standard deviation (σ) (or variance σ^2). In theory, the return (r) can take on any real number between minus infinity ($-\infty$) and plus infinity ($+\infty$). We say $r \sim N(\mu, \sigma^2)$.

Standard deviation(σ) is a statistical measure of the variability of a distribution about its mean or expected value. Investors use the standard deviation as a measure of absolute or total risk. The Coefficient of Variation (CV) is a measure of relative risk or risk per unit of return, which is the standard deviation divided by the rate of return.

The normal distribution is particularly useful because it can be described with a relatively simple equation and analyzed to reveal detailed characteristics of parts of the distribution. Since continuous probability distribution functions are defined for an infinite number of points over a continuous interval, the probability at a single point is always zero. That is, the area under the curve between two distinct points defines the probability for that interval.

Using standard normal probability tables (you can find these at the back of any introductory statistics book) we can estimate the confidence an investor has that an observation falls inside or outside the population described by the distribution.

Risk-aversion

Financial theory typically views decision makers as being risk-averse. A risk-averse decision maker considers a risky investment only if it provides compensation for risk through a risk premium.

You are risk-averse if you prefer investments with less risk, all other things being equal.

For example, you are risk-averse if you prefer to be given $5 rather than take a 50-50 gamble with pay-offs of $0 and $10. "All other things being equal" refers to the expected return.

6.2 Efficient Market Hypothesis (EMH)

6.2.1 Introduction

The previous section on risk-return trade-off discussed the first two assumptions of corporate finance theory:

Assumption 1: The returns from investments are normally distributed.

Assumption 2: Investors are risk-averse.

This section discusses the third, fourth and fifth major assumptions in finance which state that investors are **rational**, that investors are **price takers**, and that financial markets are **efficient** with respect to the use of information:

Assumption 3: Investors are rational.

Assumption 4: Investors are price takers.

Assumption 5: The Efficient Market Hypothesis (EMH) holds.

Whether you agree with these assumptions or not, they are very important concepts as most financial theories are based on them. When money is put into the stock market, it is done with the aim of maximizing the return on the capital invested. In practice, many investors try not only to make a profitable return in proportion to the risk taken, but also to outperform, or "beat", the market.

Investor rationality

Investor rationality implies that investors behave as if they were rational and possessed full knowledge of all available market information to a high degree of accuracy. Rational agents act so as to maximize their expected utility.

Rational behavior means that individuals maximize some objective function — their utility function — under the constraints that they face. As a structured assumption, the concept of rational behavior allows us to model the behavior of investors:

- Firstly, it allows us to derive optimal economic behavior in a **normative** sense — which is based on the investor behavior traditionally accepted as "normal".
- Secondly, it can be used to **explain** and **predict** actual, i.e. observed, economic behavior.

The **theory of expected utility** is the central element of the neoclassical theory of rational economic behavior.

Investors are price takers

In general, you are a price taker if you can make a buying or selling decision and your marginal output (the change in your output) is assumed not to affect the price. Hence, the price is inelastic with respect to the output so the price graph is horizontal.

In the context of investments, investors are price takers when their buying and selling won't influence the market price of the stocks. In theory, this is a result of perfect competition. In reality, it is probably more likely to be true only for individual or **retail investors** as opposed to large or institutional investors, and for frequently traded stocks as opposed to thinly traded stocks.

A firm can be considered a price taker when a change in its rate of production and sales will not significantly affect the market price of its product. Again, the underlying reason is perfect competitiveness.

Efficient market hypothesis

Market efficiency suggests that, at any given time, prices fully reflect all available information on a particular stock and/or market. Thus, according to the EMH, no investor has an advantage in predicting a return on a stock price since no one has access to information not already available to everyone else.

As prices only respond to information available in the market, and, because all market participants are privy to the same information, no one will have the ability to "beat" anyone else. In efficient markets, prices become not predictable but random, so no investment pattern can be discerned.

6.2.2 Financial market efficiency

There are three types of financial market efficiency:

- when prices are determined in a way that equates the marginal rates of return (adjusted for risk) for all producers and savers, the market is said to be **allocationally** efficient.
- when the cost of transferring funds is "reasonable", the market is said to be **operationally** efficient.
- when prices fully reflect all available information, the market is said to be **informationally** efficient.

This topic considers only the third form of market efficiency — informationally efficient markets.

Generally, there are three main factors associated with informational market efficiency:

- the **type of information** to which the market price reacts.
- the **speed** at which the market price reacts to information.
- the **degree** to which market participants over-or under-react to information.

Forms of Informational Efficiency

Based on the **type** of information available to the market, Fama (1970) distinguishes three forms of informationally efficient markets:

Weak Form

Asset prices reflect **all historical information**. It follows that it is impossible to consistently earn abnormal returns by developing a forecasting model based on past returns. Since information from past prices is available at a very low cost it makes sense that these past returns cannot be used to forecast future returns.

Most traders are of the opinion that weak-form efficiency holds over longer time horizons, but not necessarily within the day (intra-day).

Semi-strong Form

Asset prices reflect all historical price information and **all publicly available information**. This implies that it is impossible to consistently earn abnormal returns from trading based on any publicly available information.

All of this information is relatively inexpensive to collect but will not allow you to **consistently** obtain abnormal returns.

Strong Form

Asset prices reflect all historical price information, all publicly available information, and **all private information** (including information only known to insiders, such as company directors). It follows that it is impossible to consistently earn abnormal returns using any private or public information. Private information can be very costly to collect and is usually illegal to trade on. Markets cannot be strong form efficient because:

- companies need to reveal all information, which may advantage their competitors.
- there will be no need for market analysts to search for market inefficiencies. It follows that the market is efficient due to the actions of analysts who try to estimate the true value of stocks.

Characteristics of an Informationally Efficient Market

An informationally efficient market has the following characteristics:

- Price changes cannot be predicted. This implies that at any moment the price of security must reflect all relevant information known to the market. Hence, trading on information that is already public will not result in any change in asset prices.
- On average, it is impossible to profit from trading on the basis of publicly available information (arbitrage) only. The value of an asset accurately reflects the future payments to which the asset gives title, i.e. the price of the asset is equal to its fundamental (unobserved but true) value.
- Only if information arrives in the public domain that has not yet been used by the market and has not yet been incorporated into the price, will there be an opportunity for investors to make an abnormal return—provided that the transaction costs are smaller than the abnormal returns and that the investor reacts fast enough. Hence, only new and unanticipated information triggers stock price changes. Prices change due to the inflow of new information, and information flows randomly to the market. Therefore, price changes should be random and unpredictable.

6.2.3 Anomalies in Finance

Anomalies in finance are documented situations in which evidence seems to be

inconsistent with the EMH. Some popular examples are:
- the short-run underpricing of Initial Public Offerings (IPOs).
- small companies have higher returns than that expected based on the CAPM (small firm effect).
- on average, stocks have lower (negative) returns on Monday, compared to (positive) returns on other days of the week (Monday effect).
- stocks have higher returns in January, relative to other months of the year (January effect). On average, companies with high book to market value have higher returns than that expected, based on the CAPM (value effect).
- long run reversions in returns (overreaction) — buy losers, sell winners.
- post-earnings announcement drift — prices tend to drift after the announcement of earnings.

Behavioral finance is the discipline within finance which relies on psychology-based theories to explain such anomalies where rational explanations fail. Those in favor of behavioral finance argue that people behave in a way that deviates significantly and systematically from the principles of expected utility theory. It is assumed that the behavior of investors systematically influences their investment decisions as well as market outcomes. An example of such a psychology-based theory is **prospect theory**.

6.3 Portfolio Theory

In financial management, there is a trade-off between the **risk** associated with an investment and the financial **return** that it offers. The risk-return relationship is a positive one because the more risk that is assumed, the higher the required rate of return.

Risk-return trade-off shows that under the assumption of normality (Assumption 1), the expected return and the standard deviation are sufficient to completely describe the probability distribution of returns. It follows that the risk of an individual asset can be described by its **standard deviation**, which is a measure of how much the return varies around its average value.

The assumption that investors are **risk-averse** (Assumption 2) is also discussed. Hence, if two investments offer the same expected return but differ in risk, an investor would prefer the less risky investment. Investors are only prepared to accept higher risks if this is expected to lead to higher expected returns.

An asset held as part of a portfolio is less risky than the same asset held in isolation. Accordingly, most financial assets are actually held as parts of portfolios. Banks, insurance companies, mutual funds, and other financial institutions are required by law to hold diversified portfolios. Even individual investors — at least those whose security holdings constitute a significant part of their total wealth — generally hold portfolios, not the stock of only one firm.

This being the case, from an investor's standpoint the fact that a particular stock goes up or down is not very important; what is important is the return on his or her portfolio, and the portfolio's risk. Logically, then, the risk and return of an individual security should be analyzed in terms of how that security affects the risk and return of the portfolio in which it is held.

The risk-return trade-off assumption is the first item of Portfolio Theory as developed by Harry M. Markowitz (1952). He was the first to note that investors should diversify their investments due to their concern with risk and return. Markowitz thought it necessary to measure risk, suggesting variance as a method. The fact that portfolio variance also depends on security **covariance** added to the plausibility of the approach. Since there were two criteria, risk and return, he assumed that investors selected from the set of optimal risk-return combinations.

This assumption led to his computation of **mean-variance efficient frontiers** (Markowitz, 1956 and 1959).

6.3.1 The Expected Return of a Portfolio

The formula for expected return on a portfolio is very simple: the expected return on a portfolio is simply a weighted average of the expected returns on the individual securities.

6.3.2 Risk in a Portfolio Context

As you know, variance and standard deviation measure the variability of individual stocks. We now wish to measure the relationship between the return on one stock and the return on another, covariance and **correlation**. Covariance and correlation measure how two random variables are related.

Take Security A and Security B for example, the formula for covariance can be written algebraically as

$$\sigma_{AB} = \text{Cov}(R_A, R_B) = \text{Expected value of } [(R_A - \overline{R_A}) \times (R_B - \overline{R_B})]$$

Where, $\overline{R_A}$ and $\overline{R_B}$ are the expected returns for two securities, and R_A and R_B are the actual returns.

To calculate the correlation, divide the covariance by the standard deviations of both of the two securities.

$$\rho_{AB} = \text{Corr}(R_A, R_B) = \frac{\text{Cov}(R_A, R_B)}{\sigma_A \times \sigma_B} = \frac{\sigma_{AB}}{\sigma_A \times \sigma_B}$$

Because the standard deviation is always positive, the sign of the correlation between two variables must be the same as that of covariance between the two variables. If the correlation is positive, we say that the variables are positively correlated; if it is negative, we say that they are negatively correlated; if it is zero, we say that they are uncorrelated. Furthermore, it can be proved that the correlation is always between +1 and −1. This is due to the standardizing procedure of dividing by two standard deviations.

What would happen if we include more than two stocks in the portfolio? As a rule, the riskiness of a portfolio will decline as the number of stocks in the portfolio increases. If we add enough partially correlated stocks, could we completely eliminate risk? In general, the answer is no, but the extent to which adding stocks to a portfolio reduces its risk depends on the degree of correlation among the stocks: The smaller the positive correlation coefficients, the lower the risk in a large portfolio. If we could find a set of stocks whose correlations were zero or negative, all risk could be eliminated. In the real world, where the correlations among the individual stocks are generally positive but less than +1.0, some, but not all, risk can be eliminated.

6.3.3 Modern portfolio theory — Markowitz's Mean-variance Framework

Modern portfolio theory was developed by Harry Markowitz in the early 1950s.

You have seen that the standard deviation of the returns on an individual asset is a relevant measure of the riskiness of an investment only if you invest all your available funds in that single security. You find out that by combining two or more securities, the total risk of the investment can actually be reduced, without reducing the expected pay-off.

Indeed, the main aim of modern portfolio analysis is to find the most efficient portfolio. Efficient portfolios are those that have:
- the lowest risk for an expected rate of return.
- the highest expected rate of return for a given level of risk.

The assets that meet these criteria make up the efficient frontier.

6.3.4 Diversified Risk versus Market Risk

As noted above, if not impossible it is difficult to find stocks whose expected returns are negatively correlated — most stocks tend to do well when the national economy is strong and badly when it is weak. Thus, every very large portfolio ends up with substantial amount of risk, but not as much risk as if all the money is invested into one stock.

To see more precisely how portfolio size affects portfolio risk, consider Figure 6-1, which shows how portfolio risk is affected by forming larger and larger portfolios of randomly selected New York Stock Exchange (NYSE) stocks.

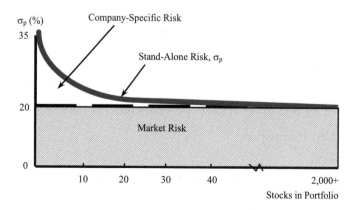

Figure 6-1 Effects of Portfolio Size on Portfolio Risk for Average Stocks

Standard deviations are plotted for an average one-stock portfolio, a two-stock portfolio, and so on, up to a portfolio consisting of all 2,000-plus common stocks that were listed on the NYSE at the time the data were graphed. The graph illustrates that, in general, the riskiness of a portfolio consisting of large-company stocks tends to decline and to approach some limit as the size of portfolio increases. A portfolio consisting of all stocks, which is called the **market portfolio**, is shown as the horizontal dashed line in Figure 6-1.

Thus, almost half of the riskiness inherent in an average individual stock can be eliminated if the stock is held in a reasonably well-diversified portfolio. Some risk always remains, however, so it is virtually impossible to diversify away from the effects of broad stock market movements that affect almost all stocks.

The part of a stock's risk that can be eliminated is called **diversifiable risk**, while the part that cannot be eliminated is called **market risk**. The fact that a large part of the riskiness of any individual stock can be eliminated is vitally important, because rational investors will eliminate it and thus render it irrelevant.

Diversifiable risk is caused by such random events as lawsuits, strikes, successful and unsuccessful marketing programs, winning or losing a major contract, and other events that are unique to a particular firm. Since these events are random, their effects on a portfolio can be eliminated by diversification — bad events in one firm will be offset by good events in another. Diversifiable risk is also known as company-specific, or unsystematic, risk.

Market risk, on the other hand, stems from factors that systematically affect most firms: war, inflation, recessions, and high interest rates. Since most stocks are negatively affected by these factors, market risk cannot be eliminated by diversification. Market risk is also known as non-diversifiable, or systematic or beta, risk, which is the risk that remains after diversification.

6.4 Beta and Capital Asset Pricing Model

We know that investors demand a premium for bearing risk; that is, the higher the risk of a security, the higher its expected return must be to induce investors to buy (or to hold) it. However, if investors are primarily concerned with the risk of their portfolios rather than the risk of the individual securities in the portfolio, how should the risk of an individual stock be measured? One answer is provided by the **Capital Asset Pricing Model** (CAPM), an important tool used to analyze the relationship between risk and rates of return. The primary conclusion of the CAPM is this: The relevant risk of an individual stock is its contribution to the risk of a well-diversified portfolio. The stock might be quite risky if held by itself, but if half of its risk can be eliminated by diversification, then relevant risk, which is its contribution to the portfolio's risk, is much smaller than its stand-alone risk.

The risk that remains after diversifying is market risk, or the risk that is inherent in the market, and it can be measured by the degree to which a given stock tends to move up or down with the market. In this section, we introduce a measure of a stock's market risk, and then an equation for determining the required rate of return on a stock, given its market risk.

6.4.1 The Concept of Beta

The benchmark for a well-diversified stock portfolio is the market portfolio, which is a portfolio containing all stocks. Therefore, the relevant risk of an individual stock, which is called its **beta coefficient**, is defined under the CAPM as the amount of risk that the stock contributes to the market portfolio. This makes sense because of the i_{th} stock's return and the return on the market. σ_i is the standard deviation of the i_{th} stock's return, and σ_M is the standard deviation of the market's return. The beta coefficient of the i_{th} stock, denoted by β_i, can be found as follows:

$$\beta_i = \frac{\sigma_i}{\sigma_M} \rho_{iM}$$

This tells us that a stock with a high standard deviation, σ_i, will tend to have a high beta. This makes sense, because if all other things are equal, a stock with high stand-along risk will contribute a lot of risk to the portfolio. Note too that a stock with a high correlation with the market, ρ_{iM}, will also have a large beta, hence be risky This also makes sense, because a high correlation means that diversification is not helping much, hence the stock contributes a lot of risk to the portfolio.

The market risk of a stock is measured by its beta coefficient, which is an index of the stock's relative volatility. Some benchmark betas follow:

$\beta=0.5$: Stock is only half as risky as the market, if held in a diversified portfolio.

$\beta=1.0$: Stock is about as risky as the market, if held in a diversified portfolio.

$\beta=2.0$: Stock is twice as risky as the market, if held in a diversified portfolio.

Theoretically, it is possible for a stock to have a negative beta. In this case, the stock's returns would tend to rise whenever the returns on other stocks fall. In practice, very few stocks have a negative beta. Keep in mind that a stock in a given period may more counter to the overall market, even though the stock's beta is positive. If a stock has a positive beta, we would expect its return to increase whenever the overall stock market rises. However, company-specific factors may cause the stock's realized return to decline, even though the market's return is positive.

A portfolio consisting of low-beta securities will have a low beta itself, because the beta of a portfolio is a weighted average of its individual securities' betas.

Betas are generally estimated from stock's characteristic line by running a linear regression between past returns on the stock in question and past returns on some market index. We define betas developed in this manner as **historical betas**. However, in most situations, it is the future beta that is needed.

6.4.2 CAPM

The capital asset pricing model (CAPM) measures the relationship between risk and required rate of return for assets held in well-diversified portfolios. In theory, CAPM is an expectational model because its inputs are expected future values. This model deals only with a single factor-systematic or market risk, as measured by beta, because it assumes diversification can greatly reduce or eliminate unsystematic risk.

$$r_i = r_{RF} + (r_M - r_{RF})\beta_i$$

The CAPM is extremely appealing at an intellectual level: It is logical and rational, and once someone works through and understands the theory, his or her reaction is usually to accept it without question. However, doubts begin to arise when one thinks about the assumptions upon which the model is based, and these doubts are as much reinforced as reduced by empirical tests. Our own views as to the current status of the CAPM are as follows:

1. The CAPM framework, which focuses on market as opposed to stand-alone risk, is clearly a useful way to think about the riskiness of assets. Thus, as a conceptual model, the CAPM is of truly fundamental importance.

2. When applied in practice, the CAPM appears to provide neat, precise answers to important questions about risk and required rates of return. However, the answers are less clear than they seem. The simple truth is that we do not know precisely how to measure any of the inputs required to implement the CAPM. These inputs should be ex ante, yet only ex post data are available.

3. Because the CAPM is logical in the sense that it represents the way risk-averse people ought to behave, the model is a useful conceptual tool.

4. It is appropriate to think about many financial problems in a CAPM framework. However, it is important to recognize the limitations of the CAPM when using it in practice.

6.5 Arbitrage Pricing Theory

The CAPM is a single-factor model. That is, it specifies risk as a function of only one factor, the security's beta coefficient. Perhaps the risk/return relationship is more complex, with a stock's required return a function of more than one factor. For example, what if investors, because personal tax rates on capital gains are lower than those on dividends, value capital gains more highly than dividends? Then, if two stocks had the same market risk, the stock paying the higher dividend would have the higher required rate of return. In that case, required returns would be a function of two factors, market risk and dividend policy.

Further, how many factors are required to specify the equilibrium risk/return relationship rather than just one or two? Stephen Ross has proposed an approach called the **Arbitrage Pricing Theory** (APT).⊖ The APT can include any number of risk factors,

---

⊖ Stephen A Ross. The Arbitrage Theory of Capital Asset Pricing [J]. Journal of Economic Theory, December 1976: 341-360.

so the required return could be a function of two, three, four, or more factors. We should note at the outset that the APT is based on complex mathematical and statistical theory that goes far beyond the scope of the fundamental of financial management. Also, although the APT model is widely discussed in academic literature, practical usage of data is limited. However, usage may increase, so students at least have an intuitive idea of what the APT is all about.

The primary theoretical advantage of the APT is that it permits several economic factors to influence individual stock returns, whereas the CAPM assumes that the effect of all factors, except those unique to the firm, can be captured in a single measure, the volatility of the stock with respect to the market portfolio. Also, the APT requires fewer assumptions than the CAPM and hence is more general. Finally, the APT does not assume that all investors hold the market portfolio, a CAPM requirement that clearly is not met in practice.

However, the APT faces several major hurdles in implementation, the most severe being that the APT does not identify the relevant factors. Thus, APT does not tell us what factors influence returns, nor does it even indicate how many factors should appear in the model. There is some empirical evidence that only three or four factors are relevant: perhaps inflation, industrial production, the spread between low-and high-grade bonds, and the term structure of interest rates, but no one knows for sure.

核心词汇
Core Words and Expressions

portfolio　组合
diversifiable risk　可分散风险
market risk　市场风险
expected return　期望收益
volatility　波动性
stand-alone risk　个别风险
random variable　随机变量
probability　概率
probability distribution　概率分布
probability distribution function　概率分布函数
normality assumption　正态假设
coefficient　系数
standard deviation　标准差
variance　方差
sensitivity analysis　敏感性分析
scenario analysis　情境分析
mean-variance world　均值-方差世界

第 6 章 风险与收益
TOPIC 6　Risk and Return

normal distribution　正态分布
efficient market hypothesis （EMH）
　有效市场假说
price taker　价格接受者
investor rationality　投资者的理性
rational behavior　理性行为
institutional investor　机构投资者
retail investor　个人投资者、散户投资者
allocationally efficient markets　配置
　有效市场
operationally efficient markets　交易
　有效市场
informationally efficient markets　信息
　有效市场
weak form　弱式
semi-strong form　半强式
strong form　强式
anomaly　异常（人或事物）
underpricing　价格低估
initial public offerings (IPO)　首次公开
　发行
Monday effect　星期一效应

January effect　一月效应
value effect　价值效应
post-earnings announcement drift　盈余
　公告后价格漂移
behavioral finance　行为金融
expected utility theory　期望效用理论
prospect theory　前景理论
portfolio theory　组合理论
mutual fund　共同基金
mean-variance efficient frontier　均值-方
　差有效边界
covariance　协方差
correlation coefficient　相关系数
New York Stock Exchange (NYSE)
　纽约证券交易所
capital asset pricing model (CAPM)
　资本资产定价模型
beta coefficient　贝塔系数
company-specific factor　公司特有风险
arbitrage pricing theory (APT)　套利定价
　理论

即 时 问 答
Quick Quiz

1. Define risk as it relates to financial decision making. Do any assets have perfect certain returns?
2. Define return. Describe the basic calculation involved in finding the return on an investment.
3. Describe the attitude toward risk of a risk-averse financial manager. Do many managers exhibit this behavior?
4. What relationship exists between the size of the standard deviation and the degree of

asset risk?

5. What is the relation between total risk, nondiversifiable risk, and diversifiable risk? Why is nondiversifiable risk the only relevant risk?
6. What is beta and what risk does it measure?
7. What is the equation for the capital asset pricing model (CAPM)? Explain the meaning of each variable.

思考与探索
Thinking and Exploration

Respond to the following comment: "Investors demand higher expected rates of return from stocks with returns that are very sensitive to fluctuations in the stock market." Is it true? Explain and qualify.

汉译英
Translation

假设你是一名出色的管理人员，拥有大好前程。现在，一家著名的且非常成功的上市公司打算雇用你做他们的首席执行官，薪酬丰厚，还有相当数量的公司股票期权。作为一个理性人，你会毫不犹豫地答应。但如果这是一家快要倒闭的公司呢？当你不能挽救公司时，你的股票期权将变得一文不值，甚至你在经理市场上的好名声也会被毁掉，你还会像先前一样痛快地答应吗？也许不会，为什么呢？

知识扩展
More Knowledge

股票市场指数

股票市场指数即股票价格指数，是由证券交易所或金融服务机构编制的表明股票行市变动的一种供参考的指示数字。由于股票价格起伏无常，投资者必然面临市场价格风险。对于具体某一种股票的价格变化，投资者容易了解，而对于多种股票的价格变化，要逐一了解，既不容易又不胜其烦。为了适应这种情况和需要，一些金融服务机构就利用自己的业务知识和熟悉市场的优势，编制出股票价格指数，公开发布，作为市场价格变动的指标。投资者据此就可以检验自己投资的效果，并用以预测股票市场的动向。同时，新闻界、工商界乃至政界领导人等也以此为参考指标，观察、预测社会政治和经济发展形势。

如果你关注每天的财经新闻,会发现有关股票市场指数的信息。不同的市场有不同的股票市场指数,如美国的标准普尔指数、道琼斯指数,中国的香港恒生指数,德国法兰克福DAX指数,法国CAC40指数,英国金融时报指数,等等。

马科维茨的投资组合理论

由于1952年的论文《投资组合选择》和1959年出版的《投资组合选择:有效分散化》一书,马科维茨被授予诺贝尔经济学奖。其主要贡献是,发展了一个概念明确的、可操作的在不确定条件下选择投资组合的理论。这个理论进一步演变成为现代财务理论的基础。该理论的主要内容是:在一定的条件下,一个投资者的投资组合选择可以简化为平衡两个因素,即投资组合的期望回报及其方差。风险可以用方差来衡量,通过分散化可以降低风险。投资组合风险不仅依赖不同资产各自的方差,而且也依赖资产的协方差。该理论的主要成就是:将大量的不同资产的投资组合选择、复杂的多维问题,约束成为一个概念清晰的、简单的二次规划问题,即均值-方差分析,并且给出了最优投资组合问题的实际计算方法。

○ **相关人物**

哈里·马科维茨(Harry M. Markowitz),1927年8月24日生于美国伊利诺伊州。他于1950年、1952年在芝加哥大学连续获得了经济学硕士、博士学位。马科维茨一生著作颇丰,有专著及合著7本,重要理论文章30余篇,研究范围涉及金融微观分析及数学、计算机在金融经济学方面的应用。他的理论也曾影响了他的同时代学者。由于其出色的、开创性的工作,马科维茨与威廉·夏普及默顿·米勒分享了1990年诺贝尔经济学奖。

资本资产定价模型(CAPM模型)

资本资产定价模型(Capital Asset Pricing Model,CAPM)由美国学者威廉·夏普、林特纳、特雷纳和莫辛等人在一般经济均衡的框架下,假定所有投资者都以这种效用函数来决策,从而导出全市场的证券组合收益率是有效的以及所谓的资本资产定价模型。在现代投资组合理论的基础上发展起来的是现代金融理论的支柱,广泛应用于投资决策和公司理财领域。夏普是马科维茨的学生,他与马科维茨一起荣获了1990年诺贝尔经济学奖。

○ **相关人物**

威廉·夏普（William Sharpe），1934年6月出生于美国马萨诸塞州的坎布里奇市。1955年和1956年，他在加州大学洛杉矶分校先后获得学士学位和硕士学位；1961年获博士学位，1961~1968年执教于华盛顿大学；1968年应邀到斯坦福大学商业研究生院工作；1973年被任命为蒂姆肯金融学教授；1980年被选为美国金融学会主席。夏普的主要贡献是在有价证券理论方面对不确定条件下金融决策的规范分析以及资本市场理论方面关于以不确定性为特征的金融市场的实证均衡理论。他的资本资产定价模型是现代金融市场价格理论的主要部分。

套利定价模型（APT模型）

套利定价理论（Arbitrage Pricing Theory，APT）由斯蒂芬·罗斯于1976年提出。他试图提出一种比传统的CAPM模型更好的解释资本资产定价的理论模型。经过十几年的发展，APT在资产定价理论中的地位已不亚于CAPM。APT与CAPM相同的假设包括：①投资者都有相同的预期；②投资者追求效用最大化；③市场是完美的；④收益由一个因素模型产生。

APT的最基本假设就是投资者都相信证券i的收益随意受k个共同因素影响，证券i的收益与这些因素的关系可以用下面这个因素模型表示出来：

$$r_i = E(r_i) + \beta_{i1}F_1 + \beta_{i2}F_2 + \cdots + \beta_{ik}F_k + \varepsilon_i$$

罗斯是基于以下两个基本点来推导APT模型的：

（1）在一个有效的市场中，当市场处于均衡状态时，不存在无风险的套利机会。

（2）对于一个高度多元化的资产组合来说，只有几个共同因素需要补偿。

证券i与这些共同因素的关系为：

$$E(r_i) = \lambda_0 + \beta_{i1}\lambda_1 + \beta_{i2}\lambda_2 + \cdots + \beta_{ik}\lambda_k$$

套利定价理论导出了与资本资产定价模型相似的一种市场关系。套利定价理论以收益率形成过程的多因子模型为基础，认为证券收益率与一组因子线性相关，这组因子代表证券收益率的一些基本因素。事实上，当收益率通过单一因子（市场组合）形成时，将会发现套利定价理论形成了一种与资本资产定价模型相同的关系。因此，套利定价理论可以被认为是一种广义的资本资产定价模型，为投资者提供了一种替代性的方法，用于理解市场中的风险与收益率间的均衡关系。套利定价理论与现代资产组合理论、资本资产定价模型、期权定价模型等一起构成了现代金融学的理论基础。

第 6 章 风险与收益
TOPIC 6　Risk and Return

○ **相关人物**

斯蒂芬·A. 罗斯（Stephen A. Ross），出生于1944年，美国著名经济学家、套利定价理论创始人，其因创立了套利定价理论而举世闻名。2017年3月3日，其在康尼狄格州家中去世，享年73岁。

如果对有效市场感兴趣，可以进一步研读的文献

研究有效市场假说的文献：

BURTON G MALKIEL. A Random Walk Down Wall Street[M]. 6th ed. New York: Norton & Co., 1995.

关于有效市场假说的评述文章：

EUGENE F FAMA. Efficient Capital Markets: A Review of Theory and Empirical Work[J]. Journal of Finance, 1970(5):25.

EUGENE F FAMA. Efficient Capital Markets: II[J]. Journal of Finance 1991(12):46.

查询 β 系数的网址：

http://moneycentral.msn.com

http://finance.yahoo.com

第 7 章
TOPIC 7

Capital Budgeting
资本预算

新闻视听
News in Media

Apple's share price: irrational? Please find how much Apple's share price risen in 2011.

本章新闻视听资料请扫二维码收听。

名人名言
Wisdom

You, academician, worry about making good decisions. In business, we also worry about making decisions good.

——Anonymous

微型案例
Mini Case

Suning Easy-to-buy buys Wanda Department Store

Suning Easy-to-buy buys all 37 department stores under Wanda Department Store to construct online and offline department store retail formats to provide users with a richer digital and scenario shopping experience.

In 2015, Suning and Wanda signed the "Strategic Cooperation Agreement for Chain Development", and carried out extensive cooperation with Wanda Square in the fields of electrical appliances 3C, maternal and child products and other professional stores. On January 29, 2018, Suning signed the Strategic Cooperation Agreement on Dalian Wanda Commercial Real Estate Co., Ltd. with Wanda Group and Wanda Commerce. It plans to invest 9.5 billion yuan or equivalent Hong Kong dollars to purchase about 31.91% of Wanda's shares held by commercial shareholders, and further deepen the cooperation with Wanda Group and Wanda Commerce on the basis of the original property leasing cooperation. Suning Easy-to-buy will strengthen quality complementarity, implement resource integration, and promote comprehensive cooperation in business areas such as commercial property development and operation, financial services and membership data.

概　　览 / Overview

Capital Budgeting is an extremely important aspect of a firm's financial management. Although a single capital asset usually comprises a small percentage of a firm's total assets, all capital assets are long-term. Therefore, a firm that makes a mistake in its capital budgeting process has to live with that mistake for a long period of time.

Today's capital expenditure decisions are even more critical than ever. Rapid technological advances, shorter product life cycles, and sophisticated competition make investment decisions vital to the success of a firm. In this topic, we show the guidelines for estimating project cash flows and various capital budgeting rules to evaluate and select independent and mutually exclusive projects, deal with conflicts among methods, and business practice. We introduce how to analyze risk of capital investments and how to make decisions under capital rationing. Also, we discuss qualitative factors that affect the selection of project and the post-audit.

正文 Text

7.1　Capital Investment Decisions

7.1.1　Nature of Capital Budgeting

Business firms regularly make decisions involving **capital goods** purchases such as equipment and structures. Capital goods are business assets with an expected use of more than one year. The fixed asset account on a firm's balance sheet represents its net investment or capital expenditures in capital goods. Capital goods represent a major portion of the total assets of today's firms. Planned future investments in capital goods make up a firm's capital budget.

An investment in capital goods requires an outlay of funds by the firm in exchange for expected future benefits over a period more than one year. The proper goal in making capital investment decisions should be maximization of the long-term market value of the firm. Managers attempt to maximize value by selecting capital investments in which the value created by the project's future cash flows exceeds the required cash outlays. **Capital budgeting** is the process used to make this decision. Specifically, capital budgeting is the process of planning, analyzing, and managing capital investments.

Proper capital budgeting analysis is critical to a firm's successful performance because sound capital investment decisions can improve cash flows and lead to higher stock prices. Yet, poor decisions can lead to financial distress and even to bankruptcy. In summary, making the right capital budgeting decision is essential to achieving the goal of maximizing shareholder's wealth.

7.1.2 Project Classifications

A capital budgeting project is a proposed long-term investment that ultimately results in capital expenditure. Firm may classify capital budgeting projects in several ways. One way to classify projects is as expansion projects or replacement projects. Another is to classify them according to the degree of their dependence on other projects into independent and mutually exclusive projects.

Expansion Projects and Replacement Projects

An **expansion project** is a capital investment designed primarily to enhance revenues by increasing operating capacity in existing products or markets or by focusing operations to expand into completely new products or markets. Expansion projects are especially important to young or growing firms that must buy new fixed assets to meet increased demand.

A **replacement project** is a capital investment designed to improve efficiency or to maintain or increase revenues by replacing deteriorated or obsolete fixed assets. Replacing outdated equipment or facilities often benefits the firm by lowering its operating costs and preserving its efficiency.

Independent Projects and Mutually Exclusive Projects

Independent projects are those in which the acceptance or rejection of one project does not prevent the acceptance or rejection of other projects under consideration. That is, implementing independent projects is unrelated to each other. Analysis can evaluate the effects of an independent project on a firm's value without having to consider its effect on other investment opportunities.

Mutually exclusive projects are those in which the acceptance of one project precludes the acceptance of others.

7.2 Guidelines for Estimating Project Cash Flows

The term cash flow refers to the actual flow of cash into (cash receipts or savings) and out of (cash payments) a firm during a given period. Cash flow and accounting profit (net income) are not necessarily the same due to the presence of certain non-cash items on the firm's income statement. Corporate managers should use cash flows, not accounting profit, because these flows directly affect the firm's ability to pay bills and buy assets.

When estimating project cash flows, there are three key guidelines to consider.

7.2.1 Identify Incremental Cash Flows

The most important guideline is to consider only those changes in a firm's cash flows that will result from a firm's undertaking a project. Specifically, what changes in the present and future cash flows are directly attributable to the decision to invest in the project? This requires comparing a firm's cash flow with and without a proposed project. Mangers are interested in the incremental cash flows generated by a project, not its total cash flows.

Incremental cash flows are the changes in cash flows that are attributable to the decision to invest in a given project. Cash flows not attributable to a new project are irrelevant to the investment decision-making process.

7.2.2 Focus on After-tax Cash Flows

The only cash flows relevant to capital budgeting are those generated by a project and still remaining after paying taxes. Considering a project's untaxed revenues overstates its benefit because the firm cannot invest all these funds in other projects or pay them out to shareholders. Some more common tax provisions influencing cash flows involve depreciation expense as well as gains and losses from the sale of existing fixed assets.

7.2.3 Postpone Considering Financing Costs

A common mistake in estimating cash flows involves the treatment of interest expense and other financial cash flows attributable to financing the project. Financing costs are payments that the company makes to the parties supplying capital to finance the project. These costs may include interest paid to lenders or dividends paid to shareholders. As a general principle, capital budgeting analyses require separating investment (capital budgeting) and financing decisions. That is, analysts should evaluate a capital budgeting project independently of the source of funds used to finance the project.

7.2.4 Other Cash Flow Considerations

Sunk Costs

A **sunk cost** is an outlay incurred before making an investment decision and represents a historical cost. Post expenditures on a project should not influence the decision whether to undertake, continue, or end a project because they are not incremental cash flows. Thus, sunk costs are not part of the evaluation process.

Opportunity Costs

Estimating project cash flows requires considering both direct outlays and opportunity costs. An **opportunity cost** is the most valuable alternative use of a resource or an asset that the firm gives up by accepting a project. By using the asset or resource in the proposed project, the firm forgoes the opportunity to employ the asset in its alternative use. The cash flows that the firm forgoes represent an opportunity cost to the proposed project.

Allocated Overhead

For internal reporting purposes, accountants often allocate existing **overhead**, such as general and administrative expenses, to each unit or division that undertakes a project. However, if the firm's current overhead remains unchanged by accepting a project, the firm should exclude this allocated overhead from the project's cash flows in the capital budgeting analysis.

Residual Value

When a project is terminated, it is likely that a portion of the initial capital outlay will be recovered. This is often termed as the project's **residual value**. A project's residual value will be the disposal value of the project's assets, less any dismantling and removal costs associated with the termination of projects.

Side Effects

Adopting and implementing new projects may have important **side effects** because they affect the cash flows of other products or divisions. Project planners should consider these potential side effects, or externalities, in the capital budgeting analysis for the project. Side effects are complements if they enhance the cash flows of existing assets and substitutes if the effect is negative.

7.3 Investment Rules

Managers use a variety of rules to evaluate and select capital investments: Net present value (NPV), Profitability index (PI), Internal rate of return (IRR), Payback period (PP), and Discounted payback period.

The basic premise of investment analysis is that an investment is worth undertaking if it creates value for its owners. Net present value (NPV) is the most appropriate approach for measuring project desirability because only this model consistently leads to shareholder's wealth maximization. In practice, analysts often use other measures to evaluate capital investments because each measure provides some relevant information not contained in any of the other methods. When compared to the NPV, each of the other profitability measures has serious flaws, especially when evaluating mutually exclusive projects.

All of these methods evaluate projects based on cash flows. Managers seek projects in which the present value of expected future cash flows exceeds the amount of the invested funds. This topic focuses on discounted cash flow (DCF) techniques, which consider the time value of money. Only the NPV, PI, and IRR methods both recognize the time value of money and consider cash flows over the entire useful life of an investment. Although these four techniques for evaluating cash flows always give the same accept-reject decision for independent projects, they can give conflicting ranking for mutually exclusive decisions. Other measures of capital investment desirability are the payback period, which considers the time value of the cash flows only until the project recovers its initial investment.

7.3.1 Net Present Value

Net present value (NPV) is the sum of the present values of the project's expected cash inflows (benefits) and cash outflows (costs). That is, the NPV is the amount of cash flow in present value terms that the project generates after repaying the invested capital. The required rate of return is the minimum percentage return acceptable to cover a project's cost of capital and risk. If we are measuring cash flows in dollars, NPV is an absolute dollar amount that represents the expected dollar change in value and therefore the expected dollar change in shareholder's wealth created by undertaking an investment. In theory, the NPV method is considered as the best approach because, as an absolute measure of a project's profitability, it leads to conceptually correct capital budgeting decisions.

7.3.2 Profitability Index

The **profitability index (PI)**, also called the benefit/cost ratio, is the ratio of the present value of an investment's expected cash inflows (benefits) to the present value of its expected cash outflows (costs). The PI shows the relative profitability of any investment, or the value increase per present value dollar of costs. In a sense, the profitability index shows how much "bang for the buck" an investment provides. For some, the profitability index as a relative measure has greater intuitive appeal than NPV criterion. PI is simply a variant of NPV because both methods use the same inputs.

7.3.3 Internal Rate of Return

The **internal rate of return (IRR)** is the rate of return that equates the present value of all cash flows to zero. This is equivalent to saying that the IRR is the rate of return for which the NPV is zero. Alternatively, the IRR is the rate of return that equates the present value of the project's costs. Thus, a project's IRR is its expected rate of return. Because IRR is a percentage, managers cannot relate the IRR directly to an absolute dollar change in value or shareholder wealth.

7.3.4 Payback Period

Financial managers are often concerned about how long a capital expenditure project takes to break even. The **payback period (PP)** is the amount of time required for an investment to generate sufficient cash flows to recover its initial cost. Underlying this method is the notion that a firm is more inclined to adopt a project if it can recover its initial outlay quickly.

7.3.5 Discounted Payback Period

To incorporate time value of money concepts, analysts sometimes use the **discounted payback period** (DPP), which is the length of time required for an investment's cumulative discounted cash flows to equal zero. Thus, the discounted payback period is the length of time required to recover the initial investment from the present value of the expected future cash flows. Due to this important distinction, the discounted payback is a more realistic measure of recouping the initial investment than the standard payback method.

7.4 Business Practice

The findings of a 1993 survey of the capital budgeting methods used by the *Fortune* 500 industrial companies are shown below:[①]

1. Every responding firm used some type of DCF method. In 1955, a similar study reported that only 4 percent of large companies used a DCF method. Thus, large firms' usage of DCF methodology increased dramatically in the last half of the 20th century.

2. The payback period was used by 84 percent of Bierman's surveyed companies. However, no company used it as the primary method, and most companies gave the greatest weight to a DCF method. In 1955, surveys similar to Bierman's found that payback was the most important method.

3. In 1993, 99 percent of the *Fortune* 500 companies used IRR, while 85 percent used NPV. Thus, most firms actually used both methods.

4. An examination of surveys done by other authors led Bierman to conclude that there has been a strong trend toward the acceptance of academic recommendations, at least by large companies.

A second 1993 study, conducted by Joe Walker, Richard Burns, and Chad Denson (WBD), focused on small companies.[②] WBD began by noting the same trend toward the use of DCF that Bierman cited, but they reported that only 21 percent of small companies used DCF versus 100 percent for Bierman's large companies. WBD also noted that within their sample, the smaller the firm, the smaller the likelihood that DCF would be used. The focal point of the WBD study was why small companies use DCF so much less frequently than large firms. The three most frequently cited reasons, according to the survey, were (1) small firms' preoccupation with liquidity, which is best indicated by payback, (2) a lack of familiarity with DCF methods, and (3) a belief that small project sizes make DCF not worth the effort.

The general conclusion one can reach from these studies is that large firms should

---

① Harold Bierman. Capital Budgeting in 1993: A Survey[J]. Financial management, Autumn 1993, 24.
② Why Small Manufacturing Firms Shun DCF[J]. Jounal of Small Business Finance, 1993: 233-249.

and do use the procedures we recommend, and that managers of small firms, especially managers with aspirations for future growth, should at least understand DCF procedures well enough to make rational decisions about using or not using them. Moreover, as computer technology makes it easier and less expensive for small firms to use DCF methods, and as more and more of their competitors begin using these methods, survival will necessitate the increased DCF usage.

7.5 Analyzing Project Risk

The effect of risk on the value of a project is normally included in the evaluation by using a required rate of return that reflects the risk of the project. However, the calculated net present value is only an estimate that relies on forecasts of the project's cash flows. In practice these forecasts will, almost certainly, turn out to be incorrect, perhaps because the volume of sales turns out to be more or less than expected, the price of the product is higher or lower than expected, or operating costs differ from the forecasts. Managers can use various techniques to analyze project risks, such as sensitivity analysis, break-even analysis and simulation.

7.5.1 Sensitivity Analysis

A project's cash flows and required rate of return are usually specified as "best estimate" or "expected values" and the resulting net present value, often referred to as the base-case net present value, is also the best estimate or expected value. **Sensitivity analysis** involves assessing the effect of changes or errors in the estimated variables on the net present value of a project. This is achieved by calculating net present values based on alternative estimates of the variables. For instance, management may wish to know the effect on net present value if a project's net cash flows are either 20 percent less than, or 20 percent greater than, those estimated. Knowledge of the sensitivity of net present value to changes or errors in the variables places management in a better position to decide whether a project is too risky to accept. Also, if management knows that the present value is sensitive to changes in particular variables, it can examine the estimates of these variables more thoroughly, or collect more data in an effort to reduce errors in forecasting.

The use of sensitivity analysis involves some problems. One of them is that frequently it is difficult to precisely specify the relationship between a particular variable and net present value. If the assumed relationship is based on past outcomes, there is always a possibility that this relationship may not hold in the future.

7.5.2 Break-even Analysis

Break-even analysis is a form of sensitivity analysis. Sensitivity analysis generally involves finding answers to "what if" questions such as: What will be the net present value of the project if sales are 10 percent less than expected? In break-even analysis, the question is turned around, in which the managers ask: How poor can sales become before the project loses money? The break-even point is the sales volume at which the present values of the project's cash inflows and outflows are equal, so that its net present value is zero.

7.5.3 Simulation

Sensitivity analysis involves changing one variable at a time and examining the effects of the changes on the profitability of a project. On the other hand, **simulation** allows a manager to consider the effects of changing all the variables whose values are uncertain. The first step in a simulation is to identify the relevant variables and to specify the probability distribution of each variable. The second step is to specify any relationships between the variables. For example, a higher sales volume may result in economics of scale in production and distribution, which should be reflected in the variable costs. The third step involves using a computer to simulate the project's cash flows.

Simulation is a potentially valuable tool that allows managers to analyze many aspects of the risks associated with a project. It is generally used for large projects where the size of the investment can justify the cost of developing the simulation model. While specifying the model can be time consuming, once it has been developed it is relatively easy to examine the effects of changing the probability distribution for one or more variables. However, users of the technique should appreciate its limitations. These include the following:

1. Simulation is a technique for processing information and presenting the results of that processing in a particular way. Therefore, the results of a simulation cannot be any more reliable than the input data and the model that specifies the relationships between variables.

2. Simulation results can be difficult to interpret. Different individuals are likely to have different opinions on whether the project should be accepted — that is, simulation does not provide an unambiguous accept/reject signal for projects.

In summary, simulation is a potentially valuable technique for analyzing the risks associated with a project, but users should be aware of its limitations.

7.6 Project Selection with Resource Constrains

Sometimes a company's managers believe that they are prevented from undertaking all acceptable projects because of a shortage of funds. **Capital rationing** is the term used to describe such a situation. It may be classified further into internal (or "soft") capital rationing and external (or "hard") capital rationing.

Internal capital rationing occurs when management limits the amount that can be invested in new projects during a specified time period. There are several reasons why management may impose a limit on capital expenditure. One reason is that management is conservative and has a policy of financing all projects from internally generated cash because it is unwilling to borrow. Similarly, management may be unwilling to issue more shares because of possible effects on the control of the company. Alternatively, imposing capital expenditure limits can be a way of maintaining financial control. For example, in large companies, managers may attempt to expand their divisions by proposing many new projects, some of which only appear to be profitable because the cash flow forecasts are very optimistic. To avoid this problem, top management may delegate authority for capital expenditure decisions to divisional managers, but retain overall control by giving each division a capital expenditure limit. The aim is to force each divisional manager to decide which of the possible projects really should be adopted.

Another possible reason is that it may be desirable to limit the rate at which a company expands because of the organizational difficulties inherent in hiring and training many additional staffs. Management may be concerned that rapid expansion will lead to inefficiency and higher costs. To avoid these problems it may limit the number of new projects that are implemented. In this case, a capital expenditure limit is used to impose the desired restriction, but it is not capital that is the scarce resource. Rather, the scarce resource is management time, and the real concern is that its constraint may result in supervision problems.

External capital rationing occurs when the capital market is unwilling to supply the funds necessary to finance the projects that a company's management wishes to undertake. In this case, the company has projects that offer positive net present values, but it cannot raise, at a cost that management considers acceptable, the funds necessary to finance them. This situation can occur if financial intermediaries are subject to controls such as limits on the volume or growth rate of their lending. However, it is difficult to see why it should occur in deregulated financial markets. Any company that has a project expected to be profitable should be able to obtain the necessary capital, no matter how small its capital budget is.

However, as discussed above, capital expenditure limits may be imposed for valid reasons that do not reflect a shortage of capital. Rather, the real constraint may be a shortage of other resources such as management time. Therefore, capital rationing can be a real phenomenon and managers may need to choose the set of projects that maximizes net present value, subject to a resource constraint. In reality, ranking of investment projects where there is capital rationing is much more complex because of the large number of investment alternatives, generally available to a company. To find solutions to such problems, mathematical programming models have been developed.

7.7 Qualitative Factors and the Selection of Projects

After the quantitative analysis has been completed, management has to decide which projects to implement. While the aim is to maximize shareholders' wealth, it does not necessarily follow that project selection decisions should be guided only by the results of the quantitative analysis. Management should also consider any qualitative factors that may affect those projects. Essentially, qualitative factors are those that management would like to induce in the quantitative analysis but is unable to include because they are difficult, if not impossible, to measure in dollars. For this reason, they are assessed separately after the quantitative analysis of the alternatives has been completed.

Qualitative factors may play a vital role in project selection. For example, suppose that quantitative analysis shows that it is cheaper for a transport company to continue using some old trunks for another year rather than replacing them now. However, management may decide to replace the old trucks now because of qualitative factors such as the desire to maintain a modern image for the company and the improved satisfaction, and consequently the improved productivity of drivers, resulting from the comfort of the new trucks.

It is essential that such qualitative factors be considered before selecting a project. However, the recognition of qualitative factors is not a general proscription for ignoring or reducing the importance of quantitative analysis. As all factors cannot be incorporated into the quantitative analysis, a comparison of alternative investment proposals is uncompleted without an assessment of the possible effects of the qualitative factors. Indeed, the influence of qualitative factors may be sufficiently important to cause management to select proposals with lower calculated net present values.

7.8 The Post-Audit

An important aspect of the capital budgeting process is the **post-audit**, which involves (1) comparing actual results with those predicted by the project's sponsors and (2) explaining why any differences occurred. For example, many firms require that the operating divisions send a monthly report for the first six months after a project goes into operation and a quarterly report thereafter, until the project's results are up to expectations. From then on, reports on the operation are received on a regular basis like those of other operations.

The post-audit has two main purposes:

1. Improve forecasts. When decision makers are forced to compose their pro-

jections to actual outcomes, there is a tendency for estimates to improve. Conscious or unconscious biases are observed and eliminated; now forecasting methods are sought as the need for them becomes apparent; people simply tend to do everything better, including forecasting, if they know that their actions are being monitored.

2. Improve operations. Businesses are run by people, and people can perform at higher or lower levels of efficiency. When a divisional term has made a forecast about an investment, its members are, in a sense, putting their reputations on the line. If costs are above the predicted levels, sales below expectations, and so on, executives in production, sales and other areas will strive to improve operations and to bring results into line with forecasts. In a discussion related to this point, one executive made this statement: "You, academician, worry about making good decisions. In business, we also worry about making decisions good."

The post-audit is not a simple process — a number of factors can cause complications. First, we must recognize that each element of the cash flow forecast is subject to uncertainty, so a percentage of all projects undertaken by any reasonably aggressive firm will necessarily go awry. This fact must be considered when appraising the performances of the operating executives who submit capital expenditure requests. Second, projects sometimes fail to meet expectations for reasons beyond the control of the operating executives and for reasons that no one could realistically be expected to anticipate. Third, it is often difficult to separate the operating results of one investment from those of a larger system. Although some projects stand alone and permit ready identification of costs of revenues, the cost savings that result from a new computer, for example, may be very hard to measure. Fourth, it is often hard to hand out blame or praise because the executives who are responsible for launching a given investment have moves on by the time the results are known. Because of these difficulties, some firms tend to play down the importance of the post-audit. However, observations of both business and governmental units suggest that the best-run and most successful organizations are the ones that output the greatest emphasis on post-audits. Accordingly, we regard the post-audit as being one of the most important elements in a good capital budgeting system.

核心词汇
Core Words and Expressions

capital expenditure　资本支出
capital budget　资本预算
financial distress　财务困境
bankruptcy　破产
expansion project　扩充项目
replacement project　更新项目
independent project　独立项目
mutually exclusive project　互不相容项目
incremental cash flows　增量现金流量
sunk cost　沉没成本
opportunity cost　机会成本
overhead　制造费用
residual value　残余价值
side effect　附加效应

net present value（NPV）　净现值
profitability index（PI）　现值指数
internal rate of return（IRR）　内部收益率，内含报酬率
payback period（PP）　回收期
discounted payback period　折现回收期
discounted cash flow（DCF）　折现现金流
Fortune 500　《财富》500 强
sensitivity analysis　敏感性分析
break-even analysis　盈亏平衡点分析
simulation　模拟
capital rationing　资本限额
post-audit　期后审计

即时问答
Quick Quiz

1. What is capital budgeting? What are the key motives for making capital expenditures? Discuss, compare, and contrast them.
2. What is the payback period? How is it calculated?
3. What is the internal rate of return (IRR) on an investment? How is it determined? What are its acceptance criteria?
4. If we say that an investment has an NPV of $1,000, what exactly do we mean?
5. What are the drawbacks to the various types of what-if analyses?
6. What are some potential sources of value in a new project?

思考与探索
Thinking and Exploration

　　If you are going to persuade your company to use the net present value rule, you must be prepared to explain why other rules do not give the correct decisions. Can you give any examples that three alternative investment criteria sometimes lead to wrong decision-making?

中国个人电脑巨头联想集团以 2.5 亿美元的高价并购了 IBM 的 PC 业务。此次并购使联想成为世界第三大 PC 制造商，年收入将超过 100 亿美元。通过并购 IBM 的 PC 业务，与 IBM 形成战略联盟，联想获得了多方面的技术，得到了全球品牌的认可，以及全球并且多样化的顾客群和世界级的遍布全球的网络分布。同时联想也提升了营运能力和获得了领先的技术。并购后，IBM 将成为联想集团的一个大股东，此次交易进一步地巩固了 IBM 在世界上成长最快的 IT 市场中的地位。

对资本预算过程研究最为全面的著作

J L BOWER. Managing the Resource Allocation Process, Division of Research, Graduate School of Business Administration, Harward University, Boston, 1970.

对资本预算实务进行总结的文献

R A POHLMAN, E S SANTIAGO, F L MARKEL. Cash flow Estimation Practice of Large Firms[J]. Financial Management, 1988(17): 71-79.

资本预算中的委托代理问题

R HIGGINS, IRWIN. Four Pitfalls in the Use of Discounted Cash Flow Techniques. Analysis for Financial Management[M]. 5th ed. New York: McGraw-Hill, 1998: 289-298.

可以到下列网站查询公司资本预算和折现率的信息：

http://www.bloomberg.com

雅虎网财经频道　http://finance.yahoo.com/

第 8 章
TOPIC 8

Capital Market and Raising Funds
资本市场与资金筹集

新闻视听
News in Media

1. Interest rates in China: A small step forward. Please find the bigger worry for China's state banks.
2. Huawei Seeking its own path.

本章新闻视听资料请扫二维码收听。

视听 8-1　　　视听 8-2

名人名言
Wisdom

You can't fool all of the people all of the time.

——Abraham Lincoln

微型案例
Mini Case

360: Backdoor listing

360 landed on the New York Stock Exchange in 2011, and announced its privatization in 2015. In July 2016, the 360 privatization transaction was successfully completed, and it was delisted from the NYSE, and the VIE structure was demolished in the same year. In March 2017, after 360 completed the shareholding system transformation, in November of the same year, it announced that it would reorganize with A-share

listed company Jiangnan Jiajie (SJEC: 601313). Two months later, the transaction was approved by the CSRC. In February 2018, 360 shares were officially listed on the Shanghai Stock Exchange through backdoor SJEC (Code: 601313). On February 1, 2018, Jiangnan Jiajie announced that it would be renamed "Three Six Zero (360)" and the stock code would be changed to "601360".

概　　览 Overview

Financial managers need to understand the environment and financial markets within business operations. Therefore, this topic describes the markets where capital is raised, securities are traded, and stock prices are established. In the process, we also focus on the content of the cost of capital. But we are not concerned with the cost of capital models and formulas.

正文 Text

8.1　Financial Markets

Firms wanting to raise funds or to invest surplus funds must enter the financial markets. Note that "markets" is plural — there are a great many different markets in an economy. A **financial market** is a mechanism for bringing together buyers and sellers of financial assets. A **financial asset** is a monetary claim on an issuer in the form of a paper asset such as stocks or bonds. In financial transactions, one party exchanges on paper asset (money) for another (securities or loans). For example, debt and equity securities are financial assets from the perspective of investors, but are claims on assets from the perspective of the issuing firm. Financial markets differ in several ways depending on the types of securities traded, trading practices, and buyers and sellers.

8.1.1　The Role of Financial Markets

Financial markets serve three important functions in a healthy economy.

1. Help channel funds from suppliers to demanders. By turning to financial markets,

firms can raise the required funds. Besides providing mechanisms for firms to raise funds, financial markets provide suppliers of capital with an opportunity to identify and invest in a suitable investment.

2. Provide a resale market. Well-functioning financial markets provide liquidity or the ability to convert an asset easily and quickly into cash at **fair market value**.

3. Set market prices and rates of return. Setting market prices is useful for two major reasons. First, the market price reflects the market's assessment of the value of a financial asset. Second, market prices typically serve as a measure of corporate performance. That is, stock prices reflect the market's view of the expected performance of a firm.

8.1.2 Types of Financial Markets

Different markets serve different types of customers, or operate in different parts of the country. So it is often useful to classify markets along various dimensions.

Money Markets vs. Capital Markets

A **money market** is a financial market for issuing and trading short-term debt securities. Money markets are decentralized markets, consisting of securities dealers who are linked by an electronic communications network. A **capital market** is a financial market for intermediate-or long-term securities. Corporations may raise funds in capital markets by selling bonds, preferred stock, and common stock. Other capital market instruments include US Treasury notes and bonds, mortgages, term loans, and leases.

Primary Markets vs. Secondary markets

The **primary market**, also called the new issue markets, is a financial market for the original sale of new securities. If Microsoft were to sell a new issue of common stock to raise capital, this would be a primary market transaction. This market is not a physical trading exchange or location, but represents a telecommunications network for selling new securities. The issuing corporation receives the proceeds from the sale of the new securities, less any related costs of the issue. The buyers, who are mainly individual and institutional investors, receive shares of a new securities issue. The initial public offering (IPO) market is a subset of the primary market. Here firms "**go public**" by offering shares to the public for the first time.

The **secondary market** is a market for trading existing securities among investors, either directly or through an intermediary. Secondary markets exist for bonds, stocks, options, future contracts, and other financial assets. The New York Stock Exchange is a secondary market, since it deals in **outstanding**, as opposed to newly issued, stocks and bonds. Firms do not use secondary market to raise external funds because these markets are resale markets. Corporations may enter the secondary market to repurchase their securities or buy securities in other companies.

Private Markets vs. Public Markets

Private markets are different from **public markets**, where transactions are worked out directly between two parties and standardized contracts are traded on organized exchanges. Bank loans and **private placements** of debt with insurance companies are examples of private market transactions. Since these transactions are private, they may be structured in any manner that appeals to the two parties. By contrast, securities that are issued in public markets (e.g., common stock and corporate bonds) are ultimately held by a large number of individuals.

Public securities must have fairly standardized contractual features to appeal to a broad range of investors because public investors cannot afford the time to study unique, nonstandardized contracts. Their diverse ownership also ensures that public securities are relatively liquid. Private market securities are, therefore, more tailor-made but less liquid, whereas public market securities are more liquid but subject to greater standardization.

Other classifications could be made, but this breakdown is sufficient to show that there are many types of financial markets. Also, note that the distinctions among markets are often blurred and unimportant, except as a general point of reference. For example, it makes little difference if a firm borrows for 11, 12, or 13 months, hence, whether we have a "money" or "capital" market transaction. You should recognize the big differences among types of markets, but don't get hung up trying to distinguish them at the boundaries.

8.1.3 Recent Trend

Financial markets have experienced many changes during the last two decades. Technological advances in computers and telecommunications, along with the globalization of banking and commerce, have led to deregulation, and this has increased competition throughout the world.

Globalization has brought the need for greater cooperation among regulators at the international level. Various committees are currently working to improve coordination, but the task is not easy. Factors that complicate coordination include (1) the differing structures among nations' banking and securities industries, (2) the trend toward financial service conglomerates, and (3) a reluctance on the part of individual countries to give up control over their national monetary policies. Still, regulators are unanimous about the need to close the gaps in the supervision of world-wide markets.

Another important trend in recent years has been the increased use of derivatives. A **derivative** is any security whose value is derived from the price of some other "underlying" asset. The market for derivatives has grown faster than any other market in recent years, providing corporations with new opportunities but also exposing them to new risks.

8.2 Investment Banks

When issuing securities to the public, a firm usually hires an investment-banking house such as Merrill Lynch, Salomon Smith Barney, Morgan Stanley Dean Witter, or Goldman Sachs to do specific services. An **investment bank** is a firm that acts as an intermediary between sellers needing additional funds and buyers with surplus funds to invest. Investment bankers can perform the functions associated with issuing securities more efficiently than issuing firms can. Unlikely other banks, investment banks neither take deposits nor make loans. Investment banks provide three major services in handing a new security issue: advising, underwriting, and marketing.

8.2.1 Advising

Investment bankers provide their financial and legal expertise to corporations wanting to sell new issues of stocks and bonds. They advise corporations on all specifics of a security to sell and its size, timing, and pricing characteristics. The investment banker also helps design new security issues with features that appeal to investors. For example, if a corporation wants to sell bonds, the investment banker helps the firm decide the bond's maturity date, coupon interest rate, collateral, payment dates, and so on. For stocks, this task involves helping a firm decide the offering size, pricing, and issuing date. Investment bankers can offer such advice because they are experts on current market conditions. They can also help firms enter the market at the right time with the right security at the right price.

8.2.2 Underwriting

Underwriting is the act of buying a new security from a company and reselling it to investors. An investment banker that acts to guarantee the sale of a new securities issue by buying the securities for subsequent resale to the public is called an **underwriter**. Because the underwriter bears the risk of not selling the entire securities issue, the issuer receives all funds needed from the sale regardless of whether the underwriter sells all the securities.

8.2.3 Marketing

Investment bankers have expertise in selling and distributing securities. Because underwriting involves risk, the investment banker forms an **underwriting syndicate** to spread the risk and to help distribute the issue to the public. The underwriter may also support the issue in the aftermarket by trying to stabilize prices around the offer date of a security through buying and selling in the open market to insure acceptance by the market. Regulations prohibit issuing corporations from stabilizing their shares to prevent them from manipulating their share price.

8.3 The Decision to Go Public

Firms often begin as proprietorships or partnerships and some of them later convert into corporations. If a company grows and prospers, the owners must decide whether to keep the company privately held or become publicly held. A **privately held company** is usually a small firm with few owners, who are often its managers. Trading shares of privately held corporations occur infrequently. By contrast, a **publicly held company** is one in which many investors own its shares but they do not actively manage the firm. Active secondary markets exist for trading shares of publicly held stock. When a privately held company sells part of its ownership to the public through a stock offering, the processing is called **going public**. New public offerings by privately held firms occur in the primary markets typically with the help of an investment banker.

When a firm makes its first equity issue available to the public, it is making an initial public offering (IPO). Microsoft had its IPO in 1986. Previously, Bill Gates and other insiders owned all the shares. In many IPOs, the insiders sell some of their shares with the company selling newly created shares to raise additional capital. Equities offered in an IPO are typically those of young, rapidly growing companies. Thus, another name for an IPO is an **unseasoned new issue**. Not surprisingly, the costs associated with an IPO are higher than for a **seasoned issue**. Several other types of IPOs include spin-offs from well-established companies and old-line, privately held companies.

Going public has both advantages and disadvantages. The decision on whether to go public depends on the relative importance of these pros and cons as they relate to a firm's characteristics. Unfortunately, only rough guidelines exist for determining whether a firm should go public and when it should do so.

8.3.1 Advantages of Going Public

These are several advantages to going public.

1. Broaden a firm's access to capital market. Going public provides firms with more capital for financing their growth and also allows a firm to enhance its debt capacity because it involves issuing new shares of common stock.

2. Increase the liquidity of a firm's stock. The shares of a privately held company are illiquid because no ready market exists for them. By going public, a firm increases the trading of its shares and, therefore, increases its liquidity.

3. Set a value for a firm's shares. Going public sets a market price for a firm's stock. The publicly traded price also provides management and shareholders with important outside information about the firm's value.

4. Increase a firm's ability to attract management. A publicly held firm can often

attract better managers by offering them incentive stock options, which allow managers to buy shares of the firm's stock at a predetermined price.

8.3.2 Disadvantages of Going Public

Despite offering many advantages, going public also has several disadvantages.

1. Dilution of control. Owner-managers of privately held companies often have greater autonomy because public ownership reduces the autonomy of management.

2. Costs. **Floatation costs** are the costs associated with floating a new issue. Their costs include both direct costs (fees paid by the issuer to the underwriters as well as filing fees, legal fees, and taxes), indirect costs (management time spent working on the new issue) and others. Another cost for IPO is underpricing, which represents "money less on the table" or losses arising from selling the stock below the correct value. One way to measure underpricing is to multiply the difference in the closing price and offering price by the number of shares sold. A publicly held company also incurs the added costs of filing annual and quarterly financial reports to the regulation officials.

3. Disclosure of operating data. Going public gives the public, including competitors, access to more information about the firm.

4. Possible inactive trading. Secondary trading of the stock may be inactive if the firm remains small after the public stock offering. A thin market can cause an artificially low market price of the common stock.

8.3.3 Different methods of Issuing New Securities

Apart from IPOs or unseasoned issues, a company that has previously issued securities to the public can make a seasoned new issue, a new equity issue of securities. Firms may issue new securities either through a public offer or a private placement.

A **public offer** is the sale of an issue of securities to the public. An IPO is a special type of public offering. Another type involves seasoned issues or securities of well-established, publicly held companies sold in the primary market. Most public offerings of debt are **cash offers**. When making a public offering of additional equity, a firm can either select a general cash offer to the public at large or offer securities on a pro rata basis to existing owners through a rights offer. A general cash offer is the public offering of securities to all interest investors. A **rights offer**, also called a privileged subscription, involves initially offering the securities to the firm's existing stockholders. Many corporate charters include a preemptive right giving existing stockholders the right to buy new shares of common stock issued in proportion to their current ownership.

If corporate management selects a general cash offer, it can structure the offering internally and then put it out for competitive offers. Alternatively, it can negotiate the offer terms directly with an underwriter. With a negotiated offer, the underwriting contract can be either a firm commitment to market all shares or a best-efforts offer, in which an investment bank does not guarantee selling all shares. Finally, the firm can register the issue with the securities regulation officials under traditional registration procedures.

8.4 Cost of Capital Concept

We can view the **cost of capital** from two major perspectives: demanders (issuers) and suppliers (investors). The cost of capital is the rate that the firm has to pay, explicitly or implicitly, the investors for their capital or the minimum **rate of return** required by the suppliers of capital. Thus, ignoring taxes and floatation costs, the cost to issuers is the return to investors. Therefore, the terms "cost of capital" and "rate of required return" could be used interchangeably. The firm's primary objective is to maximize shareholder value, and companies can increase shareholder value by investing in projects that earn more than the cost of capital. For this reason, the cost of capital is sometimes referred to as a **hurdle rate**: For a project to be accepted, it must earn more than its hurdle rate.

Various factors affect the cost of capital. Some of them are within the firm's control while others are not. For example, firms have no direct control over the level of interest rates, tax rates, and the market risk premium. Conversely, managers can affect the cost of capital of their firm. For example, investment policy decisions affect the riskiness of the firm and hence the rate of return required by creditors and stockholders who provide the funds. Capital structure decisions have an effect on the **financing mix** of the firm, which in turn affects its cost of capital. Finally, dividend policy decisions influence the amount of earnings distributed to shareholders or retained by the firm to finance future growth. Dividend policy can affect the return investors require and the firm's cost of capital.

8.4.1 Use of the Cost of Capital

The cost of capital is a central concept in financial management because it provides a way to link investment and financing decisions of a firm. An interrelationship exists between capital budgeting and cost of capital. For example, to determine the size of the capital budget, corporate managers need information about both the returns on investment opportunities and the cost of capital. Managers and analysts use estimates of the firm's cost of capital in two major ways: (1) to help identify the discount rate to be used to evaluate proposed capital investments and (2) to serve as a guideline in developing capital structure and evaluating financial alternatives.

Using the firm's overall cost of capital is appropriate for project evaluation only in those cases where the risk profile of the new project is the same as the risk profile for the firm. That is, the cost of capital embodies the average risk posture of the firm for its portfolio of operational projects. In cases where the risk profile of a specific project differs from that of the risk complexion of the firm, managers and analysts need to adjust the required discount rate to reflect this deviation. Ideally, the cost of capital for each project should reflect the risk of the project itself.

More risky projects require a higher cost of capital (discount rate, hurdle rate, or required rate of return) than less risky projects. Failing to adjust the differences in project risk would lead a firm to accept too many value-destroying risky projects and reject too many value-adding safe ones. Over time, the riskiness of the firm would increase and lead to an increase in its cost of capital. Eventually, shareholder value would suffer. An important point to remember is that the cost of capital (appropriate discount rate) depends mainly on the use of the funds, not on how and where the firm raises the capital. The specific source of financing for a project is not directly relevant.

8.4.2 Capital Components

Although some firms can finance their operations totally with common equity, most rely on other capital components that represent funds provided by various suppliers. The items on the right side of a firm's balance sheet — various types of debt, preferred stock, and common security — are called capital components. Capital components are funds that come from investors. Any increase in total assets must be financed by an increase in one or more of these capital components.

Each capital component has a component cost which is the minimum required rate of return on the component. In capital budgeting, managers and analysts should use the cost of the specific source of financing employed in a particular year as the discount or cutoff rate in project evaluation. Instead, they should view companies as ongoing concerns. Firms typically raise rate of return on the firm's overall capital. Thus, their costs of capital should be the weighted averages of the various types of funds they use.

The three major long-term components in the capital structures of most firms are straight debt, straight preferred stock, and common equity. Companies use other sources of financing to a lesser extent such as convertible debt, variable-rate debt, term loans, leases, floating-rate preferred stock, and numerous new types of securities. Estimating the cost of capital for most of these instruments is difficult. Fortunately, these financial assets usually constitute a small percentage capital of most firms.

8.4.3 Weighted Average Cost of Capital

The **weighted average cost of capital (WACC)** is the weighted average of the costs of debt and equity. WACC is the cost of capital for the firm as a whole. Since a firm uses debt and equity capital, WACC represents a mixture of the returns needed to compensate both creditors and stockholders. If the firm earns an overall rate of return on its existing assets equal to its WACC, it can maintain the market value of its stock. If the firm fails to meet this objective, the market price of its stock should decline.

Measuring a company's WACC involves two major steps: (1) estimating the cost of each capital component, and (2) determining the weights of each component. Multiplying each capital component by its weight in the capital structure and then summing the percentages produce an estimate of the WACC.

核心词汇 Core Words and Expressions

financial market　金融市场
money market　货币市场
capital market　资本市场
treasury notes　国库券
primary market　一级市场
secondary market　二级市场
option contract　期权合约
future contract　期货合约
repurchase　回购
investment bank　投资银行
Merrill Lynch　美林公司
Salomon Smith Barney　所罗门美邦投资公司
Morgan Stanley Dean Witter　摩根士丹利-添惠公司
Goldman Sachs　高盛公司
collateral　抵押
underwriting　（股份等的）承保；承销，包销
underwriter　承销商
Syndicate of underwriter　承销辛迪加
manipulate　操纵
privately held corporation　私人控股公司
publicly held company　公众控股公司
stock offering　股票发行
go public　公开上市
initial public offering (IPO)　首次公开发行
seasoned issue　适时发行、增发（seasoned 是指新股稳定发行。广泛发行给大量买者，并在二级市场有良好流动性的新发行证券）
spin-offs　分拆
pros and cons　正反两方面
incentive stock option　激励性股票期权
dilution of control　控制权稀释
autonomy　自主权，自治
floatation　发行证券；挂牌上市
floatation cost　上市成本
underpricing　抑价
unseasoned issue　首次公开发行
public offer　公开报价
private placement　私募
pro rata　按比例，成比例
rights offer　认股权发行
privileged subscription　有特权的认购
preemptive right　优先权
cash offer　现金收购
negotiated offer　议价收购
cost of capital　资本成本
hurdle rate　门槛比率，最低报酬率
rate of return　收益率
financing mix　融资组合
convertible debt　可转债
variable-rate debt　浮动利率负债

term loan　定期贷款
lease　租赁
weighted average cost of capital (WACC)
　加权平均资本成本

即时问答 Quick Quiz

1. What role do financial markets play in our economy? What are primary or secondary markets? What relationship exists between financial institutions or financial markets?
2. What is the cost of capital? What role does it play in making long-term investment decisions?
3. What is the weighted average cost of capital (WACC), and how is it calculated?
4. How do firms make initial public offerings, and what are the costs of such offerings?
5. How to measure a company's WACC?

思考与探索 Thinking and Exploration

Why are issue costs for debt issues generally less than those for equity issues? List the possible reasons. Find a debt issue and an equity issue in real world and explain.

汉译英 Translation

中国不仅是捷豹最大的市场，而且也是世界最大的汽车市场，这就是捷豹加入中国市场的原因。自 2014 年开始，人们在中国国内市场上看到越来越多汽车拥有著名的捷豹标志。捷豹与中国奇瑞汽车集团于 2012 年 11 月成立了合资公司，后者自称是中国最大的汽车出国商。上海是中国的金融中心，而这家合资工厂的拟建厂址就在上海附近，是一家带有新研发中心及新发动机厂的新汽车制造厂。

知识扩展 More Knowledge

Listing 和 floatation

Listing 和 floatation 都表示"发行证券、挂牌上市"的意思。

上市证券　listed securities
上市公司　listed company

161

Unseasoned issues 和 seasoned issues

证券市场依据是否由发行人提供出售而划分为初级市场和二级市场，初级市场又分为初发或首发（unseasoned new issue）和续发或增发（seasoned new issue）两个亚市场。初发通常被称为首次公开发行（initial public offering，IPO），是指公司第一次向公众发行并上市挂牌交易股票，故有时又称为无前例发售（unseasoned offerings）。这种股票在国外称为 unseasoned issue 或 unseasoned new issue，是一级市场的重要交易对象。

国外投资银行简介

投资银行是一国金融体系的重要组成部分，是活跃在资本市场的主要金融机构。与商业银行的区别主要体现在投资银行是一个非银行的金融机构，它不能通过发行货币或吸收存款增加货币供应量，不能办理商业银行的传统业务，如吸收活期存款、结算业务等，不参与形成一个国际支付体系。投资银行最本源的业务主要是证券承销以及在此基础上的证券经纪业务，其他任何投资银行业务都是在此基础上的延伸和发展。

下面以投资银行业最发达的美国为主，兼顾其他国家的情况，对投资银行进行分类。

（1）特大型投资银行。特大型投资银行在规模、市场、实力、客户数量、信誉等方面均达到一流的水平。在美国，美林、摩根士丹利、高盛、所罗门美邦公司等是世界公认的特大型投资银行。

在欧洲，投资银行和商业银行存在不同程度的混业经营，许多投资银行附属于商业银行。欧洲的特大型投资银行有瑞士银行旗下的瑞银华宝、德意志银行旗下的德意志摩根建富、总部设在苏黎世的瑞士信贷银行旗下的第一波士顿公司。

在日本，投资银行一般称为"证券公司"。在 1997 年亚洲金融危机之前，日本拥有世界一流的投资银行，它们分别是野村、日兴、大和与山一。这四家证券公司在资本金、员工人数、业务量和业务范围、客户数目和信誉等各项指标均居日本投资银行前列，是日本证券业的主要支柱，也是国际投资银行界的实力机构。但是，20 世纪 90 年代以来，日本经济和证券市场的长时期萧条以及 1997 年的亚洲金融危机的冲击，日本投资银行界的"四巨头"已今非昔比，其中野村创下了巨额亏损的纪录，日兴被迫与外资联合，山一倒闭，其营业网点被美林证券收购。

（2）大型投资银行。大型投资银行提供综合性服务，但与特大型投资银行相比，在信誉、实力等方面均略逊一筹。在美国，大型投资银行有普惠证券（Paine Webber）、培基证券（Prudential）等。

（3）次大型投资银行。次大型投资银行是指一些以本国金融中心为基地的、专门为某些投资者群体或较小的公司服务的投资银行，它们一般规模较小，并在组织上多采取合伙制。

（4）地区性投资银行。地区性投资银行是指专门为某一地区投资者和中小企业及地方政府机构服务的投资银行。它们一般以某一地区为基地，不在全国及世界金融中心设立总部和分支机构。

（5）专业性投资银行。专业性投资银行往往也被称为投资银行界的专卖店。它们专攻一个或几个重要业务领域，在这些领域具有优势。例如，仅经营和买卖某些行业证券（如钢铁公司股票、高科技股票、银行债券等）或仅进行技术性承销的投资银行。那些以高质量投资分析和投资研究著称，而其业务是基于这些分析和研究的投资银行，也应该属于专业性投资银行。

（6）商人银行。这里的商人银行与英国的"商人银行"概念不同，它是指专门从事兼并、收购与某些筹资活动的投资银行，这类投资银行有时也用自有资金购买证券。美国著名的商人银行有黑石集团（Blackstone Group）及 Wasserstein Perella 公司。

我国投资银行简介

根据投资银行的定义和业务经营范围，我国证券公司都可称为投资银行。在我国，证券公司是指依照《中华人民共和国公司法》（以下简称《公司法》）和《中华人民共和国证券法》（以下简称《证券法》）规定批准的从事证券经营业务的有限责任公司或者股份有限公司。设立证券公司，必须经国务院证券监督管理机构审查批准。未经国务院证券监督管理机构批准，不得经营证券业务。

1. 证券公司的业务范围

《证券法》第120条规定，经国务院证券监督管理机构核准，取得经营证券业务许可证，证券公司可以经营下列部分或者全部证券业务：证券经纪；证券投资咨询；与证券交易、证券投资活动有关的财务顾问；证券承销与保荐；证券融资融券；证券做市交易；证券自营；其他证券业务。国务院证券监督管理机构应当自受理前款规定事项申请之日起三个月内，依照法定条件和程序进行审查，作出核准或者不予核准的决定，并通知申请人；不予核准的，应当说明理由。证券公司经营证券资产管理业务的，应当符合《中华人民共和国证券投资基金法》等法律、行政法规的规定。除证券公司外，任何单位和个人不得从事证券承销、证券保荐、证券经纪和证券融资融券业务。证券公司从事证券融资融券业务，应当采取措施，严格防范和控制风险，不得违反规定向客户出借资金或者证券。同时，《证券法》第122条规定，证券公司变更证券业务范围，变更主要股东或者公司的实际控制人，合并、分立、停业、解散、破产，应当经国务院证券监督管理机构核准。

2. 证券公司的设立条件

《证券法》第 118 条规定，设立证券公司，应当具备下列条件，并经国务院证券监督管理机构批准：有符合法律、行政法规规定的公司章程；主要股东及公司的实际控制人具有良好的财务状况和诚信记录，最近三年无重大违法违规记录；有符合本法规定的公司注册资本；董事、监事、高级管理人员、从业人员符合本法规定的条件；有完善的风险管理与内部控制制度；有合格的经营场所、业务设施和信息技术系统；法律、行政法规和经国务院批准的国务院证券监督管理机构规定的其他条件。未经国务院证券监督管理机构批准，任何单位和个人不得以证券公司名义开展证券业务活动。同时，《证券法》第 121 条进行了进一步的规定，证券公司经营证券经纪，证券投资咨询；与证券交易、证券投资活动有关的财务顾问业务的，注册资本最低限额为人民币五千万元；经营证券承销与保荐，证券融资融券，证券做市交易，证券自营，其他证券业务之一的，注册资本最低限额为人民币一亿元；经营证券承销与保荐，证券融资融券，证券做市交易，证券自营，其他证券业务中两项以上的，注册资本最低限额为人民币五亿元。证券公司的注册资本应当是实缴资本。国务院证券监督管理机构根据审慎监管原则和各项业务的风险程度，可以调整注册资本最低限额，但不得少于前款规定的限额。

相 关 网 址
Useful Websites

美国《机构投资者》（*Institutional Investor*）杂志是投资界最权威的媒体之一，有美国版、欧洲版和亚洲版三种版本。其中，每年推出的投资银行排名和分析师排名是其最有特色和最有影响的栏目，跻身排行榜几乎是每个分析师的梦想。

《机构投资者》杂志的网址是 http://www.institutionalinvestor.com

中国两大证券市场：上海证券交易所（www.sse.com.cn）、深圳证券交易所（www.szse.cn）

中国两大商品交易所：大连商品交易所（www.dce.com.cn）、郑州商品交易所（www.czce.com.cn）

美国两大市场：纽约证券交易所（www.nyse.com）、纳斯达克证券交易所（www.nasdaq.com）

中国央行：中国人民银行（www.pbc.gov.cn）

美国中央银行：美国联邦储备系统（The Federal Reserve System），简称为美联储（www.federalreserve.gov）

第 9 章
TOPIC 9

Capital Structure
资本结构

新闻视听
News in Media

Amid a continuing housing crisis in the United States, the Bush administration is taking over two failing mortgage firms in an effort to limit further turmoil in the sector.

本章新闻视听资料请扫二维码收听。

名人名言
Wisdom

Give me a lever, and I will move the world.

——Paraphrase of Archimedes

微型案例
Mini Case

VAM (Value Adjustment Mechanism): Morgan Stanley vs. Yongle

Yongle Electrical was founded in 1996. The founder Chen Xiao is a businessman born in Shanghai. In the industry, Yongle Electric was once the second home appliance chain company after Gome and Suning. However, unlike Gome and Suning, which have long since expanded in the country to seize the market, Yongle Electric focuses on the penetration development in Shanghai, which has 60% market share and owns more stores than the sum of other home appliance retailers there.

After 2004, Gome and Suning accelerated nationwide expansion, and both planned to add 100 new chain stores each year, which put a lot of pressure on Yongle Electric. If Yongle Electric cannot keep up, the market gap will be widened. In contrast, Gome and Suning have been listed on Hong Kong and A shares, and have obtained effective financing channels through the capital market, while Yongle Electric has a congenital deficiency in capital supply.

In order to support the market expansion plan, Yongle began to seek the support of private equity funds, and finally obtained a 50 million joint investment of Morgan Stanley and CDH on January 1, 2005. Among them, Morgan Stanley invested 4,300 dollars, accounting for 23.53% of the shares; CDH invested 7 million dollars, accounting for 3.83% of the shares. In this financing, Chen Xiao signed a VAM agreement with capitals such as Morgan Stanley and CDH. The conditions for VAM required by Morgan Stanley and CDH are that Yongle Electric's net profit in 2007 must reach 675 million yuan. If Yongle Electric fails to realize the VAM conditions, the founder Chen Xiao must use the equity as compensation consideration. The net profit of Yongle Electric from 2002 to 2004 was 28.2 million yuan, 148 million yuan and 212 million yuan, obviously far from the target of 675 million yuan. The investor's reason is that Yongle Electric's net profit growth in the past several years has been more than 50%, and at this rate in 2007, it can achieve 675 million yuan.

On October 14, 2005, Yongle Electric was listed on the Hong Kong Stock Exchange and raised more than 1 billion Hong Kong dollars. However, the development across regions is not smooth, and the unit sales area and gross profit have both declined. On August 14, 2006, Yongle announced the semi-annual report for the year. The first half of the year ended with a profit of 15.018 million yuan, compared with a net profit of 140 million yuan in the same period in 2005, a drop of 89%. In order to avoid failure, Chen Xiao made two preparations: on the one hand, he managed to sell the company to the industry leader Gome in advance, which made it impossible to execute the gambling agreement objectively; on the other hand, he sought to acquire the industry's oldest Dazhong Electric and merge the two revenues which may be able to reach the profit target, so as not to lose the bet agreement.

Finally, on July 25, 2006, Gome and Yongle announced the merger: Gome purchased 100% of Yongle Appliances at a consideration of HK $ 5.268 billion through the "cash and stock" method. After the acquisition was completed, the original shareholders of Yongle were all transferred to Gome. As a shareholder, Chen Xiao personally held less than 4% of Gome's shares, while Yongle became a wholly-owned subsidiary of Gome and delisted from the Hong Kong Stock Exchange.

This topic investigates a firm's capital structure decision. Capital structure refers to the sources of long-term financing employed by the firm. We illustrate how a firm may use financial leverage to increase the expected returns to shareholders while decreasing risk for the shareholders. We also discuss the Modigliani-Miller theorem of capital structure irrelevance for a firm when there are no taxes or other market frictions. We then show how taxes and certain market frictions may make a firm's capital structure decision relevant in the real world. Finally, we present a checklist for capital structure decisions.

正文 Text

9.1 The Choices: Types of Financing

There are only two ways in which any business can raise money — debt or equity, which has totally different characteristics and a range of financing vehicles available within each of these categories. What's more, there is a range of securities that share some characteristics with debt and some with equity and are therefore called hybrid securities.

Equity

Although most people think of equity in terms of common stock, the equity claim on a business can take a variety of forms, depending partly on whether the firm is privately owned or publicly traded and partly on the firm's growth and risk characteristics. Private firms have fewer available choices than publicly traded firms, because they cannot issue securities to raise equity. Consequently, they have to depend either on the owner or a private entity, usually a venture capitalist, to bring in the equity needed to keep the business operating and expanding. Publicly traded firms have access to capital markets, giving them a wider array of choices.

Owner's Equity

Most businesses, including the most successful companies of our time, such as Microsoft and Wal-Mart, started off as small businesses with one or a few individuals providing the **seed money** and plowing back the earnings of the firm into the businesses. These funds, brought in by the owners of the company, are referred to as the owner's equity and provide the basis for the growth and eventual success of the business.

Venture Capital and Private Equity

As small businesses succeed and grow, they typically run into a funding constraint, where the funds that they have access to are insufficient to cover their investment and growth needs. A venture capitalist or private equity investor provides equity financing to small and often risky businesses in return for a share of the ownership of the firm.

Generally speaking, the capacity to raise funds from alternative sources and/or to go public will increase with the size of the firm and decrease with the uncertainty about its future prospects. Thus, smaller and riskier businesses are more likely to seek **venture capital** and are also more likely to be asked to give up a greater share of the value of the firm when receiving the venture capital.

Common Stock

The conventional way for a publicly traded firm to raise equity is to issue common stock at a price the market is willing to pay. For a newly listed company, this price is estimated by an investment banker and is called the **offering price**. For an existing publicly traded company, the price at which additional equity is issued is usually based on the current market price. In some cases, the common stock issued by a company is uniform; that is, each share receives a proportional share of both the cash flows (such as dividends) and the voting rights. In other cases, different classes of common stock will provide different dividends and voting rights.

Common stock is a simple security, and it is relatively easy to understand and value. In fact, it can be argued that common stock makes feasible all other security choices for a publicly traded firm because a firm without equity cannot issue debt or hybrid securities. The accounting treatment of common stock follows well-established precedent and can be presented easily within the conventional format of financial statements.

Warrants

In recent years, firms have started looking at equity alternatives to common stock. One alternative used successfully by Japanese companies in the late 1980s was **warrants**, where the holders received the right to buy shares in the company at a fixed price sometime in the future in return for paying for the warrants up front. Because their value is derived from the price of the underlying common stock, warrants have to be treated as another form of equity.

Why might a firm use warrants rather than common stock to raise equity? We can think of several reasons. First, warrants are priced based on the implied volatility assigned to underlying stock; the greater the volatility, the greater the value. To the degree that the market overestimates how risky a firm is, the firm may gain by using warrants and option-like securities. Second, warrants by themselves create no financial obligations at the time of the issue. Consequently, issuing warrants is a good way for a high-growth firm to raise funds, especially when current cash flows are low or negative. Third, for financial officers who are sensitive to the dilution created by issuing common stock, warrants seem to provide the best of both worlds — they do not create any new additional shares currently while they raise equity investment funds for current use.

Contingent Value Rights

Contingent value rights provide investors with right to sell stocks for a fixed price and thus derive their value from the volatility of the stock and the desire on the part of investors to hedge their losses. **Put options**, which are traded on option exchanges, give their holders a similar right to sell the underlying stock at a fixed price. There are two primary differences between contingent value rights and put options. First, the proceeds from the contingent value rights sales go to the firm, whereas those from the sale of listed put options go to private parties. Second, contingent value rights tend to be much more long-term than typically listed put options.

There are several reasons why a firm may choose to issue contingent value rights. The most obvious is that the firm believes it is significantly undervalued by the market. In such a scenario, the firm may offer contingent value rights to take advantage of its belief and to provide a signal to the market of the undervaluation. Contingent value rights are also useful if the market is overestimating volatility and the put price reflects this misestimated volatility. Finally, the presence of contingent value right as insurance may attract new investors to the market for the common stock.

Debt

The clear alternative to using equity, which is **residual claim**, is to borrow money. Borrowing creates an obligation to make cash flow payments in operation and provides the lender with prior claims if the firm is in financial trouble.

Bank debt

Historically, the primary source of borrowed money for all private firms and many publicly traded firms has been banks, with the interest rates on the debt based on the perceived risk of the borrower. Besides being a source of long-term borrowing for firms, banks also often offer them a flexible option to meet unanticipated or seasonal financing needs. This option is a **line of credit**, which the firm can draw on only if it needs financing. The advantage of having a line of credit is that it provides the firm with access to the funds without having to pay interest costs if the funds remain unused. Thus, it is a useful type of financing for firms with volatile working capital needs. In many cases, however, the firm is required to maintain a compensating balance on which it earns either no interest or below-market rates.

Bonds

For larger, publicly traded firms, an alternative to bank debt is to issue bonds. Generally speaking, bond issues have several advantages for these firms. The first is that bonds often carry more favorable financing terms than equivalent bank debt, largely because the risk is shared by a larger number of financial market investors. The second is that bond issues might provide a chance for the issuer to add special features that could not be added to bank debt. For instance, bonds can be convertible into common stock or be tied to commodity bonds.

Leases

A firm often borrows money to finance the acquisition of an asset needed for its operations. An alternative approach that accomplishes the same goal is to lease the asset. A lease agreement is usually categorized as either an operating lease or a capital lease. For an operating lease, the term of the lease agreement is shorter than the life of the asset, and the present value of lease payments is generally much lower than the actual price of the asset. At the end of the life of the lease, the asset reverts back to the lessor, who will either offer to sell it to the lessee or lease it to somebody else. The lessee usually has the right to cancel the lease and return the asset to the lessor. Thus, the ownership of the asset in an operating lease clearly resides with the lessor, with the lessee bearing little or no risk if the asset becomes obsolete.

A capital lease generally lasts for the life of the asset, with the present value of lease payments covering the price of the asset. A capital lease generally cannot be canceled, and the lease can be renewed at the end of its life at a reduced rate or the asset can be acquired by lessee at a favorable price. In many cases, the lessor is not obligated to pay insurance and taxes on the asset, leaving these obligations up to the lessee; the lessee consequently reduces the lease payments, lending to what are called net leases. A capital lease places the substantial risk on the shoulders of the lessee if the asset loses value or becomes obsolete. Although the differences between operating and financial leases are obvious, some lease arrangements do not fit neatly into one or another of these extremes; rather, they share some features of both types of leases. These leases are called combination leases.

Hybrid Securities

Summarizing our analysis thus far, equity represents a residual claim on the cash flows and assets of the firm and is generally associated with management control. Debt, on the other hand, represents a fixed claim on the cash flows and assets of the firm and is usually not associated with management control. There are a number of securities that do not fall neatly into either of these two categories; rather, they share some characteristics with equity and some with debt. These securities are called **hybrid securities**.

Convertible Bond

A **convertible bond** is a bond that can be converted into a predetermined number of shares at the discretion of the bondholder. Although it generally does not pay to convert at the time of the bond issue, conversion becomes a more attractive option as stock prices increase. Firms generally add conversion options to bonds to lower the interest rate paid on the bonds.

In a typical convertible bond, the bondholder is given the option to convert the bond into a specified number of shares of stock. The conversion ratio measures the number of shares of stock for which each bond may be exchanged. Stated differently, the market conversion value is the current value of the shares for which the bonds can be exchanged. The conversion premium is the excess of the convertible bond value over the conversion value of the bond.

Preferred Stock

Preferred stock is another security that shares some characteristics with debt and some with equity. Like debt, preferred stock creates a fixed dollar payment (dividend); if the firm does not have the cash to pay the dividend, it is accumulated and paid in a period when there are sufficient earnings. Like debt, preferred stockholders do not have a share of control in the firm, and their voting privileges are strictly restricted to issues that might affect their claims on the firm's cash flows or assets. Like equity, payments to preferred stockholders are not tax-deductible and come out of after-tax cash flows. Also like equity, preferred stock does not have a maturity date when the face value is due. In terms of priority, in the case of bankruptcy, preferred stockholders have to wait until the debtholders' claims have been met before receiving any portion of the assets of the firm.

9.2 The Financing Mix

The capital structure decision involves determining a firm's financing mix. Capital structure is the mix of long-term sources of funds used by the firm. The capital structures of many firms today are complex, consisting of some combination of debt, preferred stock, common stock, leases, warrants, convertible preferred stock.

Financial managers need to know how their capital structure decision affects the value of their firms. They are particularly interested in whether an optimal capital structure exists for their firm. An optimal capital structure is the financing mix that maximizes the value of the firm. The search for optimal capital structure is ongoing. Researches have led to many views. Some believe that while managers can theoretically determine a firm's optimal capital structure, they cannot determine the precise percentage of debt that will maximize the market value of the firm. Others believe that a firm's value does not depend on its financing mix (and that an optimal capital structure does not exist) or that firms do not strive to attain an optimal financing mix. In either case, managers must use informed judgment to set a desired or target capital structure.

9.3 Understanding Financial Risk

Investing in a firm's common stock involves risks. A firm's **earnings before interest and taxes (EBIT)**, also called **operating income**, often varies substantially as the general economy expands and contracts. The volatility of operating income, caused by the nature of the firm's business, refers to business risk. Many factors influence a firm's business risk, including the uncertainty of demand, the uncertainty of output prices and input costs, competitive factors, and product and other types of liability. Because business risk focuses on operating income, it ignores financing effects. Some firms, such as automobile manufacturers and other durable goods producers, have highly correlated with the business cycle. Firms in the grocery retail industry, on the other hand, typically have sales that are much less sensitive to the business cycle and have lower levels of business risk.

When firms borrow, they incur an additional risk, referred to as financial risk, which further increases the risk to the investors.

- Borrowing increases the risk of default for a firm. Interest and principal payments on debt are legal obligations for the firm. Failure to meet these payments in a timely manner may lead to default and eventual bankruptcy for the firm.
- The interest and principal payments associated with borrowing increase the volatility of a firm's earnings per share and its return on equity.

Managers sometimes overlook this latter aspect of financial risk. Because the returns to the shareholders are more volatile when firms use debt financing, the common shareholders require a higher rate of return as compensation for this increased financial risk component. Thus, while business risk refers to the volatility of a firm's operating earnings due to the nature of the firm's business, financial risk refers to the additional volatility that is translated from the operating earnings to the firm's earnings per share (EPS) and returns on equity (ROE) due to the fixed interest expenses associated with financial leverage.

9.4 Capital Structure and the Value of a Firm

Understanding the effects that **financial leverage** has on a firm's earnings per share and its return on equity is important. Yet, even more important to a financial manager is to understand the effect that financial leverage has on the value of a firm. Financial economists widely accept the premise that managers should make decisions that maximize the value of the firm's common equity. By maximizing shareholders' wealth, managers are serving the interests of the firm's owners. Under most circumstances, the premise of maximizing total firm value (debt and equity) is also consistent with maximizing shareholders' wealth. Franco Modigliani and Merton Miller (M&M) pioneered the research efforts relating to capital structure and the value of a firm. Both have won the Nobel prize in economics for their lifetime work in the area. In a seminal article, they show that in a world of perfect (or frictionless) capital markets with no corporate or personal taxes, the value of a firm is independent of its capital structure.

9.4.1 The Modigliani-Miller Theorem

The Modigliani and Miller (M&M) theorem states that in the absence of corporate and personal taxes, transaction costs, and other market imperfections, the value of a firm is independent of its capital structure. In other words, managers cannot alter the value of their firms by the capital structures that they choose. M&M argues that under a highly restrictive set of assumptions, the value of the firm is determined solely by the size and the riskiness of the real cash flows generated by the firm's assets and not by how these cash flows are divided between the debt and equity stakeholders of the firm. If managers want to increase the value of their firms, they should invest in real assets whose cash flows are sufficient to provide returns to shareholders in excess of their required returns.

One way to illustrate the M&M theorem is by showing the total cash flows in a pie chart with debt and equity claims as slices of the pie. According to the theorem, the value of a firm is determined by the size of the cash flows, or as shown in Figure 9-1 by the size of the pie. According to the M&M theorem, how the firm divides the pie between the debt and equity slices does not matter because the size of the pie (the value of the firm) remains the same.

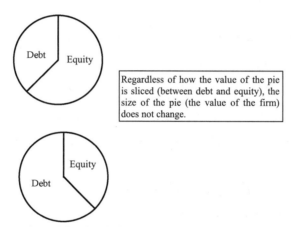

Figure 9-1 Pie models of capital structure under perfect markets with no taxes

9.4.2 The M&M Theorem in the Real World

Does the M&M theorem hold in the real world? Probably not. Miller was quoted later as saying:

The view that capital structure is literally irrelevant or that "nothing matters" in corporate finance, though sometimes attributed to us(and tracing perhaps to the very provocative way we made our point), is far from what we ever actually said about the real world applications of our theoretical propositions.

Accordingly, their results provide an important lesson. In the idealized world of M&M with no market imperfections such as taxes, capital structure does not matter.

Therefore, if capital structure decisions matter in the real world, they must be responses to market imperfections. Now we know where to investigate further. What are these market imperfections? Key imperfections or frictions that affect capital structure and value are taxes (corporate and personal), bankruptcy and financial distress costs, and information asymmetry.

The Modigliani-Miller Theorem with Corporate Taxes

The interest payments associated with corporate borrowings are a tax-deductible expense for a firm. As such, they shield taxable income from taxes. An issue is whether the tax-deductibility of the interest payments associated with corporate borrowings would affect the value of the firm. Modigliani and Miller addressed this issue by considering how capital structure affected the value of a firm under perfect capital markets with corporate taxes. The value of a levered firm is the value of an otherwise identical unlevered firm plus the value of tax shield.

Why Firms Are Not Leveraged to the Maximum

Why would financial managers miss out on such an opportunity to increase the value of the firm for their shareholders? The key reasons that managers do not use the excessive amount of debt financing suggested by M&M theorem with corporate taxes include the costs of **financial distress** and **bankruptcy**.

Costs of Financial Distress and Bankruptcy

Perhaps the strongest argument for a firm to limit its amount of debt involves the costs of financial distress and bankruptcy associated with issuing too much debt. Financial distress occurs when a firm has difficulty in meeting the contractual obligations on its debt financing. It refers to any general weakening in a company's financial condition caused by excessive financial leverage.

The extreme case of financial distress is bankruptcy, a formal legal proceeding where an overextended firm is placed under the protection of the bankruptcy court, allowing it to keep operating while developing a new plan to pay off creditors. When a firm declares bankruptcy, it will bear various legal, accounting, and administrative expenses and could be forced to sell certain assets at "fire sale" prices to meet creditors' claims. Lenders anticipate the risks of attendant costs of bankruptcy and require a higher rate of return as compensation. Thus, the firm's shareholders bear these costs of bankruptcy. The direct costs of bankruptcy do not appear to be large enough to offset the tax advantage of debt financing. Probably more significant than the actual direct costs of bankruptcy are the indirect costs of financial distress.

Actual bankruptcy is not required for a firm to face costs of financial distress. Just the threat of bankruptcy can lead to deterioration in the firm's operating performance. The costs of financial distress involve incentives for stakeholders of the firm to act in a manner that is not more beneficial to the firm. For example, rather than planning a firm's long-term strategy, top management may spend its time devising short-term strategies to stay afloat. Key employees may leave the firm in search of a more secure future. Customers may no longer want to buy the firm's products or services fearing that the firm may not be around much longer to back up the product or service. The firm's suppliers may not be willing to supply short-term credit. Finally, financial distress can also lead to several adverse incentives for a firm's management.

9.4.3 Tradeoff Theory of Optimal Capital Structure

The tax benefits of debt financing bestowed by the government and the costs of financial distress that may at some point accompany the use of financial leverage may lead to a static tradeoff that provides an optimal capital structure for a firm. According to the tradeoff theory, firms with initially little or no debt should consider adding debt to their capital structure because of the tax deductibility of the interest payments. Recall that this interest **tax shield**, which is essentially a government subsidy, increases the value of the firm. The value does not continue to increase indefinitely as the firm continues to increase its use of debt financing. At some point, the probability of being able to fully utilize the interest deduction will decrease with the uncertainty that the firm's operating earnings will exceed the interest tax deductions. Also, as a firm continues to employ higher levels of debt financing, the probability of incurring financial distress increases. Those costs of financial distress initially offset the tax advantage of debt to some degree. Yet, such costs gradually increase as debt levels rise until they begin to completely offset the tax advantage of debt. Beyond that point, issuing more debt decreases the value of the firm. So firms will borrow only up to the point where the tax benefit from another dollar of debt financing exactly equals the cost from the increased probability of financial distress. At this point, a static tradeoff exists between debt and equity financing where the firm maximizes its value.

Since the indirect costs of financial distress are difficult to measure, most financial economists agree that the optimal capital structure for a firm cannot be precisely determined. Rather, we often think of an optimal capital structure range for a firm. Managers determine this optimal capital structure range based on many factors including the firm's marginal tax rate, the amount of other non-interest tax shields, the variability of the firm's operating earnings, and the likelihood and the magnitude of the costs of financial distress for that firm.

9.4.4 Pecking Order Theory of Capital Structure

The basis for the **pecking order theory** of capital structure is the notion that managers have inside information. By contrast, Modigliani and Miller assumed that managers and investors have the same information. In finance, we often refer to this inside information which simply means that managers as insiders know more about a firm's current situation and future prospects than outsiders. Thus, investors may use capital structure decisions as a signal of management's expectations. Failure to choose the capital structure that sends the appropriate signal can result in an information asymmetry cost. This asymmetry information leads to a pecking order of financing choices.

The pecking order of financing choices for firms is as follows.

1. Managers prefer internal financing to external financing. Managers choose their target dividend payout in light of their expected future investment opportunities, seeking to avoid the need for external financing.

2. When operating cash flows and resulting profits are higher than expected and in excess of what the firm needs to fund new capital expenditures and pay dividends, managers pay off debt or invest in marketable securities. When they are less, managers draw down cash balances and sell marketable securities in order to fund new expenditures and pay dividends.

3. After drawing down cash balances and selling marketable securities, managers need to seek external financing from time to time. This is because operating cash flows and investment opportunities are often highly unpredictable.

4. When forced to raise funds externally, firms prefer to issue debt and seek to avoid issuing new shares of equity. In between these choices are hybrid securities such as convertible bonds and convertible preferred stock.

The implication of the pecking order theory of capital structure is that a firm has no optimal capital structure. At the top of the pecking order is the internal equity (reinvested earnings) and at the bottom of the pecking order is the issuance of new shares of equity (external equity). Thus, no natural tradeoff exists between debt and equity that provides a target capital structure for a firm under the pecking order theory of financing choice.

9.5 Checklist for Capital Structure Decisions

Firms generally consider the following factors when making capital structure decisions:

1. Sales stability. A firm whose sales are relatively stable can safely take on more debt and incur higher fixed charges than a company with volatile sales. Utility companies, because of their stable demand, have historically been able to use more financial leverage than industrial firms.

2. Asset structure. Firms whose assets are suitable as security for loans tend to use debt rather heavily. General-purpose assets that can be used by many businesses make good collateral, whereas special-purpose assets do not. Thus, real estate companies are usually highly leveraged, whereas companies involved in technological researches are not.

3. Operating leverage. Other things the same, a firm with less operating leverage is better able to employ financial leverage because it will have less business risk.

4. Growth rate. Other things the same, faster-growing firms must rely more heavily on external capital. Further, the floatation costs involved in selling common stock exceed those incurred when selling debt, which encourages rapidly growing firms to rely more

heavily on debt. At the same time, however, these firms often face greater uncertainty, which tends to reduce their willingness to use debt.

5. Profitability. One often observes that firms with very high rates of return on investment use relatively little debt. Although there is no theoretical justification for this fact, one practical explanation is that very profitable firms such as Intel, Microsoft, and Coca-Cola simply do not need to do much debt financing. Their high rates of return enable them to do most of their financing with internally generated funds.

6. Taxes. Interest is a deductible expense, and deductions are most valuable to firms with high tax rates. Therefore, the higher a firm's tax rate, the greater the advantage of debt.

7. Control. The effect of debt versus stock on a management's control position can influence capital structure. If management currently has voting control (over 50 percent of the stock) but is not in a position to buy any more stock, it may choose debt for new financings. On the other hand, management may decide to use equity if the firm's financial situation is so weak that the use of debt might subject it to serious risk of default, because if the firm goes into default, the managers will almost surely lose their jobs. However, if too little debt is used, management runs the risk of a takeover. Thus, control considerations could lead to the use of either debt or equity because the type of capital that best protects management will vary from situation to situation. In any event, if management is at all insecure, it will consider the control situation.

8. Management attitudes. Because no one can prove that one capital structure will lead to higher stock prices than another, management can exercise its own judgment about the proper capital structure. Some managements tend to be more conservative than others, and thus use less debt than the average firm in their industry, whereas aggressive managements use more debt in the quest for higher profits.

9. Lender and rating agency attitudes. Regardless of managers' own analyses of the proper leverage factors for their firms, lenders' and rating agencies' attitudes frequently influence financial structure decisions. In the majority of cases, the corporation discusses its capital structure with lenders and rating agencies and gives much weight to their advice. For example, one large utility was recently told by Moody's and Standard & Poor's that its bonds would be downgraded if it issued more debt. This influenced its

decision to finance its explanation with common equity.

10. Market conditions. Conditions in the stock and bond markets undergo both long-and short-run changes that can have an important bearing on a firm's optimal capital structure. For example, during a recent credit crunch, the junk bond market dried up, and there was simply no market at a "reasonable" interest rate for any new long-term bonds rated below triple B. Therefore, low-rated companies in need of capital were forced to go to the stock market or to the short-term debt market, regardless of their target capital structures. When conditions where eased, however, these companies sold bonds to get their capital structures back on target.

11. The firm's internal condition. A firm's own internal condition can also have a bearing on its target capital structure. For example, suppose a firm has just successfully completed an R&D program and it forecasts higher earnings in the immediate future. However, the new earnings are not yet anticipated by investors, hence are not reflected in the stock price. This company would not want to issue stock — it would prefer to finance with debt until the higher earnings materialize and are reflected in the stock price. Then it could sell an issue of common stock, retire the debt, and return to its target capital structure. This point was discussed earlier in connection with asymmetric information and signaling.

12. Financial flexibility. Firms with profitable investment opportunities need to be able to fund them. An astute corporate treasurer made this statement:

Our company can earn a lot more money from good capital budgeting and operating decisions than from good financing decisions. Indeed, we are not sure exactly how financing decisions affect our stock price, but we know for sure that having to turn down a promising venture because funds are not available will reduce our long-run profitability. For this reason, my primary goal as treasurer is to always be in a position to raise the capital needed to support operations.

We also know that when times are good, we can raise capital with either stocks or bonds, but when times are bad, suppliers of capital are much more willing to make funds available if we give them a secured position, and this means debt. Further, when we sell a new issue of stock, this sends a negative "signal" to investors, so stock sales by a mature company such as ours are not desirable.

Putting all these thoughts together gives rise to the goal of maintaining financial flexibility, which from an operational viewpoint means maintaining adequate reserve borrowing capacity. Determining an "adequate" reserve borrowing capacity is judgmental, but it clearly depends on the factors, such as the firm's forecasted need for funds, predicted capital market conditions, management's confidence in its forecasts, and the consequences of a capital shortage.

核心词汇 Core Words and Expressions

value adjustment mechanism 估值调整机制，即投资界所称的"对赌"
hybrid security 混合证券
venture capitalist 风险资本家
publicly traded firm 公开上市公司
owner's equity 所有者权益
venture capital 风险资本
newly listed company 新上市公司
investment banker 投资银行家
offering price 发行价格
voting right 投票权
warrant 认股权证
underlying common stock 标的普通股
option-like security 类期权证券
contingent value rights 或有价值权
put option 卖出期权
option exchange 期权交易
put price 卖出价
residual claim 剩余索取权
line of credit 信贷额度（公司与一般商业银行所签订的契约，表示在一定条件及条款下，公司可贷得的定额款项）
bank debt 银行借款
lease 租赁
operating lease 经营性租赁
capital lease 融资性租赁
lessor 出租人
lessee 承租人
convertible debt 可转债
convertible bond 可转换债券
conversion ratio 转换比率
market conversion value 市场转换价值
conversion premium 转换溢价
preferred stock 优先股
financing mix 融资结构
convertible preferred stock 可转换优先股
optimal capital structure 最优资本结构
desired or target capital structure 目标资本结构
earnings before interest and taxes (EBIT) 息税前盈余
operating income 经营收益

business risk　经营风险
financial risk　财务风险
financial leverage　财务杠杆
financial economist　财务经济学家
Modigliani and Miller(M&M) theorem　MM 定理
transaction cost　交易成本
market imperfection　市场不完全性
real assets　实物资产
perfect capital market　完全资本市场
levered firm　杠杆企业
unlevered firm　无杠杆企业
tax shield　税盾
tradeoff theory　权衡理论
interest deduction　利息抵减
pecking order theory　排序理论
internal financing　内部融资
external financing　外部融资
general-purpose assets　一般目的资产
special-purpose assets　特殊目的资产
operating leverage　经营杠杆
Moody's and Standard & Poor's　穆迪和标准普尔
financial flexibility　财务灵活性
reserve borrowing capacity　保留借款能力

即 时 问 答 / Quick Quiz

1. What is a firm's capital structure? What ratios assess the degree of financial leverage in a firm's capital structure?
2. Explain the differences between:
   a) Real and financial assets
   b) Capital budgeting and financing decisions
   c) Closely held and public corporations
   d) Limited and unlimited liabilities
   e) Corporation and partnership
3. Briefly describe the agency problem that exists between owners and lenders. Explain how and why investors may view the firm's financing actions as signals.
4. How does asymmetric information affect the firm's capital structure decisions? Explain how and why investors may view the firm's financing actions as signals.
5. What is the major benefit of debt financing? How does it affect the firm's cost of debt?
6. Define business risk, and discuss the three factors that affect it. What influence does business risk have on the firm's capital structure decisions? Define financial risk, and explain its relationship to the firm's capital structure.

思考与探索 / Thinking and Exploration

What are the main differences between corporate debt and equity? Why do some firms try to issue equity in the guise of debt?

汉译英 / Translation

2020年1月15日，比亚迪股份有限公司（下称"比亚迪"，002594.SZ）发布公告称，公司向合格投资者公开发行面值总额不超过100亿元的公司债券一事已被中国证监会核准。本次发债，比亚迪将采用分期发行方式，首期发行自中国证监会核准发行之日起12个月内完成；其余各期债券发行，自中国证监会核准发行之日起24个月内完成。

根据比亚迪第六届董事会第三十三次会议通过的《关于发行公司债券的议案》，比亚迪本次发行债券采取储架式发行（即一次核准，多次发行的再融资制度）方式，即面向合格投资者公开发行一般公司债券、绿色公司债券、可续期公司债券及各类专项债券等。债券期限为不超过10年（含10年）。比亚迪表示，本次债券募集资金拟用于补充营运资金、偿还公司借款及其他符合法律法规之用途。发行后公司累计债券余额不得超过公司最近一期期末净资产的40%。

比亚迪似乎比较偏爱通过发行债券进行融资。据Wind统计，2019年以来，比亚迪先后至少发行各种债券16次。比亚迪2018年报数据显示，其一年内到期的应付债券达70.77亿元。截至2019年第三季度末，比亚迪资产负债率达68.48%，位于所属行业较高水平。一般而言，只有公司信誉良好，才能获准发行公司债。比亚迪的资产负债率虽然比较高，但其现金流状况仍算健康，偿债能力也还不错。

知识扩展 / More Knowledge

弗兰科·莫迪利亚尼与默顿·米勒

弗兰科·莫迪利亚尼（Franco Modigliani）与默顿·米勒（Merton Miller）分别于1985年和1990年获得了诺贝尔经济学奖。莫迪利亚尼教授获得诺贝尔经济学奖不是因为MM理论，而是因为他第一个提出储蓄的生命周期假设，这一假设被广泛应用于研究家庭和企业储蓄。1990年10月，米勒获得了诺贝尔经济学奖。他的获奖标志着经济学对公司理财学学术地位的确认。瑞典皇家科学院对米勒的学术贡献做了高度评价，认为他的获奖成就是 MM 理论对公司财务理论做出的奠基性贡献。

莫迪利亚尼 1918 年 6 月 18 日出生在意大利罗马的一个犹太家庭里，1939 年 8 月移民美国。1942 年，莫迪利亚尼赴哥伦比亚大学的巴尔德学院担任经济学和统计学讲师。1944 年，莫迪利亚尼取得了新社会研究学院授予的社会科学博士学位，同年，他以高级讲师的身份回到新学院，并在纽约世界事务研究所担任副研究员。在此期间，莫迪利亚尼还做出了储蓄研究方面的第一个贡献，即著名的杜森贝-莫迪利亚尼假说。1948 年秋，莫迪利亚尼荣获声誉很高的芝加哥大学政治经济学奖学金，被聘为当时居于领导地位的经济研究委员会的研究顾问。1960 年，莫迪利亚尼成为麻省理工学院的访问教授（期间曾在西北大学任教一年），此后就一直留在麻省理工学院。

米勒 1923 年 5 月 16 日出生于美国的麻省波士顿，1943 年在哈佛大学获得文学学士学位，1952 年于霍浦金斯大学获得博士学位，2000 年 6 月去世，享年 77 岁。他的学术研究活动开始于 20 世纪 50 年代初期进入卡内基工学院（即现在的卡内基-梅隆大学）之后。在那里，他遇到了他学术生涯中最为重要的伙伴，即 1985 年获得诺贝尔经济学奖的莫迪利亚尼教授。1961 年之后，米勒教授任教于芝加哥大学。在 20 世纪 80 年代以前，米勒教授的工作主要集中于公司理财方面，奠定了他作为理财学一代宗师的地位。学界普遍认为，米勒教授在奠定现代公司财务理论的基础上所做的开创性工作，彻底地改变了企业制定投资决策与融资决策的模式。现代公司财务理论不仅对金融和商务领域中存在的问题给予了深刻描述，而且也使其渐趋成型。很少有经济理论分支能够如此贴近企业管理的实际决策过程。

"MM 理论"的学术贡献

1958 年 6 月，莫迪利亚尼与米勒在《美国经济评论》杂志上合作发表了论文"资本成本、公司理财与投资理论"[⊖]，这篇文章提出了著名的"MM 理论"，开启了现代公司理财理论的先河，为以后在这个领域的理论与经验进展准备了条件。美国经济学联合会对 MM 理论做出了很高的评价，认为 MM 理论的影响远远超出了公司理财学的领域，它为包括布莱克-斯科尔斯期权定价在内的证券组合理论中许多重要的突破铺平了道路，这些发展反过来又对投资管理实践和公司财务理论产生了巨大的影响。

"MM 理论"首次从理论上以一种全新的论证方法对企业价值、资本成本、财务决策等问题进行了严谨的、科学的分析。"MM 理论"的基本含义是：任何企业的价值，无论其是否存在负债，都与其资本结构无关，而取决于其生产经营活动创造现金

⊖ Modigliani F, Miller M H. The Cost of Capital, Corporation Finance and the Theory of Investment. American Economic Review June 1958 (48): 261-296.

流量的能力。这意味着企业实现理财目标——企业价值最大化、投资者财富的最大化的途径是通过科学的投资决策、合理的风险控制,进而创造理想的经营活动现金流量。与投资决策相比较,其他的财务决策比如融资决策、股利政策、营运资本政策等均为派生的、从属的、次要的财务决策。理财目标的实现归根结底要依赖于企业投资决策的水平,因而,对投资决策进行分析、判断的过程,就是对企业价值进行长远规划的过程;而投资决策实现的过程,就是企业价值最大化目标实现的过程。MM 的股利无关论实际上是对 MM 企业价值理论的进一步补充。

在现代财务理论的发展过程中,MM 的无关理论——资本结构无关论与股利无关论具有极其核心的作用。这两种无关论绝非仅仅是对公司资本结构决策、股利政策等所做的政策性分析,而是在理论上对企业价值、资本成本、资本结构、现金流量、风险等重要的财务概念所做的深入的、系统的分析。没有哪一位理财学家像莫迪利亚尼与米勒教授那样对现代财务理论中的基本概念做出如此精密而科学的研究,从而奠定了现代公司理财理论的基石。

相 关 网 址
Useful Websites

利用以下网站查询我国上市公司财务报告信息,考察你所感兴趣的上市公司的资本结构情况:

  上海证券交易所 www.sse.com.cn
  巨潮资讯网 www.cninfo.com.cn
  雅虎财经 http://finance.yahoo.com

第 10 章
TOPIC 10

Dividend Policy
股利政策

新闻视听
News in Media

At the end of the year, big banks are facing a dilemma — to reward or not to reward. Please listen to the report carefully and find out the details.

本章新闻视听资料请扫二维码收听。

名人名言
Wisdom

Why do corporations pay dividends? Why do investors pay attention to dividends? Perhaps the answers to these questions are obvious. Perhaps the answers are not so obvious. I claim the answers to these questions are not obvious at all. The harder we look at the dividend picture, the more it seems like a puzzle, with pieces that just don't fit together…What should the individual investor do about dividends in his portfolio? We don't know. What should the corporation do about dividend policy? We don't know.

——Fischer Black, "The Dividend Puzzle"

The prime purpose of a business corporation is to pay dividends to its owners.

——Benjamin Graham and David Dodd, *Security Analysis*

A cow for her milk, a hen for her eggs, and a stock, by heck, for her dividends.

An orchard for fruit, bees for their honey, and stocks, besides, for their dividends.

——John Burr Williams, *The Theory of Investment Value*

Apple's stock buyback

Since Apple said in January that it would bring back most of the $252 billion it held abroad under the new tax law, investors have wondered what the company would do with the enormous cash pile.

Apple said it would buy back an additional $100 billion in stock , by far the largest increase in its already historic record of returning capital to investors. The company didn't provide a timeline for the repurchases. Apple also increased its dividend by 16 percent to 73 cents a share, pushing past Exxon Mobil to become the largest dividend payer, according to S&P Dow Jones Indices.

Apple's stock buyback fits into a broader trend of companies using the financial windfall from President Trump's tax cut to reward shareholders. Share buybacks, which are reaching record levels, are great for investors, including executives and employees, because they reliably lift stock prices by limiting the supply of shares for sale.

But critics say the actions can take money away from potential investments in hiring or research and development, and can increase economic inequality because they typically benefit wealthier people.

Once a company makes a profit, they must decide on what to do with those profits. They could continue to retain the profits within the company, or they could pay out the profits to the owners of the firm in the form of dividends. Once the company decides on whether to pay dividends, they may establish a somewhat permanent dividend policy, which may in turn impact on investors and perceptions of the company in the financial markets. What they decide depends on the situation of the company now and in the future. It also depends on the preferences of investors and potential investors.

In this topic, we focus on dividend policy because it is the principal mechanism by which corporations disburse cash to shareholders. We also discuss other related matter such as share repurchase.

正文 Text

10.1 Dividends and Dividend Policy

Companies that earn a profit can do one of three things: pay that profit out to shareholders, reinvest it in the business through expansion, debt reduction or share repurchases, or both. When a portion of the profit is paid out to shareholders, the payment is known as a dividend.

During the first part of the twentieth century, dividends were the primary reason investors purchased stock. It was literally said on Wall Street, "the purpose of a company is to pay dividends". Today, the investor's view is a bit more refined; it could be stated, instead, as, "the purpose of a company is to increase my wealth." Indeed, today's investor looks to dividends and capital gains as a source of increase.

Microsoft, for example, did not pay a dividend until it had already become a $350 billion company, long after making the company's founders and long-term shareholders multi-millionaires or billionaires.

Dividend policy is an important topic because dividends represent major cash outlays for many corporations. Dividends are at the heart of the difficult choice that management must make in allocating their capital resources: reinvesting the money within the company or distributing it to shareholders. Although paying dividends directly benefits stockholders, it also affects the firm's ability to retain earnings to exploit growth opportunities. Dividend policy provides guidelines for balancing the conflicting forces surrounding the dividend payment versus retention decision.

Dividend policy refers to the payout policy that management follows in determining the size and pattern of distributions to shareholders over time. The dividend policy question centers on the percentage of earnings that a firm should not pay out. A dividend is a direct payment from a corporation to its stockholders. Corporations commonly pay dividends in cash, but occasionally they pay dividends in stocks, property, or some other asset. The dividend payout ratio is the percentage of earnings paid to shareholders in cash.

10.1.1 Dividend Payout Procedure

A corporation's board of directors is ultimately responsible for a firm's dividend policy. This policy could vary from zero to 100 percent payout of earnings. A corporation has no legal obligation to declare a dividend. After the board declares a dividend, the declared cash dividend becomes a liability and the corporation has a legal obligation to make the payment. Once the board sets the dividend, the procedure for paying the dividend is routine. In chronological order, the four important dates associated with a dividend payment are as follows.

1. **Declaration date**. The declaration date is the day the Board of Director's announces its intention to pay a dividend. On this day, the company creates a liability on its books; it now owes the money to the stockholders. On the declaration date, the Board will also announce a date of record and a payment date.

2. **Ex-dividend date**. The ex-dividend date is the cut-off date for receiving the dividend. That is, the ex-dividend date is the first date on which the right to the most recently declared dividend no longer goes along with the sale of the stock. Companies and exchanges report the ex-dividend date to remove any ambiguity about who will receive a dividend after the sale of a stock. Investors who buy the stock before the ex-dividend date are entitled to the dividend, while those who buy shares on or after the ex-dividend date are not.

3. **Record date**. The record date is the date on which an investor must be a share-

holder of the record to be entitled to the upcoming dividend only if they have bought the stock for at least two business days before the record date. This rule allows time for the transfer of the shares and gives the company a sufficient notice of the transfer to ensure that new stockholders receive the dividend. Therefore, a stock sells ex-dividend for two business days, not calendar days, before the record date. The board of directors sets the record date, which is typically several weeks after the declaration date.

4. **Payment date**. The payment date is the date when the firm mails the dividend checks to the shareholders of a record. This date is usually several weeks after the record date.

10.1.2 Types of Dividends

There are several ways to classify dividends. First, dividends can be paid in cash or as additional stock. Stock dividends increase the number of shares outstanding and generally reduce the price per share. Second, the dividend can be a regular dividend, which is paid at regular intervals (quarterly, semi-annually, or annually), or a special dividend, which is paid in addition to the regular dividend. Most of China's listed firms pay regular dividends every year. Finally, firms sometimes pay dividends that are in excess of the retained earnings they show on their books. These are called **liquidating dividends**.

Cash Dividends

Regular **cash dividends** are those paid out of a company's profits to the owners of the business (i.e. the shareholders). A company that has preferred stock issued must make the dividend payment on those shares before a single penny can be paid out to the common stockholders. The preferred stock dividend is usually set whereas the common stock dividend is determined at the sole discretion of the Board of Directors.

Stock Dividends

A **stock dividend** is a pro-rata distribution of additional shares of a company's stock to owners of the common stock. A company may opt for stock dividends for a number of reasons including inadequate cash on hand or a desire to lower the price of the stock on a per-share basis to prompt more trading and to increase liquidity (i.e., how fast an investor can turn his holdings into cash). Why does lowering the price of the stock increase liquidity? On the whole, people are more likely to buy and sell a $50 stock than a $5,000 stock; this usually results in a large number of shares trading hands each day.

A **stock split** is not a stock dividend in essence. In cases of stock splits, a company may double, triple or quadruple the number of shares outstanding. The value of each share is merely lowered; economic reality does not change at all. It is, therefore, completely irrational for investors to get excited over stock splits.

One of the more interesting theories of corporate dividend policy is that managements should opt for stock dividends over all other kinds. This will allow investors who want their earnings retained in the business (and not taxed) to hold on to the additional stock paid out to them. Investors who want current income, on the other hand, can sell the shares they receive from the stock dividend, pay the tax and pocket the cash — in essence, creating a **"do-it-yourself" dividend**.

Property Dividends

A **property dividend** is caused when a company distributes property to shareholders instead of cash or stock. Property dividends can literally take the form of railroad cars, cocoa beans, pencils, gold, silver, salad dressing or any other item with tangible value. Property dividends are recorded at market value on the declaration date.

10.2 The Dividend Puzzle

The questions of "why do corporations pay dividends?" and "why do investors pay attention to dividends?" have puzzled both academicians and corporate managers for many years. Despite many researchers intend to resolve the dividend puzzle, dividend policy remains one of the most judgmental decisions that managers must make.

At the heart of the dividend puzzle is whether dividend policy affects share prices. Some financial experts contend that dividend policy does not affect the value of a firm's common stock. Others believe that dividend policy has a strong impact on stock price. Despite the dividend puzzle, many firms pay cash dividends and managers typically behave as though dividend policy is relevant. We present below the major opposing views about the relevancy of dividend policy.

10.2.1 Dividend Irrelevance Theory

One school of thought called dividend irrelevance theory argues that what a firm pays in dividends is irrelevant and that stockholders are indifferent about receiving dividends. Thus, it does not matter whether a firm pays dividends or not. According to this view, there is no optimal dividend policy.

The notion that dividends are irrelevant comes from the pioneering work of Nobel laureates Miller and Modigliani (M&M). Under restrictive assumptions, they provide a compelling and widely accepted argument for dividend irrelevance. M&M's dividend irrelevance theory is based on a perfect capital market. Once we leave M&M's idealized world of economic theory and enter the real world, the issue of dividend irrelevance becomes debatable.

10.2.2 Dividend Relevance Theory

Another school of thought on dividends argues that dividend policy is relevant. If dividend policy matters, its relevance mostly results form various market imperfections. What are these market imperfections or frictions?

To accommodate the world in which market imperfections exist, academicians have developed various theories to explain why firms pay dividends. We focus on explanations involving the major market imperfections but also discuss other minor market frictions that potentially make the dividend decision relevant.

The Tax-preference Explanation

In perfect capital markets, there are no taxes. In the real world, taxes do exist and may differ among investors. One of the earliest explanations of why dividend policy matters involves the tax effect. Tax-adjusted models assume that investors expect higher pretax returns from dividend-paying stock because of the future tax liability on dividends. According to the tax-preference argument, investors who receive favorable tax treatment on capital gains may prefer stocks with low dividend payout.

The Signaling Explanation

In perfect capital markets, all parties have equal and costless access to the same information. Such markets are symmetrically informed markets. In practice, information asymmetry exists. Information asymmetry suggests that corporate managers have an information advantage over other interested parties. If managers, as corporate insiders, have information that others do not have, they may use a change in dividends as a way to signal this private information and thus reduce information content of dividends. In turn, investors may use dividend announcements as information to assess a firm's stock price. Thus, signaling models assume that dividend policy conveys important information to the market about the quality of a company. Managers have an incentive to signal this private information to the investment public when they believe that the current market value of their firm's stock is below its intrinsic value. If managers accurately convey favorable information about firm, which is unknown to the investors, the firm's stock price is likely to increase. Yet, investors are aware that management has an incentive to provide false signals if this will temporally increase the price of the stock. In addition, dividend changes may not be perfect signals. Thus, management faces a signaling problem of transmitting information that is believable to the market.

The Agency Explanation

Another view of dividend relevance is agency theory. This theory derives from the conflict of interests between corporate managers (agents) and outside shareholders (principals). Management may decide to retain earnings and subsequently use the money inappropriately rather than paying out dividends to shareholders. Thus there are conflicts between management and shareholders. These are conflicts which lead to **agency costs**. **Agency theory** posits that the dividend mechanism provides an incentive for managers to reduce these agency costs related to the **principal/agent relationship**. That is, agency theory models contend that dividend policy mitigates agency conflicts between managerial and stockholder priorities.

One way to reduce agency costs is to increase dividends. According to the **free cash flow hypothesis**, dividend payments can reduce the potential misuse of free cash flow generated by companies. Thus, paying dividends reduces the discretionary funds that managers could use and forces the firm to seek more external financing. Raising costly outside capital subjects the firm to the scrutiny of the capital market for new funds and reduces the possibility of suboptimal investment. This monitoring by outside suppliers of capital also helps to ensure that managers act in the best interest of outsider shareholders. Thus, dividend payments may serve as a means of monitoring management performance and ensuring behavior consistent with shareholder wealth maximization. Thus, shareholders are willing to accept the higher personal taxes associated with dividends in exchange for the increase in monitoring that the professional investment community provides.

10.3 Factors Influencing the Dividend Decision

To determine a proper dividend policy, management must consider many different and often conflicting and overlapping factors. We classify these factors into three broad groups:

- Shareholder factors.
- Firm factors.
- Other constraints.

The importance of these factors differs from firm to firm. The problem that management faces is to balance the importance of each factor.

10.3.1 Shareholder Factors

Different perceptions and preferences may affect shareholders' views about dividend policy.

Income Needs

Some investors, such as retirees, depend on dividend income to help pay their living expenses. They want firms to provide large and stable dividends. An omission or cut in dividends could cause hardship for them. M&M says that shareholders can create **homemade dividends** by liquidating their share of ownership in a company. Yet, some shareholders are averse to creating homemade dividends because selling shares involves paying brokerage fees and perhaps taxes if they sell shares at prices above their original investment. In practice, homemade dividends are not perfect substitutes for cash dividends.

Risk Preferences

The attitudes of shareholders about risk may affect their preferences for dividend policies. When a firm chooses to keep say $1 per share of earnings instead of paying that amount out as a dividend, investors should expect to benefit in the future by selling that stock at a price that is at least $1 higher than the dividend paid. Waiting to sell stock at a higher price is risky. Therefore, cautious investors may prefer to receive the cash dividend now, rather than take a chance on the future sale price of the stock. A common term for this preference is the **"bird-in-hand" argument**.

Tax Status

When stockholders receive dividends, they must declare them as income and pay taxes on them in the year received. Investors in high tax brackets often prefer small dividends. Retaining earning may lead to an increase in a firm's stock price and to a postponement in the taxed shareholders pay on capital gains. By deferring the payment of taxes on capital gains, shareholders reduce the present value of their future tax payments.

Dilution of Ownership

When firms can support their need for common equity financing by using retained earnings, they can avoid issuing new common stock and, therefore, avert diluting each stockholder's proportionate ownership of the firm.

10.3.2 Firm Factors

Stage of Life Cycle

A firm's dividend policy often follows the life cycle of the firm. A firm's dividend cycle consists of several stages.

- Start-up and initial public offering (IPO) stages. Market imperfections and frictions lead to a policy of paying no dividends.
- Rapid growth stage. Companies tend to pay no or very low dividends.
- Maturity and decline stage. At these stages, a growing to generous dividend payout policy tends to prevail.

External Financing Costs

When issuing costs are high, firms often prefer to use retained earnings as a source of capital rather than to raise funds externally.

Access to Funds and Reserves

Firms with greater access to external funds can have most stable and higher dividend payments because they are less dependent on internally generated funds to finance growth. The amount of a firm's financial reserves can also affect the amount of dividends. Firms with larger amount of financial reserves can have higher dividend payments.

Profitability and Earning Stability

Profitable firms with stable earnings are more likely to assume the risk of having higher dividend payouts than those firms with more volatile earnings.

10.3.3 Managerial Preferences and Constraints

Although management should keep the best interests of shareholders in mind when making dividend decisions, managerial preferences may also influence such decisions. For example, the firm may desire to smooth dividends and to avoid dividend reductions, if possible.

Some bond indentures and loan agreements contain provisions limiting the payment of dividends. The main reason for limiting dividend distributions is to protect creditors.

10.4 Dividend Policies

With the input of senior management, the company's board of directors set a corporation's dividend policy. Management faces the challenge of balancing many conflicting forces to arrive at an appropriate dividend policy. Changing dividend policy can have a short-term impact on the firm's stock price. Firms often prefer to pay the same dividend as in the prior period unless strong justification exists for making a change. Most companies' boards are reluctant to cut their dividends unless conditions force them to do so or to increase their dividends unless the new dividend is sustainable.

One concern is that decreasing or eliminating a dividend may convey negative information to the financial market that adversely affects a firm's stock price. The market usually interprets an increase in dividends as a lasting commitment to pay out future cash flows to shareholders.

10.4.1 Residual Dividend Policy

With a **residual dividend policy**, a firm pays dividends from earnings left over after meeting its investment needs while maintaining its target capital structure. This passive approach assumes that investors prefer the firm to keep and reinvest earnings. This may be true when the return that firms can earn on additional equity exceeds the return that investors can earn by investing the cash themselves. Management recognizes that selling new common stock is an alternative to using retained earnings as a source of common equity. Using this more expensive source of equity will increase the firm's cost of capital and may result in accepting fewer profitable projects.

10.4.2 Stable Dollar Dividend policy

A **stable dollar dividend policy** is one where the company maintains the same dividend per share each period unless it believes that future earnings can sustain a higher dividend. By following this policy, the firm pays a variable fraction of earnings as dividends, which results in a changing dividend payout. Dividends may grow over time if management views the new dividend as sustainable. In such cases, increases in regular cash dividends would normally make the earnings increases lag.

10.4.3 Constant Dividend Payout Ratio

A **constant dividend payout ratio** is a policy of paying a fixed percentage of earnings as dividends. Since a firm's earnings vary, such a policy results in unstable and unpredictable dividends. Few firms follow a constant payout ratio because highly volatile dividends may adversely affect stock prices.

10.4.4 Low Regular plus Specially Designated Dividends

A **policy of low regular plus specially designated dividends** is one in which a firm maintains a low regular cash dividend but pays a specially designed cash dividend if warranted based on the firm's earnings performance. Such a policy represents a compromise between paying a stable dividend per share and maintaining a constant payout ratio. Such a policy gives the firm flexibility but leads to some uncertainty among shareholders.

10.5　Stock Repurchases

There are a number of ways in which a company can return wealth to its shareholders. Although stock price appreciation and dividends are the two most common ways of doing this, **share repurchase** is an another useful, but often overlooked, way for companies to share their wealth with investors.

A share repurchase, also known as a **stock buyback**, is a company's buying back its shares from the marketplace. You can think of a buyback as a company investing in itself, or using its cash to buy its own shares. The idea is simple: because a company can't act as its own shareholder, repurchased shares are absorbed by the company, and the number of outstanding shares on the market is reduced. When this happens, the relative ownership stake of each investor increases because there are fewer shares, or claims, on the earnings of the company.

Rapid growth in share repurchases during the 1990s appeared to be a global phenomenon. Many countries that previously prohibited share repurchases, such as Germany and Japan, also introduced provisions that allowed companies to repurchase shares. Share repurchases also grew dramatically in countries like US, Canada, UK and Australia where repurchases had long been permitted.

10.5.1　Ways of Repurchases

The company wants to purchase outstanding shares of its stock, that is, shares held by the public outside of its control. Typically, it can do this in one of the two ways.

Tender Offer

Shareholders may be presented with a **tender offer** by the company to submit, or tender, a portion or all of their shares within a certain time period. The tender offer will stipulate both the number of shares the company is looking to repurchase and the price range it is willing to pay (almost always at a premium to the market price). When investors take up the offer, they will state the number of shares they want to tender along with the price they are willing to accept. Once the company has received all of the offers, it will find the right mix to buy the shares at the lowest cost.

Open Market

The second alternative a company has is to buy shares on the **open market**, just as an individual investor would, at the market price. It is important to note, however, that when a company announces a buyback it is usually perceived by the market as a positive thing, which often causes the share price to shoot up.

10.5.2 The Reasons for Stock Buybacks

There are several reasons a company may want to buy back shares of its own stock, some of them for the benefit of stockholder, while others have less altruistic purposes.

Here are some of the reasons, both good and bad, why a company might do a stock buyback:

1. If a company is sitting on a large sum of cash and must decide how to invest it, one of the options is to distribute part of it to shareholders.

Companies can do this either of two ways: as dividends or buying up outstanding shares. If the company chooses to buy up shares, stockholders benefit even if they don't sell by the reduction in outstanding shares.

2. If a company's stock is suffering from low financial ratios, buying back stock can give some of the ratios a temporary boost.

Key ratios like earnings per share (EPS) and price earnings ratio (PE) look better because they are based on the number of outstanding shares. Reduce the number of shares and even though earnings don't change, the EPS looks better.

3. Another reason companies buy back stock is to cover large **employee stock option programs (ESOP)**. The effect of these programs, which were out of control during the tech boom of the late 1990s, is to dilute the stock and shareholder's equity. Buying back shares reduces dilution and increases shareholder value.

4. Some companies buy back shares as protection against unfriendly takeovers from other companies. By gathering outstanding shares off the open market, the company makes it more difficult for a raider to take control.

核心词汇 Core Words and Expressions

share repurchase　股票回购
dividend payout ratio　股利支付比率
chronological　按时间顺序排列的
declaration date　股利宣布日
ex-dividend date　除息日
record date　股权登记日
payment date　股利支付日
regular dividend　正常股利
liquidating dividend　清算股利
cash dividends　现金股利
stock dividends　股票股利
stock split　股票分割
"do-it-yourself" dividend　自制股利
property dividend　财产股利
dividend irrelevance theory　股利无关论
intrinsic value　内在价值
free cash flow hypothesis　自由现金流假说

homemade dividends　自制股利
brokerage fee　经纪费
dilution of ownership　所有权稀释
residual dividend policy　剩余股利政策
target capital structure　目标资本结构
stable dollar dividend policy　固定股利政策
constant dividend payout ratio　固定股利支付率政策
low regular plus specially designated dividends　低正常股利加额外股利政策
stock price appreciation　股价增值
stock buyback　股票回购
tender offer　（美）要约收购；（英）takeover bid
open market　公开市场
employee stock option program (ESOP)　员工股票期权计划

即时问答 Quick Quiz

1. Describe the residual theory of dividends. Does following this approach lead to a stable dividend? Is this approach consistent with dividend relevance? Explain.
2. Describe, compare, and contrast the basic arguments relative to the irrelevance or relevance of dividend policy given by: (a) Miller and Modigliani (M&M), and (b) Gordon and Lintner.

3. Briefly describe each of the following factors affecting dividend policy: (a) shareholder factors; (b) firm factors; (c) managerial preferences and constraints.
4. What is a stock dividend? Why do firms issue stock dividends?
5. What is a stock split? What is a reverse stock split? Compare a stock split with a stock dividend.
6. What is the logic behind repurchasing shares of common stock to distribute excess cash to the firm's owners?

思考与探索
Thinking and Exploration

The stock market reacts positively to increases in dividends and negatively to decreases in dividends. Please explain.

汉译英
Translation

格力可谓是家电企业中分红最慷慨的企业之一。Wind 数据显示，1996 年上市以来格力共分红 19 次，现金分红金额达到 417 亿元，分红率达 40.96%。自 2012 年董明珠就任董事长以来，格力的分红力度不断增强。格力的股利支付率从 40.4% 提升到 70.22%，仅用了 4 年。一向以高分红在资本市场上备受关注的格力电器，却突然宣布"不分红了"，其于 2017 年 4 月 25 日晚间对外公布的年报中利润方案为：不派发现金红利，不分红股，不以公积金转增股本。对此，格力给出的理由是：公司需为多元化拓展做好相应的资金储备，并将其用于智能装备等新产业的研发和推广。

知识扩展
More Knowledge

我国上市公司关于呈报的时间要求和分配的具体程序

目前，我国上市公司每年必须提供四次定期的公开财务报告：每年 1~4 月，必须公布上一年度年报；每年 4 月份，必须公布当年的第一季度季报；每年 7~8 月份，必须公布当年上半年的中期报告；每年 10 月份，必须公布当年第三季度季报。

上市公司进行分配的具体程序是：首先，董事会在公布"年度报告"或"中期报告"时，公布分配预案以及召开股东大会的日期；其次，股东大会开会讨论、通过分配预案，并授权董事会具体实施；最后，董事会公布分配方案，确定股权登记日、除息日、新增股与现金红利到账日以及配股的最后缴款日。

我国股票回购的现行模式及法律规定

1999年,申能股份有限公司以每股2.51元的价格回购10亿国有法人股。按照《公司法》的规定,股本在4亿元以上的公司,其向社会公开发行的流通股应在15%以上,申能股份公司回购前,国有股占80.25%,流通A股只占9.57%,回购股票注销后,由于国有股所占比例下降到68.16%,流通A股则相对上升到15.37%,符合《公司法》的要求。

2000年,云南云天化股份有限公司以每股2.83元的价格回购其控股母公司持有的法人股2亿股并注销。回购后,云南云天化股份有限公司的流通A股比例则上升为27.16%。

以上两起国有股回购均采用了协商购买方式,通过公司与具有绝对控股地位的国家股或国有法人股股东协商,用现金回购股票并注销。

在我国,原则上是不允许股票回购的,但《公司法》第142条规定,公司不得收购本公司股份。但是,有下列情形之一的除外:①减少公司注册资本;②与持有本公司股份的其他公司合并;③将股份用于员工持股计划或者股权激励;④股东因对股东大会作出的公司合并、分立决议持异议,要求公司收购其股份;⑤将股份用于转换上市公司发行的可转换为股票的公司债券;⑥上市公司为维护公司价值及股东权益所必需。公司因第①项、第②项规定的情形收购本公司股份的,应当经股东大会决议;公司因第③项、第⑤项、第⑥项规定的情形收购本公司股份的,可以依照公司章程的规定或者股东大会的授权,经三分之二以上董事出席的董事会会议决议。公司依照规定收购本公司股份后,属于第①项情形的,应当自收购之日起十日内注销;属于第②项、第④项情形的,应当在六个月内转让或者注销;属于第③项、第⑤项、第⑥项情形的,公司合计持有的本公司股份数不得超过本公司已发行股份总额的百分之十,并应当在三年内转让或者注销。上市公司收购本公司股份的,应当依照《中华人民共和国证券法》的规定履行信息披露义务。上市公司因第③项、第⑤项、第⑥项规定的情形收购本公司股份的,应当通过公开的集中交易方式进行。

显然,修订后的《公司法》放松了股份公司股票回购的限制,增强了股票回购的可操作性,允许将回购的股份用于奖励公司员工,使得建立"库存股"在我国有章可循。

《公司法》对股份回购条款主要进行了三方面的修订:

一是增加了股份回购的情形。《中华人民共和国公司法修正案》(以下简称《修正案》)规定的股份情形包括:用于员工持股计划,上市公司为配合可转换公司债券、认股权证的发行用于股权转换的,上市公司为维护公司信用及股东权益所必需的,法律、行政法规规定的其他情形等。特别是增加了"上市公司为维护公司信用及股东权益所必需",为上市公司回购股票提供了更多灵活性。

二是完善了实施股份回购的决策程序。《修正案》简化了程序要求,对于实施员工持股计划或者股权激励,上市公司配合可转债、认股权证发行用于股权转换,以及为维护公司信用及股东权益等情形实施股份回购的,可以依照公司章程的规定或者股东大会的授权,经董事会三分之二以上董事出席,并经全体董事过半数同意,收购不超过已发行股份总额百分之十的股份。

三是建立了库存股制度。现行《公司法》不允许将购回股份以库存方式持有,因股权激励回购的股份也要在一年内转让。《修正案》明确,因实施员工持股计划或者股权激励,上市公司配合可转债、认股权证发行用于股权转换以及为维护公司信用及股东权益回购本公司股份后,可以转让、注销或者将股份以库存方式持有。同时,为限制公司长期持有库存股,影响市场的股份供应量,明确规定以库存方式持有的,持有期限不得超过三年。

我国股票分割与公积金转增股本的特殊情况

在我国,目前各股份公司的股票面值均为 1 元/股。在新股发行时,发行价均大大高于股票面值,使得资本公积金数倍于股本。比如,公司按 15 元/股的价格发行股票,其股本只有 1 元/股,但资本公积金却高达 14 元/股。在这种情况下,再对 1 元/股的面值进行分割也显得意义不大。因此,我国上市公司对股票分割实际上多是采用资本公积金转增股本的形式来进行。虽然,严格地说,资本公积金转增股本并不属于股票分割,但它的确起到与股票分割同样的作用,即股票数量增加的作用。所不同的是,不是分割股票面值,而是摊薄的每股资本公积。

在我国实务中,上市公司往往把资本公积金转增股本与股利分配混在一起,所谓盈利分配公告中的 10 送 2 转 3 就是如此,它表明,公司盈利分配政策为 10 股送 2 股股票股利,另外再用资本公积金转增 3 股股票。由于我国上市公司发行股票时存在大量的资本公积金,因此,在公司上市初期,不少公司均有能力大比例转增股票,以致让不少股票投资者将它视为了一种盈利分配。因此,在我国,虽然不存在对面值进行分割的股票分割情形,但是资本公积金转增股本普遍存在,二者仅仅是表现形式不同而已。

有关现金股利和股票红利的一些资料:
www.dripcentral.com

第 11 章
TOPIC 11

Working Capital Management
营运资本管理

新闻视听
News in Media

Internet bookstores are becoming more and more popular. It is time for traditional bookstores to learn from the internet bookstores. Please listen to the report carefully and find out the difference in management of the two kinds of bookstores.

本章新闻视听资料请扫二维码收听。

名人名言
Wisdom

Cash is the life blood of a business.

——Anonymous

微型案例
Mini Case

Jingdong is a Chinese e-commerce company headquartered in Beijing. It was founded by Liu Qiangdong in July, 1998, and its retail platform went online in 2004. It started as an online magneto-optical store, but soon diversified, selling electronics, mobile phones, computers and similar items. The company changed its domain name to 360buy.com in June, 2007 and then to JD.com in 2013. JD.com was listed on Nasdaq in the U.S. in May, 2014.

JD has triggered a price war at the beginning of entering the market and brought a revolution to the 3C market which refers to computer, communication and consumer electronics. JD provides low price at the same time ensuring product quality, aiming to provide the best service. It quickly established brand advantages and market position, forming a strong ability to negotiate with suppliers, and using the time difference of accounts payable in operation which is known as commercial credit. At the same time, JD's B2C model allows JD to occupy a large number of consumers' prepayments by delivering goods after payment by the consumer. In this way, JD makes a perfect use of other people's money, resulting in a large number of cash flow from operating activities. With this part of the funds, JD does not need a large quantity of external financing and can save a lot of financing costs which helps it to strengthen the management of operations, introduce new and better products and consolidates its market position.

概　览 Overview

Working capital management involves the relationship between a firm's short-term assets and its short-term liabilities. The goal of working capital management is to ensure that a firm is able to continue its operations and that it has sufficient ability to satisfy both maturing short-term debt and upcoming operational expenses. The management of working capital involves managing cash, accounts receivable and inventories.

正文 Text

11.1　Introduction to Working Capital Management

Working capital management is the administration of the firm's current assets and current liabilities. Gross working capital refers to a firm's current assets used in operations, including cash and marketable securities, accounts receivable, and inventory.

TOPIC 11 Working Capital Management

Net working capital is current assets minus current liabilities. An effective working capital management policy requires that managers find appropriate investment levels of cash, marketable securities, receivables, and inventories and the appropriate level and mix of short-term financing.

Managers need to understand how to develop effective working capital policies to ensure growth, profitability, and long-term success for their firms. Firms experiencing rapid growth may easily fall into a growth trap with insufficient levels of current assets to support increasingly higher levels of sales. In such cases, a firm values by managing current assets and current liabilities in a way that balances profitability and risk. Determining the firm's optimal investment in working capital involves a trade-off between liquidity and profitability. Financial managers should minimize the costs associated with working capital without jeopardizing the liquidity need for continuing operations.

Approaches to Working Capital Management

Managers must maintain sufficient liquidity to ensure the firm can meet its maturing short-term obligations. On the other hand, excessive investment in current assets enhances liquidity but lowers profitability and reduces shareholder wealth. Managers have different philosophies or approaches for handling this risk-return relationship in working capital management. A relaxed or conservative approach is one that relies on greater levels of current assets; a restricted or aggressive approach relies much less heavily on investments in cash, marketable securities, and inventories. A moderate approach falls between these two.

11.2 Cash Management

Cash management is a sophisticated and important aspect of working capital management. When we refer to cash management, we are referring to the management of cash and marketable securities. Cash is the currency and coin the firm keeps on hand in cash registers, petty cash drawers, or in checking accounts at commercial banks. Marketable securities are short-term investments in securities that the firm can quickly convert into cash. Because of their strong liquidity, marketable securities are often referred to as near cash or near-cash assets. Cash and near-cash assets comprise the liquid assets of a firm. The objective of cash management is to keep the investment in cash as low as possible while maintaining the firm's efficient operations. Cash management involves three major decision areas:

- Determining appropriate cash balances.
- Investing idle cash.
- Managing collections and disbursements.

11.2.1 Three Motives for Holding Cash

Speculative Motive

Firms have a **speculative motive** to hold cash so that they can take advantage of bargain purchases that may arise, attractive interest rates, and favourable exchange rate fluctuations.

Precautionary Motive

The **precautionary motive** for holding cash arises from the need for a safety supply of cash to act as a financial reserve. While a precautionary need for maintaining liquidity probably exists, given that the value of money market instruments is relatively certain and liquid and that substantial cash holdings to satisfy the precautionary are generally unnecessary.

Transaction Motive

Firms need cash on hand to pay wages, trade debts, taxes, and dividends. They collect cash from product sales, asset sales, and financing. Firms need a level of cash holdings because cash inflows and cash outflows are not perfectly synchronized. The advent of electronic funds transfers and other high-speed paperless payment methods have greatly reduced the transaction demand for cash.

Firms also hold cash as **compensating balances** at commercial banks to compensate for banking services the firm receives.

When estimating the optimal cash balance level for a firm, we should take into consideration the opportunity cost of holding cash and the transaction costs incurred when selling marketable securities to increase cash balances. The opportunity cost of holding cash refers to the return the firm could earn if it invests the cash in marketable securities instead of holding cash. When the firm sells marketable securities, it incurs transactions costs that primarily include fees paid to brokerage firms who conduct the sales transaction.

11.2.2 Determining Appropriate Cash Balances

This decision involves determining the minimum levels of cash that the firm needs to provide liquidity while minimizing the total costs of holding in an investment in cash. We examine two models available for determining the firm's optimal cash balances — the Baumol and the Miller-Orr cash management models.

The **Baumol cash management model** is a method used to determine a firm's optimal cash balance level assuming that cash disbursements are spread evenly over time, the opportunity cost of holding cash is constant, and the company pays a fixed transactions cost each time it converts securities to cash. Another assumption of the model is that a firm can predict its future cash requirements with certainty. Instead of assuming cash balances decline uniformly over time, the **Miller-Orr cash management model** assumes that daily cash flows fluctuate randomly from day to day. Thus, this probabilistic model incorporates the uncertainty of future cash flows. Factors other than those considered in the Baumol and the Miller-Orr cash management models may also affect a firm's optimal level of cash balances.

If the firm has a compensating balance requirement, its average cash balance is the greater of the balance needed for transactions and the compensating balance amount.

A firm's optimal level of marketable securities can be determined by subtracting the cash balances from the total liquidity amount desired. Some firms, however, hold large portfolios of marketable securities that exceed what they need for liquidity purpose. Others with foreign operations invest cash in marketable securities abroad to avoid paying income taxes on the amount earned.

11.2.3 Investing Idle Cash

Firms typically invest temporary surplus cash in short-term marketable securities.

When investing in excess cash, firms often consider several important factors when choosing among a variety of short-term securities available. These factors include marketability, maturity, default risk, and taxes.

- **Marketability** is the ease of converting an asset or security to cash with minimum possible loss. Money market instruments vary in terms of marketability with US Treasury Bill being among the most marketability (liquidity).
- **Maturity** is the length of time remaining before the issuer repays the security. As we know, securities with longer maturities have great invest rate risk. That is, their prices are more sensitive to changes in interest rates. Many firms do not invest in securities with maturities greater than 90 days to avoid substantial price declines if interest rates increase.
- **Default risk** is the probability that the lender will not make full interest and principal payments when due. Firms typically invest temporary idle cash only in short-term securities that have negligible default risk.
- **Taxes** refer to the amount of taxes that the holder pays on short-term securities.

11.2.4 Types of Money Market Securities

Firms generally invest any temporary surplus cash in money market securities which are short-term highly marketable securities with a low risk of default. In US, the most common money market securities include the US Treasury Bills, tax exempt instrument, certificates of deposits, commercial paper, and repurchase agreements.

- **US Treasury Bills** are short-term debt obligations of the US government with initial maturities of 30, 90, or 180 days. Treasury Bills sell at a discount to par value and do not make coupon invest payments.
- **Short-term tax exempt instruments** are short-term debt securities which are attractive to many investors because they are exempt from federal taxes.
- **Commercial paper** is unsecured short-term debt obligations issued by corporations, banks, and finance companies with maturities ranging from a few days to 270 days.
- **Negotiable certificates of deposit (CDs)** are short-term loans to commercial

banks with denominations of $100,000 or more.

- **Bankers' acceptances are drafts (orders to pay)** drawn on a bank to a customer who has an account at that bank.
- **Repurchase agreement** is an agreement between a seller and a buyer, usually of US government securities, in which the seller agrees to repurchase the securities at an agreed higher price at a stated time. Maturities are short, usually overnight or just a few days. These agreements have little risk because of their short maturity and the promise of the borrower to repurchase the securities at a fixed price.

11.2.5 Managing Collections and Disbursements

A third decision of cash management involves minimizing cash balances by accelerating receipts and slowing disbursements. Managing collections and disbursement requires a thorough understanding of float. Float is the amount of money represented by checks outstanding and in the process of collection.

Float arises from a delay in the payment system. The three principal sources of delay are:

1. **Mail float**: the time when a check is in the mail.

2. **Processing float**: the time required to process a check after it is received.

3. **Clearing time float**: the time required for a check to clear through the banking system and to reduce the paying firm's account.

Paying firms have an incentive to delay in all three areas, while receiving firms want to speed up the process.

Accelerating Collections

The objective of accelerating collections is to increase the speed of payment receipt without incurring excessive costs. By speeding up collections, the firm can free cash to reduce its total financing requirement. We introduce two methods to speed up collections: using a lockbox system and concentration banking.

Use a **lock-box system**. Under a lockbox system, customers send incoming checks to a special post office box that a local bank maintains. A local bank collects the checks sent to a lockbox several times per day and deposits the checks directly into the firm's account. Thus, the purpose of a lockbox system is to eliminate processing float. In addition, a lockbox system can reduce the firm's internal processing costs because the bank handles the clerical work for a fee.

Use **concentration banking**. The firm's customers make payments at a firm's regional offices rather than its corporate headquarters. The regional offices then deposit the checks into their local bank accounts. The firm periodically transfers surplus funds from the regional banks to a concentration account at one of the company's concentration banks. Thus, the purpose of concentration banking is to accelerate the flow of funds by instructing customers to remit payments to strategic collection centers.

Slowing Disbursement

The objective of slowing disbursement is to delay paying supplies and other creditors without jeopardizing the firm's credit standing or incurring any finance charges.

Centralize payables. Firms can gain better control over their disbursements by centralizing their payables into a single or small number of accounts, usually maintained at the company's headquarters. Firms can minimize their use of cash by sending payments at the end of any cash discount periods or the final due date of no cash discount available.

Establish a zero balance system. Firms can use a **zero balance account (ZBA)** system with their bank. Under a ZBA system, one master disbursement account services multiple subsidiary accounts. Each day, the bank automatically transfers enough funds from the master disbursement account to the subsidiary accounts to cover all checks that holders have presented to that bank on that day. Idle cash is eliminated from subsidiary accounts as a zero balance is maintained in each subsidiary account. Only the master account maintains a cash balance.

11.3 Accounts Receivable Management

Many firms sell goods or provide services on a credit basis. **Accounts receivable** represent money owned to a company from the sale, on credit, of goods or services in the normal course of business. **Trade credit** refers to credit sales made to other businesses, whereas **consumer credit** refers to credit sales made to individuals. Trade credit terms may provide a discount for prompt payment, whereas consumer credit terms are unlikely to have this feature. Although firms grant credit to stimulate sales, they also incur costs when granting credit. The costs include the bad debt expense that a firm incurs if the customer does not pay, and the interim financing needed until the customer pays the account.

Financial managers should make decisions referred to as the company's **credit and collection policies**. The establishment of a **credit policy** involves four elements:

1. Is the company prepared to offer credit?

2. Assuming that credit is to be offered, what standards will be applied in the decision to grant credit to a customer?

3. How much credit should a customer be granted?

4. What credit terms will be offered?

When credit has been offered and accepted, the company must then seek to ensure that the promised amount is received. Inevitably, some account will prove difficult to collect and the company will need to take steps to recover the amount owing — that is, the company will adopt a **collection policy**. This requires the manager to determine which procedures will be used to encourage payment and for how long these procedures should be followed.

11.3.1 Credit Policy

Four elements of credit policy are mentioned above. They are now considered further.

The Decision to Offer Credit

In principle, a company must decide whether it will sell on a strictly "cash only" basis or whether some credit will be extended. In practice, an individual company will often have little choice but to extend credit. If competitors provide credit to customers, it is likely that the company will also have to extend credit if it is to retain its customers' business. The reason is simple: an offer of credit is equivalent to a price reduction and, naturally, a lower price tends to increase demand.

Selection of credit-worthy customers

A company will usually offer similar terms to all its credit-worthy customers, but it must first decide which of its customers will be granted credit and which will be refused — that is, so it needs information about the riskiness of extending credit to a particular customer at a particular time. In reaching a decision about granting credit, one of the best guides is often the company's own experience with the customer.

One technique that is a useful aid in deciding whether to grant credit is the Five Cs of Credit. Credit analysts generally consider five factors when determining whether to grant credit: character, capacity, capital, collateral, and conditions.

1. Character involves the customer's willingness to pay off debts. It is usually the most important aspect of credit analysis. An applicant's prior payment history is generally the best indicator of his/her character.

2. Capacity represents the customer's ability to meet its obligations. A typical measure of capacity is the customer's liquidity ratios and cash flow from operations.

3. Capital refers to the relative amounts of the customer's debt and equity financing. Credit granting firms often consider the customer's debt-to-equity ratio and times interest earned ratio.

4. Collateral refers to the customer's assets that are available for use in securing the credit.

5. Conditions refer to the impact of economic trends that may affect the customer's ability to repay debts.

Credit Terms

A company's credit terms specify a credit period, and may also specify a discount period(s) and a discount rate(s). The **credit period** is the period that elapses between the date when the purchasing company is invoiced and the date when payment is due. The **discount period** is the period that elapses between the date when the purchasing company is invoiced and the date when the discount is foregone. The **discount rate** expresses, in effect, the price reduction that the purchasing company will receive if it pays within the discount period.

Typical examples of credit terms are as follows:

n/30: There is no discount and the credit period is 30 days. After the expiration of the credit period, the purchaser is in default.

2/10, n/30: The discount rate is 2 percent, the discount period is 10 days and the credit period is 30 days.

11.3.2 Collection Policy

A company that never has a bad debt almost certainly has a sub-optimal credit policy — that is, if a more lenient policy were adopted, then the increase in sales would more than offset the losses imposed by a few bad debts. For most companies, some bad debts are inevitable. Notwithstanding this fact, it is also true that in most cases some attempts to collect overdue debts are worthwhile. These efforts are referred to as the company's **collection policy**.

An important aspect of a firm's collection policy involves the monitoring of its accounts receivable to detect troubled accounts and past-due accounts. A common method used to monitor accounts receivable is an aging schedule. An aging schedule classifies the firm's receivables by the number of days outstanding (the age of the receivable). It provides useful information about the quality of a firm's receivables. Other tools for managing accounts receivable are the average age of accounts receivable and the bad debt loss ratio (the proportion of the total receivables that are not paid).

The critical problem in collection policy is the need to recognize when an account warrants special attention. Obviously, it is not sensible to institute legal action on a $10 account that is 2 days overdue. But what is the account for $10 million, rather than $10? Is action warranted if a $100 account is 30 days overdue? If so, what action should be taken? There are no hard and fast answers to these questions. However, most busi- nesses adopt a set of procedures. Generally, attempts to collect an account that is overdue begin with a standard reminder notice, followed by personal letters and telephone calls. Eventually, visits may be made in person. The last resort is a legal action, but this can be very expensive and may involve lone delays. An alternative is to employ a debt collection agency, but this can be expensive too. It may also sometimes pay a business to accept a partial payment, rather than continue with attempts to collect the full amount owed.

As the amount spent on collection activities increases, it is to be expected that bad debt losses will be reduced and the average collection period will be shorter. However, these relationships are unlikely to be linear. For example, an initial small level of expenditure is unlikely to have any marked effect in reducing bad debts, or in shortening the average collection period, while additional expenditure is likely to have a much greater effect. However, beyond a certain level of collection expenditure, the benefits will diminish until eventually a saturation point is reached. The relationship between the average collection period and the level of collection expenditure is likely to be similar.

Collection policy involves a trade-off between the costs of collection, and the benefits of lower bad debt losses and a shorter average collection period, which in turn will result in a reduction in the company's investment in accounts receivable. Comparing these costs and benefits to determine a preferred policy is likely to involve considerable judgment. Also, in determining a collection policy, it is important to take account of the effect of the collection policy on sales, as a more forceful collection procedure may adversely affect sales. For example, if collection procedures begin too early, customers may be offended and switch to alternative suppliers.

11.4 Inventory Management

Effective inventory management involves turning over inventory as quickly as possible without losing sales from inventory stockouts. Inventory management is important for two major reasons. On one hand, inventory represents a sizable investment from some firms and affects their profitability. On the other hand, managers often cannot correct errors in inventory management quickly because inventory is the firm's least liquid current asset.

11.4.1 Successful Inventory Management

Successful inventory management involves balancing the costs of inventory with the benefits of inventory. Many business managers fail to fully appreciate the true costs of carrying inventory, which include directing not only costs of storage, insurance and taxes, but also the cost of money tied up in inventory.

This fine line between keeping too much inventory and not enough is not the manager's only concern. Others include:

1. Maintaining a wide assortment of stock — but not spreading the rapidly moving ones too thin;

2. Increasing inventory turnover — but not sacrificing the service level;

3. Keeping stock low — but not sacrificing service or performance;

4. Obtaining lower prices by making volume purchases — but not ending up with slow-moving inventory;

5. Having an adequate inventory on hand — but not getting caught with obsolete items.

The degree of success in addressing these concerns is easier to gauge for some than for others. For example, computing the inventory turnover ratio is a simple measure of managerial performance. This value gives a rough guideline by which managers can set goals and evaluate performance, but it must be realized that the turnover rate varies with the function of inventory, the type of business and how the ratio is calculated (whether on sales or cost of goods sold).

Average inventory turnover ratios for individual industries can be obtained from trade associations.

11.4.2　The Purchasing Plan

One of the most important aspects of inventory control is to have the items in stock at the moment they are needed.

This includes going into the market to buy the goods early enough to ensure delivery at a proper time. Thus, buying requires advance planning to determine inventtory needs for each time period and then making the commitments without procrastination.

For retailers, planning ahead is very crucial. Since they offer new items for sale months before the actual calendar date for the beginning of the new season, it is imperative that buying plans be formulated early enough to allow for intelligent buying without any last minute panic purchases. The main reason for this early offering for sale of new items is that the retailer regards the calendar date for the beginning of the new season as the merchandise date for the end of the old season. For example, many retailers view March 21 as the end of the spring season, June 21 as the end of summer and December 21 as the end of winter.

Part of purchasing plan must include accounting for the depletion of the inventory. Before a decision can be made as to the level of inventory to order, you must determine how long the inventory you have in stock will last.

For instance, a retail firm must formulate a plan to ensure the sale of the greatest number of units. Likewise, a manufacturing business must formulate a plan to ensure enough inventories are on hand for the production of a finished product.

In summary, the purchasing plan details:

1. When commitments should be placed.
2. When the first delivery should be received.
3. When the inventory should be peaked.
4. When reorders should no longer be placed.
5. When the item should no longer be in stock.

Well planned purchases affect the price, delivery and availability of products for sale.

11.4.3 Inventory Management Techniques

Managers commonly use four inventory management techniques: the ABC system, the economic order quantity (EOQ) model, the just-in-time (JIT) system, and the materials requirement planning (MRP) system. We discuss them in turn.

The ABC System

Under the **ABC inventory management system**, a firm divides its inventory into A, B, and C groups. The firm places these items with the largest dollar investment in the A group, while the A group often includes as little as 20 percent of its total investment in inventory. The B group includes inventory items that account for the next largest inventory investment, and the C group includes a large number of inventory items that represent a relatively small inventory investment. Monitoring inventory levels differ among the three groups. Because of its high value in terms of investment, the A group logically receives the most extensive monitoring. Managers track items in the A group using a perpetual inventory system that allows for immediate, hourly, or daily inventory tracking or counts. Mangers track items in the B group less frequently, often on a weekly basis. Items in the C group receive even less attention.

Economic Order Quantity (EOQ) Model

The **economic order quantity (EOQ)** is the order size for inventory that minimizes total inventory cost. The basic EOQ model assumes that items are removed from inventory at a constant rate. Total annual costs are equal to the ordering costs plus carrying costs. The order quantity that minimizes total costs is the economic order quantity (EOQ).

Just-In-Time (JIT) System

Materials arrive exactly when needed in the production process in a **just-in-time system (JIT)**. Japanese firms popularized JIT inventory systems in the 1980s when high-interest rates increased the opportunity costs of carrying high levels of inventory. JIT systems require managers to carefully plan and schedule inventory for the production process. Firms rely heavily on extensive cooperation from relatively few suppliers as they usually require frequent deliveries of the exact amounts needed in a specific order. Thus, delivery schedules, quantities, quality, and instantaneous communication with suppliers are essential factors in a JIT system. Because of the extensive planning involvement, firms usually limit the number of suppliers. An effective JIT system can greatly reduce a firm's inventory carrying costs.

Material Requirements Planning (MRP) Systems

Material requirements planning systems (MRP) are computer-based systems for ordering and scheduling production of inventories that essentially work backward through the production process. Once managers determine finished goods inventory levels, they can determine the appropriate levels of work-in-process inventories needed for the finished goods. Then they can decide on the quantity of raw materials they need to have on hand. MRP systems are most effective for complicated products that require numerous components to create the finished product.

核心词汇
Core Words and Expressions

working capital management　营运资本管理
marketable security　短期有价证券
net working capital　净营运资本
jeopardize　危害
relaxed or conservative approach　稳健策略
restricted or aggressive approach　激进策略
moderate approach　适中策略
speculative motive　投机动机
precautionary motive　预防动机
transaction motive　交易动机
compensating balance　补偿性余额
Baumol cash management model　鲍莫尔现金管理模型
Miller-Orr cash management model　米勒-欧尔现金管理模型
marketability　可销售性
US Treasury Bill　美国短期国库券
maturity　（债券、票据等）到期
default risk　违约风险
tax exempt instrument　短期免税证券
commercial paper　商业票据
repurchase agreement　回购协议
negotiable certificates of deposit (CD)　大额可转让存单
bankers' acceptance　银行承兑汇票
disbursement　支出，支付
float　浮游量，浮差
mail float　邮寄浮游量
processing float　内部处理浮游量
clearing time float　清算浮游量
lock-box system　加锁信箱系统
concentration banking　集中银行法
slowing disbursement　延期支付
centralize payables　集中支付
zero balance account (ZBA)　零余额账户
accounts receivable　应收账款
trade credit　交易信用
consumer credit　消费者信用
credit and collection policy　信用与收款政策
credit term　信用条件
credit period　信用期限
discount period　折扣期限
discount rate　折扣率
aging schedule　账龄表
average age of accounts receivable　应收账款平均账龄
bad debt loss ratio　坏账损失率
saturation point　饱和点

procrastination 延迟

perpetual inventory system （存货）永续盘存制

economic order quantity (EOQ) 经济订货量

just-in-time (JIT) system 准时制

material requirements planning (MRP) system 物料需求计划系统

即时问答
Quick Quiz

1. Briefly describe each of the following techniques for managing inventory
   (a) ABC system
   (b) materials requirement planning (MRP) system
   (c) just-in-time (JIT) system
2. List and describe the three motives for holding cash. Which is the most common motive?
3. Briefly list the five C's of credit and discuss their role in the credit selection activity.
4. What is meant by credit terms? What are three components of credit terms?
5. What does a firm's accounts receivable represent? What is meant by a firm's credit policy?
6. Briefly describe the key features of each of the following techniques for slowing down disbursements:
   (a) centralize payables
   (b) zero-balance accounts

思考与探索
Thinking and Exploration

To maximize shareholder wealth, management should aim to set the level of the firm's cash holdings such that the marginal benefit of the incremental dollar of cash would equal the marginal cost of those holdings. There are two main benefits from holding liquid assets. First, it allows companies to avoid the transaction costs associated with raising funds or liquidating assets to make current payments. Second, the firm can use its liquid assets to finance its activities and investments when other sources of funding are not readily available or are excessively costly. (Tim Opler, Lee Pinkowitz, Rene Stulz, and Rohan Williamson, "Corporate Cash Holdings," Journal of Applied Corporate Finance 14,

Spring 2001, P. 55.)

Please discuss the following questions.

1. What are the reasons for holding cash?

2. Can you list as many as actions of increasing, decreasing or no change in company's cash balance?

汉译英 Translation

苏宁作为我国零售行业的龙头企业,要想在零售业中占据一定的市场份额,必须采用一种低成本的、高效的营运资本管理方法。因此,苏宁运用OPM(Other People's Money)式战略进行营运资本管理,满足企业在规模扩张过程中对资金的大量需求,为企业带来利润的快速增长和良好发展。

OPM 战略指企业充分利用做大规模的优势,增强与供应商讨价还价的能力,将占用在存货和应收账款的资金及其资金成本转嫁给供应商的运营资本管理战略。简言之,OPM 战略本质上是一种创新的盈利模式,是"做大做强"的生动实践。

通过运用 OPM 战略,苏宁形成"规模扩张—销售规模提升—账面浮存现金上升—低成本资金用以继续扩张规模—进一步提升零售渠道价值—压榨供应商—更多的账面浮存现金"的流动资金内循环体系。

知识扩展 More Knowledge

准时制

准时制(Just-in-time,JIT)是存货在需要时才取得并进入生产过程的一种存货管理和控制的方法。

1950 年,时任日本丰田汽车公司机械厂厂长的大野耐一在美国超级市场中得到启发,顾客可以在超级市场一次选购多种商品(多品种),而每种只买很少的量(小批量),超级市场的配送系统可以迅速补充顾客买走的商品。大野耐一认为,可以把供需关系引入工业公司内部,在汽车生产过程中可以把后道工序视为购物顾客,前道工序视为超级市场的配送系统,前道工序应按后道工序的要求"在必要的时间提供必要量的必要零件"。从 1950 年开始构思和实验,到 1962 年,丰田公司才全面推广这种生产方式,其后,丰田又在承包其外购零部件的厂家全面推广,其间经历了 20 年时间的反复改进，直到 20 世纪 70 年代，丰田的"秘密武器"才为世人所知，这种生产方式被称为"看板管理"或"准时制"（即在刚好需要时存货才被取得并进入生产，各种类型的存货都将被减少到一个最低限度）。

在准时制下，通过"看板"将公司供、产、销的各个环节在时间上和数量上紧密衔接起来，尽可能实现不多不少，不早不迟，"恰好"满足顾客需要。但这种方式绝不是提倡"零存货"。20 世纪 70 年代，由于"准时制"的极大成功，丰田公司一度把库存压得很低，结果在 80 年代初的一次地震后当市场需求突然大增时，丰田由于不能及时供货而蒙受损失。此后丰田公司适度增加了存货。实践证明，库存为零的做法在市场稳定的情况下，在中小公司也许是能够做到的，但对大公司则是不现实的。

一般来说，"准时制"要求有一套十分准确的生产和存货系统，高效率的采购、十分可靠的供应商和一个有效率的存货处理系统。尽管存货不可能减少到零，但"准时制"还是减少存货的极其严格的存货控制观点之一。当然，"准时制"的目标不仅是减少存货，还包括不断提高生产率、产品质量和生产弹性。

物料需求计划

准时制采取人工看板管理和后工序向前工序拉动方式传递生产信息，物料需求计划则采取计算机管理和前工序向后工序推动方式传递生产信息，虽然管理手段和方式不同，但它们的出发点和结果是大致相同的。

物料需求计划（Material Requirements Planning，MRP）为解决小批量多品种生产难题利用计算机介入管理的尝试，美国计算机应用和管理专家维特（W.Wight）、普劳士（W.Plosh）和奥里奇（Orliky）等为此做出重大贡献。物料需求计划也是从市场需求开始的，根据市场需求制定成品生产计划，即主生产计划，再用计算机对主生产计划进行分解，制定出物料需求计划，所需物料需求计划就是各个工序上的必要时间、必要量的必要物料（零部件或原材料）。和准时制相比，物料需求计划使各工序进入生产状况之前对生产任务就已明确，并由计算机下达生产指令，因此在实际生产控制时，仍可像大规模生产那样由前向后推进。

以摩托罗拉中国公司天津移动电话厂生产来说，顾客订货单进入工厂后，由生产部门编制主计划并输入计算机，计算机根据常规分解主计划，确定各种型号移动电话生产所需物料，并每天确定当日计划，各生产线根据计算机当日下料单领料并生产。在生产过程中，生产工程师根据物料情况，有时需要做出调整，并将信息反馈给"中央系统控制"部门，此部门对计算机计划进行修改。同时，计算机系统与厂内各部门联网，每日供料情况、生产情况以及所发生的财务情况随时传递给各部门。

将准时制与物料需求计划相比较可以看出,这两个系统都是从市场需求出发,都需要有明确的成品计划并由此推出合理的物料供给与库存;其目的都是为小批量多品种生产而设计的,以寻求最大限度地减少浪费、降低成本。它们的区别在于,MRP是个更有发展性的系统,它更适合全系统更大范围的配合协调;而准时制的现场灵活性更强,更适合生产线的内部协调,较适合更小批量的生产。

相 关 网 址
Useful Websites

如果你对营运资本管理的软件感兴趣,可以登录网站:www.decisioneering.com

刊载有关营运资本管理文章的英文杂志网站:

www.americanbanker.com

www.treasuryandrisk.com

关于现金管理的网站:

www.nacha.org(提供有关电子支付的资料)

关于信用管理的网站:

www.creditworthy.com

www.nacm.com

第 12 章
TOPIC 12

International Financial Management
国际财务管理

新闻视听
News in Media

Toyota was recalling for sticking accelerator pedals in worldwide. It would cost the automaker hundreds of millions to fix, and millions more to rescue its reputation. This news will explain the whole issue to you.

本章新闻视听资料请扫二维码收听。

名人名言
Wisdom

The globe is not a level playing field.

——Anonymous

微型案例
Mini Case

Huawei was founded in 1987. The company's initial development kept in step with the national policies. However, due to the fact that China was basically under a fixed exchange rate system before the exchange rate reform, the operators' awareness of preventing foreign exchange risks is not strong enough. With the implementation of the floating exchange rate since 2005, the foreign exchange risk faced by the company's operations increased, and the exchange rate changes brought certain loss of profit to the company. The company began to take some measures to hedge and avoid foreign exchange risks.

However, from the analysis of the subject of net exchange loss from Huawei's financial statements over the years, it can be seen that the company's foreign exchange risk management capability needs to be improved. In 2014, the company's net exchange loss was 2.135 billion yuan. In 2015, the net exchange loss increased by 2.26 billion yuan to 4.362 billion yuan. In 2016, the company's net exchange loss continued to increase to 5.223 billion yuan. The company's net exchange losses continued to rise sharply for three years. Although it has a lot to do with the company's overseas business development, it can be seen that the company has not managed foreign exchange risks effectively.

概　　览 Overview

Financial management decisions of most firms are not confined to domestic borders. In this topic, we discuss special factors that must be considered in international corporate financial management. We begin with a review of the global economy, looking at recent international agreements that affect financial decisions. We will also examine the foreign exchange market where firms expand operations and transactions. Finally, we discuss issues related to financial decisions and multinational capital budgeting.

正文 Text

12.1　Introduction

Financial management decisions of most firms are not confined to domestic borders. Many financing and investment decisions involve economies and firms outside a firm's own domestic borders either directly through international transactions or indirectly through the effects of international issues on the domestic economy. **International**

TOPIC 12　International Financial Management

financial management is the management of a firm's assets and liabilities considering the global economy in which the firm operates. Many firms derive a large part of their income from international operations.

12.1.1 The Global Economy

Countries trade with each other, exporting and importing, because they are specialized in one or more areas. This ability to specialize makes for more efficient production and ultimately greater output. Countries will produce and export goods and services for which they have a comparative or competitive advantage and countries will import goods and services for which other countries have a comparative or competitive advantage.

comparative or competitive advantage may originate from a country's natural resources (such as petroleum), its human resources (such as education), its capital investment (which may or may not be aided by the government), or its laws or regulations that may promote certain activities.

Many advocate **free trade**, which is trading among countries without barriers such as export or import quotas and tariffs (taxes on imported goods). The benefits of free trade include enhanced competition, which ultimately benefits consumers. However, for countries for which there are few or no comparative or competitive advantages, free trade may not be beneficial, and such countries may impose barriers to protect their own companies. These barriers may affect foreign companies' investment and financing decisions in that country.

Throughout history, most countries have exercised some protectionism. However, trends throughout the twentieth century reduced protectionism. One such agreement is the **General Agreement on Tariffs and Trade (GATT)**, which was originally signed by 23 countries in 1947. GATT is basically a forum for negotiating the reduction in trade barriers on a multilateral basis — that is, many countries/regions agree to such reductions at one time. Through time, other countries/regions joined in GATT. On April 15, 1994, the **Marrakesh Agreement**, signed in Marrakech, Morocco, established the **World Trade Organization**, which came into being upon its entry into force on

January 1, 1995. The Marrakesh Agreement developed out of the General Agreement on Tariffs and Trade.

Monetary cooperation is facilitated through the **International Monetary Fund (IMF)**, an agency of the United Nations, which began operations in 1947. The objective of the IMF is to promote monetary cooperation and encourage international trade. An important function of the IMF is to facilitate trade through a system of payments for current transactions. Further, the IMF strives to reduce and eliminate restrictions on foreign exchange. In 2001, there were 184 members of the IMF.

Two recent major agreements affect trade among major industrialized nations: the European Union (EU) and the North American Free Trade Agreement (NAFTA). The **European Union** is an organization, consisting of 15 European countries in 1996, whose goal is to increase economic cooperation and integration among its member countries. The European Union was established with the **Maastricht Treaty** in November 1993, which was then ratified by the member nations, forming the **European Economic Community (EEC)**. Under this treaty, citizens of the member countries gain mobility because immigration and customs requirements are reduced. An objective of this union was the development of a common currency for all member nations. The European countries that did not join the European Union remained in its predecessor, the **European Free Trade Association (EFTA)**, which was formed to reduce trade barriers and to enhance economic cooperation. A January 1994 agreement eliminated trade barriers between the EU and the EFTA by creating the **European Economic Area** and creating the largest free trading area in the world.

The **North American Free Trade Agreement** is a pact among Canada, Mexico, and the United States for the gradual removal of trade barriers for most goods produced and sold in North America. This pact became effective on January 1, 1994, and makes North America the world's second-largest free trade zone. It is expected that this pact will expand to encompass Latin American countries, but the economic requirements imposed upon those included countries may be difficult for some countries to satisfy, as least in the near term.

Most of the significant trade pacts involve major industrial nations. However, because many of the future growth opportunities are in lesser developed nations, barriers to free trade exist and are important considerations in many aspects of financial decision making.

12.1.2 Multinational Corporations

Corporations that have significant foreign operations are often referred to as international corporations or multinationals.

Corporations expand beyond their domestic borders for many reasons, including:

To gain access to new markets

Growth in the domestic market may slow, but there may be opportunities to grow in other countries.

To achieve production efficiency

By shifting operations to other lower-cost nations, a company can reduce its operating costs.

To gain access to resources

Companies that rely on natural resources, such as oil companies, establish access to these resources by establishing subsidiaries in other countries. This assures these companies of their basic materials to maintain uninterrupted operations.

To reduce political and regulatory hurdles

Shifting operations to other countries may be necessary to overcome the many hurdles established by nations to protect their domestic businesses. For example, in the 1970s Japanese auto firms established manufacturing and assembly plants in the United States to avoid import quotas imposed by the United States.

To diversify

Over any given period of time, the level of business activity may be different in different countries. This results in opportunities to reduce the overall fluctuations in a firm's business revenues and/or costs by doing business abroad. For example, in the 1980s, the Japanese economy was flourishing, while the U.S. economy was in a recession; in contrast, during the early 1990s, the Japanese economy did poorly, while the U.S. economy was prospering.

To gain access to technology

As technology is developed in other countries, a firm may expand operations in other countries, say, through joint ventures, to assure access to patents and other developments that ensure its competitiveness both domestically and internationally.

International corporations must consider many financial factors that do not directly affect purely domestic firms. These include foreign exchange rates, different interest rates from country to country, complex accounting methods for foreign operations, foreign tax rates, and foreign government intervention.

The basic principles of corporate finance still apply to international corporations; like domestic companies, they seek to invest in projects that create more value for the shareholders than they cost and to arrange financing that raises cash at the lowest possible cost. That is, the net present value (NPV) principle holds for both foreign and domestic operations. However, it is usually more complicated to apply the NPV principle to foreign operations.

12.2 Foreign Exchange Market

The foreign exchange market is the market where one country's currency is traded for another's. It has no physical marketplace but rather is a communications network linking banks and other dealers in foreign exchange. The foreign exchange market is an over-the-counter market. Traders are located in the major commercial and investment banks around the world. They communicate using computer terminals, telephones and other telecommunication devices. One element in the communications network for foreign transactions is the Society for Worldwide Inter-bank Financial Telecommunications (SWIFT). It is a Belgian not-for-profit cooperative. A bank in New York can send messages to a bank in London via SWIFT's regional processing centers. The connections are through data-transmission lines.

A company wishing to buy or sell foreign currency may do so through one of the banks or other dealers. Apart from exporting or importing goods and services, reasons for using the foreign exchange market include borrowing foreign currency, lending foreign currency, buying or selling foreign assets, and speculating on exchange rate movements.

12.2.1 Exchange Rates

An important outcome of the transactions that occur in the foreign exchange market is the set of prices known as exchange rates. The exchange rate is the number of units of a given currency that can be purchased for one unit of another country's currency; the exchange rate tells us about the relative value of any two currencies. The exchange rate can be quoted in term of the number of units of the domestic currency relative to a unit of the foreign currency (referred to as a **direct quotation**), or in terms of the number of units of the foreign currency relative to a unit of the domestic currency (referred to as an **indirect quotation**). In practice, almost all trading of currencies takes place in terms of the U.S. dollar. For example, both the Eurodollars and British pound will be traded with their price quoted in U.S. dollars. If the quoted price is the price in dollars of a unit of foreign exchange, the quotation is said to be direct (or American) terms. For example, US$1.50=£1 is a direct term. The financial press frequently quotes the foreign currency price of a U.S. dollar. If the quoted price is the foreign currency price of a U.S. dollar, the quotation is indirect (or European). For example, £0.67= US$1.

There are two reasons for quoting all foreign currencies in terms of the U.S. dollar. First, it reduces the number of possible cross-currency quotes. For example, with five major currencies, these would potentially be 10 exchange rates. Second, it makes triangular arbitrage more difficult. If all currencies were traded against each other, it would make in-consistencies more likely.

Consider the exchange rate of U.S. dollars and Swiss francs. From the perspective of the U.S. firm, the exchange rate would be the number of U.S. dollars needed to buy a Swiss franc. If the rate is 0.70, this means that it takes $0.70 to buy one Swiss franc, 1CHF. From the perspective of the Swiss firm, the rate is US$0.70/1CHF = 1.428,6; that is, it takes 1.428,6 Swiss francs to buy one U.S. dollar.

Countries have different policies concerning their currency exchange rate. In the **floating exchange rate system**, the currency's foreign exchange rate is allowed to fluctuate freely by supply and demand for the currency. Another type of policy is the **fixed exchange rate system**, where the government intervenes to offset changes in exchange rates caused by changes in the currency's supply and demand. The third type of policy is a **managed floating exchange rate system**, which falls somewhere between the fixed and floating systems. In the managed floating rate system, the currency's exchange rates are allowed to fluctuate in response to changes in supply and demand, but the government may intervene to stabilize the exchange rate in the short-run, avoiding short-term wild fluctuations in the exchange rate.

The international foreign currency market has undergone vast changes since the gold standard was abolished in 1971. Prior to August 1971, the value of the U.S. dollar was tied to the value of gold (fixed at $35 per ounce) and the value of other countries' currency was tied to the value of the U.S. dollar. In other words, the world's currencies were on a type of fixed exchange rate system. Since August 1971, the values of the U.S. dollar and other currencies have been allowed to change according to supply and demand.

The value of a country's currency depends on many factors, including the imports and exports of goods and services. As the demand and supply of countries' currencies rise and fall, the exchange rates, which reflect the currencies' relative values, change if rates are allowed to "float". For example, if a Swiss company purchases U.S. goods, the Swiss company must buy U.S. dollars to purchase the goods, thus creating demand for U.S. dollars. If a U.S. company purchases Swiss goods, the U.S. company must buy Swiss francs, thus creating demand for Swiss francs. If there is an increased demand for U.S. dollars, the price of the dollar relative to the Swiss franc increases the U.S. dollar appreciates and the Swiss franc depreciates. But this system does not go unchecked — countries' central banks may buy or sell currencies to affect the exchange rates, thus managing the rate changes. Usually, the role of the central banks is to smooth out any sudden fluctuations in exchange rates.

Another factor that affects the relative value of currencies is the movement of investment capital from one country to another. If interest rates are higher in one country, investors may buy the currency of that country in order to buy the interest-bearing securities in that country. This shifting of investment capital increases the demand for the currency of the country with a higher interest rate.

When a currency loses value relative to other currencies, we say that the currency has "depreciated" if the change is due to changes in supply and demand, or has been "devalued" if the change is due to government intervention. If the currency gains value relative to other currencies, we say that the currency has "appreciated" or been "revalued".

12.2.2 Currency Risk

The uncertainty of exchange rates affects a financial manager's decisions. Consider a U.S. firm making an investment that produces cash flows in British pounds, £. Suppose you invest £10,000 today and expect to get £12,000 one year from today. Further suppose that £1 = $1.48 today, so you are investing $1.48 times 10,000 = $14,800. If the British pound does not change in value relative to the U.S. dollar, you would have a return of 20%:

$$Return = \frac{£12,000 - £10,000}{£10,000} \text{ or } \frac{\$17,760 - \$14,800}{\$14,800} = 20\%$$

But what if one year from now £1 = $1.30 instead? Your return would be less than 20% because the value of the pound has dropped in relation to the U.S. dollar. You are making an investment of £10,000, or $14,800, and getting not $17,760, but rather $1.30 times £12,000 = $15,600 in one year. If the pound loses value from $1.48 to $1, your return on your investment is:

$$Return = \frac{\$15,600 - \$14,800}{\$14,800} = \frac{\$800}{\$14,800} = 5.41\%$$

Currency risk, also called **exchange-rate risk**, is the risk that the relative values of the domestic and foreign currencies will adversely change in the future, changing the value of the future cash flows. Financial managers must consider currency risk in investment decisions that involve other currencies and make sure that the returns on these investments are sufficient compensation for the risk of changing values of currencies.

The buying and selling of foreign currency takes place in the foreign exchange market, which is an over-the-counter market consisting of banks and brokers in major world financial centers. Trading in foreign currencies may be done in the spot market, which is the buying and selling of currencies for immediate delivery, or in the **forward**

market, which is the buying and selling of contracts for future delivery of currencies. If a U.S. firm needs euros in 90 days, it can buy today a contact for the delivery of euros in 90 days.

Forward contracts can be used to reduce uncertainty regarding foreign exchange rates. By buying a contract for euros for 90 days from now, the firm is locking in the exchange rate of U.S. dollars for euros. This use of forward contracts in this manner is referred to as **hedging**. By hedging, the financial manager can reduce a firm's exposure to currency risk.

12.2.3　Types of Transactions

Three types of trades take place in the foreign exchange market: spot, forward, and swap. **Spot trades** involve an agreement on the exchange rate today for settlement in two days. The rate is called the spot-exchange rate. **Forward trades** involve an agreement on exchange rates today for settlement in the future. The rate is called the forward-exchange rate. The maturities for forward trades are usually 1 to 52 weeks. A **swap** is the sale (purchase) of a foreign currency with a simultaneous agreement to repurchase (resell) it sometime in the future. The difference between the sale price and the repurchase price is called the swap rate.

12.3　Exchange Rate Parity

We now discuss links among four important variables: interest rates, inflation rates, spot exchange rates and forward exchange rates. In this analysis, it is assumed that market participants are risk-neutral and that there are no barriers or frictions (such as taxes or transaction costs) in any market.

12.3.1　Interest Rate Parity

Market forces determine whether a currency sells at a forward premium or discount, and the general relationship between spot and forward exchange rates is specified by a concept called "interest rate parity".

Interest rate parity holds that investors should earn the same return on security investments in all counties after adjusting for risk. It recognizes that when you invest in a country other than your home country, you are affected by two forces — returns on the investment itself and changes in the exchange rate. It follows that your overall return will be higher than the investment's stated return, if the currency in which your investment is denominated appreciates relative to your home currency. Likewise, your overall return will be lower if the foreign currency you receive declines in value.

Interest rate parity is expressed as follows:

$$\frac{Forward\ exchange\ rate}{Spot\ exchange\ rate} = \frac{1+K_h}{1+K_f}$$

Here, both the forward and spot rates are expressed in terms of the amount of home currency received per unit of foreign currency, and K_h and K_f are the periodic interest rates in the home country and the foreign country, respectively. If this relationship does not hold, then currency traders will buy and sell currencies — that is, engage in arbitrage — until it does hold.

Interest rate parity shows why a particular currency might be at a forward premium or discount. Note that a currency is at a forward premium whenever domestic interest rates are higher than foreign interest rates. Discounts prevail if domestic interest rates are lower than foreign interest rates. If these conditions do not hold, then arbitrage will soon force interest rates back to parity.

12.3.2 Purchasing Power Parity

We have considered the relationship between spot and forward exchange rates. However, we have not yet addressed the fundamental question: What determines the spot level of exchange rates in each country? While exchange rates are influenced by a multitude of factors that are difficult to predict particularly on a day-to-day basis over the long-run market forces work to ensure that similar goods sell for similar prices in different countries after taking exchange rates into account. This relationship is known as **"purchasing power parity" (PPP)**.

Purchasing power parity, sometimes referred to as the **law of one price**, implies that the level of exchange rates adjusts so as to cause identical goods to cost the same amount in different countries.

Here is the equation for purchasing power parity:

$$Spot\ rate = \frac{P_h}{P_f}$$

where P_h——the price of the good in the home country.

P_f ——the price of the good in the foreign country.

Note that the spot market exchange rate is expressed as the number of units of home currency that can be exchanged for one unit of foreign currency.

PPP assumes that market forces will eliminate situations in which the same product sells at a different price overseas. And it also assumes that there are no transportation or transaction costs, or import restrictions, all of which limit the ability to ship goods between countries. In many cases, these assumptions are incorrect, which explains why PPP is often violated. An additional complication, when empirically testing to see whether PPP holds, is that products in different countries are rarely identical. Frequently, these are real or perceived differences in quality, which lead to price differences in different countries. Still, the concepts of interest rate and purchasing power parity are critically important to those engaged in international activities. Companies and investors must anticipate changes in interest rates, inflation and exchange rates, and they often try to hedge the risks of adverse movements in these factors. The parity relationship is extremely useful when anticipating future conditions.

12.3.3 Unbiased Forward Rates

If market participants are risk-neutral and there are no transaction costs, the market will set the forward rate equal to the spot rate which is expected to be observed on the maturity date of the forward contract. If this result doesn't hold, then risk-neutral speculators would trade in foreign currency until the forward rate is equal to the expected spot rate.

12.3.4 Inflation, Interest Rates, and Exchange Rates

Relative inflation rates, or the rates of inflation in foreign countries compared with those in the home country, have many implications for multinational financial decisions. Obviously, relative inflation rates will greatly influence future production costs at home and abroad. Equally important, inflation has a dominant influence on relative interest rates and exchange rates. Both of these factors influence the methods chosen by multinational corporations for financing their foreign investments, and both have an important effect on the profitability of foreign investments.

The currencies of countries with higher inflation rates than that of the United States by definition depreciate over time against the dollar. Countries where this has occurred include Mexico and all the South American nations. On the other hand, the currencies of Switzerland and Japan, which have had less inflation than the United States, have appreciated against the dollar. In fact, a foreign currency will, on average, depreciate or appreciate at a percentage rate approximately equal to the amount by which its inflation rate exceeds or is less than our own.

Relative inflation rates also affect interest rates. The interest rate in any country is largely determined by its inflation rate. Therefore, countries currently experiencing higher rates of inflation than the United States also tend to have high-interest rates. However, this is not always a good strategy. Because the lower interest rate could be more than offset by losses from currency appreciation. Similarly, multinational corporations should not necessarily avoid borrowing in a country, where interest rates have been very high, because future depreciation could make such borrowing relatively inexpensive.

12.4 Multinational Capital Budgeting

Although the same basic principles of capital budgeting analysis apply to both foreign and domestic operations, there are some key differences. First, cash flow estimation is more complex for overseas investment. Most multinational firms set up separate subsidiaries in each foreign country in which they operate, and the relevant cash flows for the parent company are the dividends and royalties paid by the subsidiaries to the parent. Second, these cash flows must be converted into the parent company's currency. Hence they are subject to exchange rate risk.

Dividends and royalties are normally taxed by both foreign and home country governments. Furthermore, a foreign government may restrict the amount of the cash that may be repatriated to the parent company. For example, some governments place a ceiling, stated as a percentage of the company's net worth, on the amount of cash dividends that a subsidiary can pay to its parent. Such restrictions are normally intended to force multinational firms to reinvest earnings in the foreign country, although restricttions are sometimes imposed to present large currency out-flows, which might disrupt the exchange rate.

Whatever the most country's motivation for blocking repatriation of profits, the result is that the parent corporation cannot use cash flows blocked in the foreign country to pay dividends to its shareholders or to invest elsewhere in the business. Hence, from the perspective of the parent organization, the cash flows relevant for foreign investment analysis are the cash flows that the subsidiary is actually expected to send back to the parent. The present value of those cash flows is found by applying an appropriate discount rate, and this present value is then compared with the parent's required investment to determine the project's NPV.

In addition to the complexities of the cash flow analysis, the cost of capital may be different for a foreign project from for an equivalent domestic project, because foreign projects may be more or less risky. A higher risk could arise from two primary sources — exchange rate risk and political risk. A lower risk might result from international diversification.

Exchange rate risk relates to the value of the basic cash flows in the present company's home currency. The foreign currency cash flows to be turned over to the parent must be converted into U.S. dollars by translating them at expected future exchange rates. An analysis should be conducted to ascertain the effects of exchange rate variations, and on the basis of this analysis, an exchange rate risk premium should be added to the domestic cost of capital to reflect this risk. It is sometimes possible to hedge against exchange rate fluctuations, but it may not be possible to hedge completely, especially on long-term projects. If hedging is used, the costs of doing so must be subtracted from the project's cash flows.

Political risk refers to potential actions by a host government that would reduce the value of a company's investment. It includes at one extreme the expropriation without compensation of the subsidiary's assets and also includes less drastic actions that reduce the value of the parent firm's investment in the foreign subsidiary, including higher taxes, tighter repatriation or currency controls, and restrictions on prices charged.

12.5　International Financial Decision

An international firm can finance foreign projects in three basic ways:

1. It can raise cash in the home country and export it to finance the foreign project.

2. It can raise cash by borrowing in the foreign country where the project is located.

3. It can borrow in a third country where the cost of debt is the lowest.

If a Chinese firm raises cash for its foreign projects by borrowing in China, it has an exchange-rate risk. If the foreign currency depreciates, the Chinese parent firm may experience an exchange-rate loss when the foreign cash flow is remitted to China. Of course, the Chinese firm may sell foreign exchange forward to hedge this risk. However, it is difficult to sell forward contracts beyond one year.

Firms in China may borrow in the country where the foreign project is located. This is the usual way of hedging long-term foreign exchange risk.

Another alternative is to find a country where interest rates are low. However, foreign interest rates may be lower because of lower expected foreign inflation. Thus, financial managers must be careful to look beyond nominal interest rates to real interest rates.

12.6　Working Capital Management

Political risk, foreign currency risk, and restrictions on repatriation affect the working capital management of firms with international operations. In addition, there is a host of unique issues that arise concerning working capital.

Cash management requires working with one or more global center banks that can assist in the transfer of funds across borders. These global center banks specialize in seeking out the best rates of foreign exchange. To avoid having numerous cash balances, each being denominated in a different currency, companies can pool these cash balances in cooperation with a global bank. Cross-currency pooling systems essentially offset credits in one currency with debits in another, allowing the company to earn interest on the net credit balance without having to physically convert currencies. For example, if a company has a credit balance (that is, a deposit) in British pounds and a debt balance in Singapore dollars (that is, a deficiency), without cross-currency pooling the company would have to borrow Singapore dollars on a short-term basis and would earn interest (most likely at a lower rate) on its British pounds. With cross-currency pooling, the two balances are netted and the company earns interest or pays interest on the net amount only, resulting in savings. The two currencies are translated at the going exchange rate, but no actual exchange takes place — avoiding transactions costs.

Accounts receivable management is especially important in the international setting because extending credit is an important part of doing business in developing countries. Many growth opportunities exist in the developing countries and granting credit is sometimes the only way to do business. The evaluation of credit is more difficult in developing countries because in most cases reliable, historical financial information is not available. This means that the evaluation of credit must rely on other information.

Inventory management is more complex because the geographical range is expanded, often requiring inventory to be maintained at one or more locations in foreign countries. This geographical span also requires more lead time in ordering and, perhaps, more time in getting the goods to customers. Another consideration is the possible restrictions or costs of moving inventory from one country to another because of import or export taxes. Still another consideration is that some countries impose taxes on property, which includes inventory, as of some specific date. For example, a country may impose a tax on all property owned on March 1st; this may inspire companies to move inventory out of that country prior to this date and to move inventory into that country after that date.

12.7 Hedging Currency Risk

Given the existence of currency risk, the natural question is how a firm can hedge this risk. There are four derivative instruments that firms can use to protect against adverse foreign exchange rate movements: (1) currency forward contracts, (2) currency futures contracts, (3) currency swaps, and (4) currency option contracts. We discuss one by one as follows.

12.7.1 Currency Forward Contracts

A forward contract is a financial derivative in which one party agrees to buy the underlying asset, and another party agrees to sell that same underlying asset at a designated price and date in the future. Forward contract in which the underlying asset is foreign exchange is called a currency forward contract.

Most currency forward contracts have a maturity of less than two years. For longer-dated forward contracts, the bid-ask spread for a forward contract increases; that is, the size of the spread for a given currency increases with the maturity. Consequently, forward contracts become less attractive for hedging long-dated foreign currency exposure.

Forward contracts, as well as futures contracts, can be used to lock in a foreign exchange rate. In exchange for locking in a rate, the hedger forgoes the opportunity to benefit from any advantageous foreign exchange rate movement. Futures contracts that are creations of an exchange have certain advantages over forward contracts for types of underlying assets. For foreign exchange, however, the forward market is the market of choice rather than futures contracts.

12.7.2 Currency Futures Contracts

There are U.S.-traded currency futures contracts for the major currencies traded on the International Monetary Market (IMM), a division of the Chicago Mercantile

Exchange, as well as other exchanges. The maturity cycle for currency futures is March, June, September, and December. The longest maturity is one year. Consequently, as in the case of a currency forward contract, currency futures are limited with respect to hedging long-dated foreign-exchange risk exposure.

12.7.3 Currency Swaps

When issuing bonds in another country where the bonds are not denominated in the base currency, the issuer is exposed to currency risk. One way to hedge this risk is to use currency futures contracts or currency forward contracts. While these derivative instruments allow an issuer to lock in an exchange rate, they are difficult to use in protecting against the currency risk faced when issuing a bond or when facing other long-term liabilities. The reason is that a currency futures or forward contract is needed to protect against each payment that must be made by the issuer. So, if a bond is issued with a maturity of 20 years and interest payments are made annually, 20 currency futures or forward contracts must be used for each year when payment is to be made.

The major problem is that currency futures contracts have settlement dates that go out only one year and therefore cannot be used. Currency forward contracts can be obtained from a commercial bank for longer terms. However, they become expensive because dealers in this market charge a larger spread for long-dated forward contracts.

Today, when an issuer wants to protect itself against bonds denominated in a foreign currency, the treasurer will use a currency swap. A swap is an agreement whereby two counterparties agree to exchange payments. In an interest rate swap, only interest payments are exchanged. In a currency swap, there is an exchange of both interest and principal.

12.7.4 Currency Option Contracts

In contrast to a forward or futures contract, an option gives the buyer the opportunity to benefit from favorable exchange rate movements but establishes a maximum loss. The option price is the cost of establishing such a risk/return profile.

There are two types of foreign currency options traded on exchanges: options on the foreign currency and futures options. The latter is an option to enter into a foreign exchange futures contract which has the same effect in hedging exposure to currency risk.

There is also an over-the-counter (OTC) market for options on currencies. The markets for these products are made by commercial banks and investment banking firms. OTC options are tailor-made products to accommodate the specific needs of corporate clients. While options on the major currencies are traded on the exchange, an option on any other currency may be purchased in the OTC market.

There are variations on the standard call and put options in the OTC market. These options are called **exotic options**. Two common types of exotic options on currencies used by firms are the lookback currency option and the average rate currency option.

A **lookback currency option** is an option where the option buyer has the right to obtain the most favorable exchange rate that prevails over the life of the option. For example, consider a two-month lookback call option to buy yen when the exchange rate between the U.S. dollar and Japanese yen is $1 for 105 yen on Day 0. Suppose that the next day, Day 1, the exchange rate changes to $1 for 110 yen — the option buyer has the right to exchange $1 for 110 yen. Suppose that on Day 2 the exchange rate changes to $1 for 108 yen. The option buyer still has the right to exchange $1 for 110 yen. Regardless of what happens to the exchange rate over the 60 days, the option buyer gets to exercise the option at the exchange rate that prevails and gives the largest number of yen for $1 (or, equivalently, at the lowest price per yen).

An **average rate currency option**, also called an **Asian currency option**, has a payoff that is the difference between the strike exchange rate for the underlying currency and the average exchange rate over the life of the option for the underlying currency. In the case of a call option, if the average exchange rate for the underlying currency is greater than the stoke exchange rate, then the option seller must make a payment to the option buyer. The amount of the payment is:

Payoff for average rate currency call option

= (Average exchange rate − Stoke exchange rate) × Underlying units

In the case of a put option, if the stoke exchange rate for the underlying currency is greater than the average exchange rate, then the option seller must make a payment to the option buyer that is equal to:

Payoff for average rate currency put option

= (Stoke exchange rate − Average exchange rate)× Underlying units

核心词汇 Core Words and Expressions

international financial management　国际财务管理

free trade　自由贸易

General Agreement on Tariffs and Trade (GATT)　关贸总协定

Marrakesh Agreement　马拉喀什协议

World Trade Organization　世界贸易组织

European Union (EU)　欧盟

International Monetary Fund (IMF)　国际货币基金组织

Maastricht Treaty　欧洲联盟条约，又称马斯特里赫特条约

European Economic Community (EEC)　欧洲经济共同体，又称欧洲共同市场

European Free Trade Association (EFTA)　欧洲自由贸易联盟，又称"小自由贸易区"

European Economic Area (EEA)　欧洲经济区协定

North American Free Trade Agreement (NAFTA)　北美自由贸易协议

multinational corporation　跨国公司

international corporation　跨国公司

Society for Worldwide Inter-bank Financial Telecom-munications (SWIFT)　环球同业银行金融电信协会

exchange rate　汇率

direct quotation　直接标价

indirect quotation　间接标价

cross-currency quote　交叉标价

Swiss Francs　瑞士法郎

floating exchange rate system　浮动汇率制度

fixed exchange rate system　固定汇率制度

managed floating exchange rate system　有管制的浮动汇率制度

depreciate　贬值

appreciate　升值

currency risk　外汇风险

exchange-rate risk　汇率风险

forward market　远期市场

hedging　避险，套期保值

spot trade　即期交易

forward trade　远期交易

swap　互换，掉期

interest rate parity　利率平价

forward rate 远期汇率	currency futures contract 货币期货合约
spot rate 即期汇率	currency swap 货币互换
forward premium 远期升水	currency option 货币期权
forward discount 远期贴水	over-the-counter (OTC) market 场外交易市场
purchasing power parity 购买力平价	exotic option 特种期权
law of one price 一价定律	lookback currency option 回顾式货币期权
unbiased forward rate 无偏差远期汇率	
cross-currency pooling system 外汇交叉组合系统	average rate currency option 均价期权
currency forward contract 远期外汇合约	Asian currency option 亚式期权

即时问答 Quick Quiz

1. What explains the difference between the forward exchange rate and the spot rate?
2. Why do interest rates in different countries differ?
3. How do different rates of inflation in two countries affect each country's interest rate as well as the exchange rate between the currencies of those countries?
4. What does absolute PPP say? According to relative PPP, what determines the change in exchange rates?
5. How can a firm hedge short-run exchange rate risk? Long-run exchange rate risk?

思考与探索 Thinking and Exploration

Suppose a Chinese company import components from German. Assembles them, and then sells the finished product in China. It also has a Chinese company which buys raw materials in China and exports its output to German.

How is each company likely to be affected by a fall in the value of the US dollar? How could each company hedge itself against exchange risk?

汉译英 Translation

宝马公司（以下简称"宝马"）于1916年在德国创建，是一家以生产汽车为主导，同时生产飞机引擎、越野车和摩托车的跨国公司。宝马在国际化的过程中，大部分产品销往国际市场，而在德国本土销售产品不足 17%，中国、印度、俄罗斯和东欧部分地区对宝马产品的需求不断增加。为了避免将汇兑成本传递给客户，宝马必须通过汇率管理降低相应的财务费用以降低成本。

从策略上来说，宝马选择了两种策略来进行汇率风险的控制。一种策略是"自然对冲"，即将某种货币的收入在当地使用，例如在当地建立工厂、采购原材料、雇用人工等。"自然对冲"可以有效地降低企业经营成本，但是这种方式无法覆盖所有的汇率管理敞口。因此，宝马还采用了第二种策略，通过地区性的金融中心进行常规金融工具对冲，例如新加坡、美国和英国等。

知识扩展
More Knowledge

几个最主要的国际经济性机构

与"国际财务管理"相关的最主要的国际机构包括：

- 国际货币基金组织（International Monetary Fund，IMF，http://www.imf.org）
- 世界银行（World Bank，http://www.worldbank.org）
- 世界贸易组织（World Trade Organization，WTO，http://www.wto.org）

建立上述三个世界性组织的设想是在 1944 年 7 月举行的布雷顿森林会议上提出的，当时设想在成立世界银行和国际货币基金组织的同时，成立一个国际性贸易组织，从而使它们成为二战后左右世界经济的"货币-金融-贸易"三位一体的机构。目前，世界贸易组织与世界银行、国际货币基金组织一起，并称为当今世界经济体制的"三大支柱"。

国际货币基金组织

国际货币基金组织是政府间国际金融组织，1945 年 12 月 27 日正式成立，1947 年 3 月 1 日开始工作，1947 年 11 月 15 日成为联合国的专门机构，在经营上有其独立性，其总部设在华盛顿。该组织的宗旨是通过一个常设机构来促进国际货币合作，为国际货币问题的磋商和协作提供方法；通过国际贸易的扩大和平衡发展，把促进和保持成员方的就业、生产资源的发展、实际收入的高水平作为经济政策的首要目标；稳定国际汇率，在成员方之间保持有秩序的汇价安排，避免竞争性的汇价贬值；协助成员方建立经常性交易的多边支付制度，消除妨碍世界贸易的外汇管制；在有适当保证的条件下，基金组织向成员方临时提供普通资金，使其有信心利用此机会纠正国际收支的失调，而不采取危害本国或国际繁荣的措施；按照以上目的，缩短成员方国际收支不平衡的时间，减轻不平衡的程度等。

该组织临时委员会是世界两大金融机构之一国际货币基金组织的决策和指导机构。该委员会将在政策合作与协调，特别是在制定中期战略方面充分发挥作用。委员会由24名执行董事组成。国际货币基金组织每年与世界银行共同举行年会。

中国是该组织创始国之一。1980年4月17日，该组织正式恢复中国的代表权。中国在该组织中的份额为33.852亿特别提款权，占总份额的2.34%。中国共拥有34 102张选票，占总投票权的2.28%。中国自1980年恢复在货币基金组织的席位后单独组成一个选区并派一名执行董事。1991年，该组织在北京设立常驻代表处。

世界银行

世界银行是国际复兴开发银行（International Bank for Reconstruction and Development，IBRD）的简称，它是一个国际组织，其一开始的使命是帮助在二战中被破坏的国家的重建。今天它的任务是资助国家克服穷困，其资金来自成员方缴纳的基金和世界银行债券。在1944年7月1日到7月22日的布雷顿森林会议上参加国决定建立世界银行，1945年12月27日，在参加国签署其条约后世界银行正式成立。

世界银行的使命是战胜贫困和提高发展中国家人民的生活水平。它是个向低收入和中等收入国家提供贷款、政策建议、技术援助和知识分享服务以减轻贫困的开发银行。世界银行的主要帮助对象是发展中国家，帮助它们建设教育、农业和工业设施。它向成员方提供优惠贷款，同时世界银行向受贷国提出一定的要求，比如减少贪污或建立民主等。

世界银行的工作经常受到非政府组织和学者的严厉批评，有时世界银行内部的审查也对其某些决定提出质疑。往往世界银行被指责为美国或西方国家施行有利于它们自己的经济政策的执行者，此外往往过快、不正确的、按错误的顺序引入的或在不适合的环境下进行的市场经济改革对发展中国家的经济反而造成破坏。

世界贸易组织

1994年4月15日，在摩洛哥的马拉喀什市举行的关贸总协定乌拉圭回合部长会议决定，成立更具全球性的世界贸易组织，简称"世贸组织"（World Trade Organization，WTO），以取代成立于1947年的关贸总协定（GATT）。

世贸组织是一个独立于联合国的永久性国际组织，1995年1月1日正式开始运作，负责管理世界经济和贸易秩序，总部设在瑞士日内瓦莱蒙湖畔。1996年1月1日，它正式取代关贸总协定临时机构。世贸组织是具有法人地位的国际组织，在调解成员争端方面具有更高的权威性。它的前身是1947年订立的关贸总协定。与关贸总协定相比，世贸组织涵盖货物贸易、服务贸易以及知识产权贸易，而关贸总协定只适用于商品货物贸易。目前，世贸组织的贸易量已占世界贸易的95%以上。

1995年7月11日，世贸组织总理事会会议决定接纳中国为该组织的观察员，中国于2001年11月加入该组织。

世贸组织成员分为四类：发达成员、发展中成员、转轨经济体成员和最不发达成员。2006年11月7日世界贸易组织关于接纳越南加入该组织的工作全部完成，11月28日，越南国会批准关于越南加入世界贸易组织的议定书。在这项议定书获得批准30天后，越南正式成为世贸组织第150个成员。

几个重要的区域性组织与协定

马拉喀什协议（Marrakesh Agreement）即《建立世界贸易组织的马拉喀什协议》（Marrakech Agreement Establishing the World Trade Organization，WTO Agreement），它是关贸总协定乌拉圭回合谈判达成的协议，1995年1月1日生效。根据该协议成立了世界贸易组织。

马斯特里赫特条约（Maastricht Treaty）即《欧洲联盟条约》，1991年12月9～10日，第46届欧洲共同体首脑会议在荷兰的马斯特里赫特（Maastricht）举行。经过两天辩论，会议通过并草签了《欧洲经济与货币联盟条约》同《政治联盟条约》，即《马斯特里赫特条约》。该条约是对《罗马条约》的修订，它为欧共体建立政治联盟同经济与货币联盟确立了目标与步骤，是欧洲联盟成立的基础。

欧洲自由贸易联盟（European Free Trade Association，EFTA），又称"小自由贸易区"。1960年1月4日，奥地利、丹麦、挪威、葡萄牙、瑞典、瑞士和英国在斯德哥尔摩签订《建立欧洲自由贸易联盟公约》，即《斯德哥尔摩公约》。该公约经各国议会批准后于同年5月3日生效，欧洲自由贸易联盟正式成立，简称欧贸联，总部设在日内瓦。欧贸联的宗旨是：在联盟区域内实现成员之间工业品的自由贸易和扩大农产品贸易；保证成员国之间的贸易在公平竞争的条件下进行；发展和扩大世界贸易并逐步取消贸易壁垒。其主要任务是：逐步取消成员国内部工业品的关税和其他贸易壁垒，以实现"自由贸易"；对其他国家的工业品仍各保持不同的关税率；扩大农产品的贸易；不谋求任何形式的欧洲政治一体化。

欧洲联盟（European Union，EU）是由欧洲共同体（European Communities）发展而来的，是一个集政治实体和经济实体于一身、在世界上具有重要影响的区域一体化组织。1991年12月，欧洲共同体马斯特里赫特首脑会议通过《欧洲联盟条约》，通称《马斯特里赫特条约》（简称《马约》）。1993年11月1日，《马约》正式生效，欧盟正式诞生，总部设在比利时首都布鲁塞尔。

欧洲经济区协定（European Economic Area，EEA）于 1994 年 1 月 1 日生效，2004 年扩大范围之后，协定的有效范围包括 25 个欧盟成员国[○] 和"欧洲自由贸易区协定"（EFTA）成员国冰岛、列支敦士登和挪威。虽然瑞士也是"欧洲自由经济区协定"的成员国，但是没有加入"欧洲经济区协定"。

北美自由贸易协议（North American Free Trade Agreement，NAFTA）是美国、加拿大及墨西哥三国在 1992 年 8 月 12 日签署的关于三国间全面贸易的协议。与欧盟性质不一样，NAFTA 不是凌驾于国家政府和国家法律之上的一项协议。北美自由贸易协议于 1994 年 1 月 1 日正式生效。

环球同业银行金融电信协会

环球同业银行金融电信协会（SWIFT）是国际银行同业间的国际合作组织，成立于 1973 年，目前全球大多数国家大多数银行已使用 SWIFT 系统。SWIFT 的使用，为银行的结算提供了安全、可靠、快捷、标准化、自动化的通信业务，从而大大提高了银行的结算速度。SWIFT 需要会员资格。我国的大多数专业银行都是其成员。SWIFT 的客户包括银行、保险公司、证券公司、投资商、经纪人以及清算公司。

相 关 网 址
Useful Websites

经济合作与发展组织（Organization for Economic Cooperation and Development）：
www.oecd.org

欧洲中央银行（European Central Bank）：
www.ecb.int

美国联邦储备系统（U.S. Federal Reserve System）：
www.federalreserve.gov

美联储经济数据（Federal Reserve Economic Data Database）：
https://www.stlouisfed.org/

欧洲证券交易所联合会（Federation of European Securities Exchanges）：
https://www.euronext.com/en

国内外汇牌价可以从中国银行网站上查找，网址为：
https://www.boc.cn/

国际上各种主要货币之间的汇率可以到下列网站上查找：

○ 英国已于 2020 年正式脱欧。

http://www.x-rates.com

http://www.bloomberg.com/

各国中央银行网址可以通过搜索引擎查询：

http://www.bis.org/cbanks.htm

国际市场情况可以通过下列网站查找：

http://finance.yahoo.com

参考文献

[1] DAMONDARAN A. Applied Corporate Finance: A user's Manual [M]. 2nd ed. NJ: John Wiley & Sons, Inc., 2005.

[2] BENRUD, ERIK. Understanding Financial Management: A Practical Guide [EB]. Ebook Library: Blackwell Publishing Ltd., 2005.

[3] BERGEVIN P. Financial Statement Analysis: An Integrated Approach [M]. NJ: Prentice Hall, 2002.

[4] DEANGELO, HARRY, DEANGELO L. The Irrelevance of the MM Dividend Irrelevance Theorem [J]. Journal of Financial Economics, 2006, (2): 293-315.

[5] BRIGHAM E F, EHRHARDT M C. Financial management: theory and practice [M]. 11th ed. Ohio: South-Western ; London : Thomson Learning, 2005.

[6] PEIRSON G, BROWN R, EASTON S, et al. Business Finance [M]. 9th ed. NSW: McGraw-Hill Australia Pty Limited, 2006.

[7] FABOZZI, FRANK J. Financial Management and Analysis [M]. NJ: John Wiley & Sons, 2003.

[8] HARRY M. Portfolio Selection [J]. Journal of Finance, 1952, 7 (1):77-91.

[9] HARRY M. Portfolio Selection: Efficient Diversification of Investments [M]. NJ: John Wiley & Sons, 1959.

[10] JEFF M. International Financial Management [M]. Ohio: South Western, 2003.

[11] SABINE M. Corporate Finance: Flotation, Equity Issues and Acquisitions [M]. 3rd ed. Bath Press, Bath LexisNexis Butterworths, 2003.

[12] JENSEN M C, MECKLING W H. Theory of the firm: managerial behavior, agency costs and ownership structure [J]. Journal of Financial Economics, 1976, 3(4): 305-360.

[13] MERTON M H. Debt and Taxes [J]. Journal of Finance, 1977(5): 261-276.

[14] STEWART M C. Determinants of Corporate Borrowing [J]. Journal of Financial Economics.

[15] BREALY R A, MYERS S C. Principle of Corporate Finance [M]. 7th ed. NY: McGraw-Hill, 2003.

[16] LEONARD S, ROBIN S. Financial Statement Analysis: A valuation Approach [M]. NJ: Prentice Hall, 2003.

[17] ROSS S A, WESTERFIELD R W, JAFFE J. Corporate finance [M]. 7th ed. NY: McGraw-Hill, 2004.

[18] 郭永清. 财务报表分析与股票估值[M]. 北京：机械工业出版社，2017.

[19] 帕利普，希利. 经营分析与估值[M]. 刘媛媛，译. 大连：东北财经大学出版社，2014.

[20] 姜国华. 财务报表分析与证券投资[M]. 北京：北京大学出版社，2008.

[21] 刘淑莲. 公司理财[M]. 北京：北京大学出版社，2013.

[22] 佩因曼. 财务报表分析与证券估值（原书第5版）[M]. 朱丹，屈腾龙，译. 北京：机械工业出版社，2016.

[23] 肖星. 上市公司财务问题及其分析[M]. 北京：中国计划出版社，2002.

[24] 张然. 基本面量化投资：运用财务分析和量化策略获取超额收益[M]. 北京：北京大学出版社，2017.

[25] 张先治，陈友邦. 财务分析[M]. 大连：东北财经大学出版社，2019.

[26] 张新民. 战略视角下的财务报表分析[M]. 北京：高等教育出版社，2017.